# DECENTERING SOCIAL THEORY

# POLITICAL POWER AND SOCIAL THEORY

Series Editor: Julian Go

Recent Volumes:

POLITICAL POWER AND SOCIAL THEORY    VOLUME 25

# DECENTERING SOCIAL THEORY

## EDITED BY

## JULIAN GO

*Boston University, Boston, MA, USA*

United Kingdom – North America – Japan
India – Malaysia – China

Emerald Group Publishing Limited
Howard House, Wagon Lane, Bingley BD16 1WA, UK

First edition 2013

Copyright © 2013 Emerald Group Publishing Limited

**Reprints and permission service**
Contact: permissions@emeraldinsight.com

**British Library Cataloguing in Publication Data**
A catalogue record for this book is available from the British Library

ISBN: 978-1-78190-726-9
ISSN: 0198-8719 (Series)

ISOQAR certified
Management System,
awarded to Emerald
for adherence to
Environmental
standard
ISO 14001:2004.

Certificate Number 1985
ISO 14001

INVESTOR IN PEOPLE

# CONTENTS

# LIST OF CONTRIBUTORS

| | |
|---|---|
| *Sinem Adar* | Department of Sociology, University of South Florida, Tampa, FL, USA |
| *Patricia Hill Collins* | Department of Sociology, University of Maryland, College Park, MD, USA |
| *Raewyn Connell* | Faculty of Education and Social Work, University of Sydney, Sydney, NSW, Australia |
| *Mustafa Emirbayer* | Department of Sociology, University of Wisconsin, Madison, WI, USA |
| *Fatma Müge Göçek* | Department of Sociology, University of Michigan, Ann Arbor, MI, USA |
| *Sujata Patel* | Department of Sociology, University of Hyderabad, Hyderabad, India |
| *Besnik Pula* | Center for the Study of Social Organization, Princeton University, Princeton, NJ, USA |
| *Raka Ray* | Department of Sociology, University of California at Berkeley, Berkeley, CA, USA |
| *Isaac Ariail Reed* | Department of Sociology, University of Colorado at Boulder, Boulder, CO, USA |

# SENIOR EDITORIAL BOARD

# STUDENT EDITORIAL BOARD

Cara Bowman

Zophia Edwards

Kiri Gurd

Adrienne Lemon

David Levy

Megan O'Leary

# EDITORIAL STATEMENT

*Political Power and Social Theory* is a peer-reviewed annual journal committed to advancing the interdisciplinary understanding of the linkages between political power, social relations, and historical development. The journal welcomes both empirical and theoretical work and is willing to consider papers of substantial length. Publication decisions are made by the editor in consultation with members of the editorial board and anonymous reviewers. For information on submissions, please see the journal web site at www.bu.edu/sociology/ppst.

# EDITOR'S INTRODUCTION

To "decenter" theory could mean at least one of two things. The first refers to the movement of "theory" (in the general sense of abstract, logically connected concepts) to the margins of our concern, thereby making empirical research more central. The second refers to moving certain *types* of theory to the margins and making other types more central. This second meaning is the one guiding this volume of PPST. In some ways this volume thus continues the theme of the previous volume (Volume 24 on *Postcolonial Sociology*).

The first two essays (by Sinem Adar and Besnik Pula) take up familiar theoretical concepts deployed to analyze political relations in Europe and the North (e.g., "democracy" in Adar's case and the "state" in Pula's case) and see their workings in less familiar contexts – less familiar, that is, to the original theories at stake. The essays in the second part (by Fatma Müge Göçek and Sujata Patel) make similar moves, however by rethinking the scholarship and knowledge production on the Ottoman empire and India (respectively).

The final part offers a forum on Raewyn Connell's *Southern Theory* (Polity Press, 2007). Connell's book is among the most important statements on the inequality of social science production and the tendency of academic thought in the North to subjugate knowledges from the Global South. The commentaries by Mustafa Emirbayer, Patricia Hill Collins, Raka Ray, and Isaac Ariail Reed illuminate the strengths and challenges of this provocative project.

I am grateful to the commentators for sharing their thoughts and to Raewyn Connell for agreeing to do this forum. Finally, thanks to Thomas Dark and the rest of the Emerald team for their work on this volume.

Julian Go
May 2013
Boston, MA

# PART I
# RESEARCH ARTICLES

# AMBIGUITIES OF DEMOCRATIZATION: NATIONALISM, RELIGION, AND ETHNICITY UNDER AKP GOVERNMENT IN TURKEY

Sinem Adar

## ABSTRACT

*This chapter explores the impact of the seemingly new recognition of non-Muslims in Turkey, a historically marginalized minority. In the 2000s, the ruling AKP party, a religiously and socially conservative party, made a number of symbolic gestures toward the increasing recognition of these communities. This chapter explores this ethnographically and historically by looking at the political effects of AKP's democratization attempts on the Rum Orthodox ("Greek") community in Istanbul. It argues that these attempts paralleled a similar language of democracy within the community particularly in the aftermath of the government's permission to run elections in the non-Muslim community institutions (vakıfs), following a period of time during which no elections had been held in these institutions. At the same time, these attempts occasioned old and new forms of hierarchies within the community, which emerged as a result of*

Decentering Social Theory
Political Power and Social Theory, Volume 25, 3–36
Copyright © 2013 by Emerald Group Publishing Limited
ISSN: 0198-8719/doi:10.1108/S0198-8719(2013)0000025007

*the competing claims within it to its representation. These seemingly
ambiguous effects of democratization within the Rum community
emerged in the gap between the AKP's democracy discourse that claims
universal inclusion and its highly selective practice of democracy. This
was so because the AKP preserved the ethnoreligious definition of
national identity even while it readopted the historical legacies of the
Ottoman millet system that managed society along religious confessional
lines. These findings contribute to the existing theories on democratization by highlighting the inextricable link between inclusion and exclusion
that emerges in the gap between the discursive claims of democracy
toward universal inclusion and the selective actualization of these claims
in practice. Such selective inclusion that is inherent to the politics of
democracy is managed differently in different contexts due to the hybrid
forms of state recognition of the population.*

# INTRODUCTION

The "Turkish model of democracy," under the leadership of the Justice and
Development Party (*Adalet ve Kalkınma Partisi*, "AKP" thereafter) from
the time of its ascension after the 2002 elections, emerged as a contested
topic in popular media, especially in the aftermath of the Arab Spring. On
one hand there has been growing public sympathy toward AKP's seemingly
inclusive and liberal policies, particularly toward religious and ethnic
minorities, especially during its first two mandates (2002–2011). The party's
adamant support of Turkey's EU membership, its strong criticism of
military hegemony in Turkish politics, and its strong commitment to
neoliberal economic policies earned AKP the reputation of being the
moderate among Islamist parties. In fact, AKP has become a poster child
for the idea that Islam and democracy are compatible, as noted in a 2008
article in *The Economist*.[1]

On the other hand, since the 2011 elections there has been a significant
and puzzling shift in AKP's seemingly democratic inclinations. Severe
limitations were imposed on freedoms of speech and expression. The
language of dialogue and rights adopted in relation to resolution of the
Kurdish problem was dropped and was replaced by militaristic language. A
recent commentary published in *Foreign Affairs* of June 27, 2012, posed the
current political situation as a paradox of "simultaneously embracing and
abusing democracy."

This chapter explores this paradox by examining the political effects of the AKP's democratization attempts during the period from 2002 through 2011 on the internal politics of the community of Rum Orthodox ("Greek")[2] in Istanbul. The Rum Orthodox is one of the officially recognized religious minority communities in Turkey. Here I would like to caution that this chapter is not concerned with the claims of or debate about the compatibility of Islam and democracy. Instead it explores the gap between democracy claims and practices, not as a function of a particular religion, culture, or civilization, but from a historical sociological perspective. It argues that the paradox of democracy stems from the selective inclusion that emerges in the gap between the discourse of democracy and its practices. The peculiarities of selective inclusion are shaped and in turn shape the historical matrix of state–society relations.

Using historical and ethnographic evidence collected during fieldwork in Istanbul during 2008 and 2011, this chapter argues that the AKP's attempts at democratization during its first two mandates occasioned a strong democracy discourse within the Rum Orthodox community. This discourse was also accompanied by the practice of democracy, particularly in the aftermath of the government's permission to run elections in the non-Muslim community institutions (*vakıfs*), following a period of time during which no elections had been held in these institutions. The actual possibility of holding elections created new spaces for inclusion within the community, while at the same time intensified intra-communal hierarchies stemming from increasingly salient old and new claims to its representation.

These seemingly ambiguous effects of democratization within the Rum Orthodox community emerged in the gap between the AKP's democracy discourse and its practice of democracy. Despite its discursive claims of universal inclusion, the AKP's democracy practice remained highly selective. In the specific case of non-Muslims, it almost solely focused on the communal institutions and the return of the confiscated communal properties. A more substantive debate critiquing the existing notions of national identity that excluded non-Muslims from the nation was missing. This was so because the AKP preserved the ethnoreligious definition of national belonging even while it readopted the historical legacies of the Ottoman *millet* system that managed society along religious confessional lines.

This chapter is organized as follows: the first section develops an analytical framework by applying Rancière's (2004) understanding of politics to the existing theories of democracy to better understand democratization along the nexus of discourse–practice. A brief summary of the fieldwork follows as the second section. The third section is an analysis of the historical matrix of state relations with non-Muslim communities through the lens of the analytical framework outlined in the first section. The fourth section explores the AKP's democracy discourse during the period from 2002 through 2011 whereby the fifth section sheds the light on the parallel effects on democratization within the Rum Orthodox community during this period. The last section analyzes the increasingly salient old and new claims within the community to its representation, and their impacts on intra-communal political hierarchies.

# DEMOCRATIZATION AS DISCOURSE AND PRACTICE

The literature of democracy is broad, encompassing highly philosophical abstractions as well as empirical demonstrations. Regardless of whether the focus is on the ontological basis of democracy, its procedures, or its practices, existing theories reflect a strong belief in the centrality of the relationship between the state and the individual agent. Democracy as "the government of all people," which concentrates the "sovereignty in man" is a project of universal inclusion that expands individual freedoms and equality within the society (Huber, Rueschemeyer, & Stephens, 1997; Stephens, 1989; Tilly, 2007). Solidarity in representative democracies is ensured through the legally enforced social contract between the state and its citizens, who are both "the addressees and authors of law" (Habermas, 2001, p. 65).

Recent studies on democracy extend these contractual interpretations from the realm of procedure to the realm of practice. Democracy is learned through face-to-face interactions in associational life (Putnam, 2001). It is practiced through the active involvement of subaltern, marginalized individuals, especially, in decision-making processes despite continuous interruptions by power struggles and hierarchies (Baiocchi, 2005; Baiocchi, Heller, & Silva 2011; Heller, 2001; Houtzager & Acharya, 2011; Rao & Woolcock, 2007). Central to this shift toward democracy as a set of practices is the increasing emphasis on the communicative realm in democratization (Baiocchi, 2012). The formation of public opinion through deliberation (Habermas, 1991) and struggles within different regulatory institutions, such as the media and the legal system, for the civil incorporation of out groups (Alexander, 2006) highlight the inextricable link between communicative frameworks, institutions, and practice.

Existing theories of democratization are based on an ontological belief in the centrality of the relationship between the state and the individual citizen vis-à-vis the democratization process, whether this is constituted in a set of procedures, practices, or discursive frameworks. The chief premise in this relationship is the emancipation of individual citizens from the constraining power of their ascribed identities. In fact, democratization becomes the continuous enlargement and secularization of "public politics" (Tilly, 2007) or the "civil repair" of non-civil spheres (Alexander, 2006) in ways that enhance universal inclusion and solidarity (Dahl, 1989).

This chapter approaches the belief in the necessity of freedom from ascribed identities through democratization with some caution. The roots of this skepticism are not about the ideal of democracy as a universally inclusive project but instead concern the ontological basis of universal inclusion itself and its relation to particularisms (Young, 1989). Does universalism absolutely and necessarily imply elimination of particularisms? If not, how can the universally inclusive democratic project be reconciled with preserving particulars that are most often defined by ascribed identities (Benhabib, 1996; Laclau & Mouffe, 1985; Young, 2000)?

These highly philosophical, abstract questions provide a starting point for understanding the political effects of democratization on marginalized populations. Democratization is understood in this chapter as a twofold process. On one hand, it is the aspiration to redefine the existing categories of belonging within the society toward universal inclusion. On the other hand, it is about rearranging existing forms of state–society relations in ways to ensure the equal access of individual citizens to the state while simultaneously allowing their differences to coexist. At the intersection of these two components of the democratization process lie different forms of state recognition of the population as individual citizens and/or community members.

Under the lens of the state, that which constitutes society is seldom neutral and homogenous yet it is defined through categories. Categorization is a tool of dividing and compartmentalizing (Bourdieu, 1985). In other words, categorizing society is a struggle over boundary making (Brubaker, 1992; Wacquant, 1997; Wimmer, 2008) between the nation, an aggregation of individual citizens who legitimately constitute a "community of equals" (Rancière, 2004) that is imagined (Anderson, 1983), and the rest. Those who fall outside the boundaries of the nation are most often recognized by the state as members of communities such as the poor, ethnic and religious minorities, and women. As such, they are exposed to various forms of discrimination on the basis of ascribed identities such as race (Mills, 1997), gender (Young, 1997), and ethnicity and religion (Taylor, 1998). In extreme cases, they are the victims of ethnic cleansings and genocides (Mann, 2005).

Rancière (2004) positions this struggle for categories of inclusion and exclusion at the very heart of what constitutes politics in democracies. This view is not concerned with democracy from a normative standpoint. Instead it conceptualizes democracy as the praxis of inclusion and exclusion. The ideal of universal inclusion is continuously interrupted by the exclusionary practices of democracy. Discursive claims for universal inclusion, therefore, do not necessarily overlap with the actualization of these claims because of the inextricable link between inclusion and exclusion.

Such a gap between a democracy discourse and its practice does not necessarily imply complete closure. It rather points toward a selective inclusion that needs to be managed in particular ways. I intentionally use the word "manage" despite its technocratic connotations to refer to the relational nexus between state and society. This relational nexus is an institutionally structured political project. It includes but is not necessarily circumscribed by the legally enforced social contract between the state and its individual citizens. Management of society is contingent on governing ideologies, beliefs, and sociopolitical conjunctures. It shapes and is shaped by state recognition of society as individual citizens and/or community members.

It is in these situations with hybrid forms of state recognition that democratization opens up spaces to new claims for inclusion within the society. It also simultaneously invokes old and new claims for representation within marginalized communities, which lead to new forms of hierarchies. In his analysis of the role of democracy in the rise of Hindu nationalism in India, Hansen (1999, p. 9) emphasizes the emergence of such claims between Hindus and Muslims during democratization, and notes that the "*claims of cultural collectivities and identities are dominant forms of political identity in India and other post-colonial states*, [and] does not make them 'deformities' in relation to the liberal Western political trajectories, but rather results of the specific historicities and 'vernacularization' of democratic discourses and procedures in the post-colonial world" (emphasis added).

A thorough understanding of how and on what basis such claims emerge requires an understanding of how the relationship between the state and different parts of society evolved historically. For instance, how can one understand and assess the process of democratization in Bolivia, where an independent judicial system for indigenous communities was legalized in 2010, one of the aims of which was to defend individual and communal rights? Or, what does the lack of a unified legal system in Lebanon imply for democracy, especially with respect to personal status matters such as marriage, divorce, and inheritance? Similarly, consider the examples of Turkey and Egypt where a certain category of "foreignness" – in spite of its different connotations – is attributed to non-Muslims (excluding Coptic Christians in Egypt). However, this seeming similarity in categorizations belies the fact that the management of these categories is completely different in these two contexts: recognition of non-Muslims in a limbo between individual citizens and members of a religious community in Turkey versus recognition of non-Muslims in Egypt as communal members.

I argue here, contrary to Hansen's view, that the importance of these hybrid forms of state recognition in understanding democratization is not limited to postcolonial states especially in the context of increasing immigration to the Western countries. Take for instance the debates on headscarves in France. Taylor (2002, p. 13) draws attention to the contradictory situation in which "head-scarves were refused, but other French girls often wear, e.g., a cross around their necks, and this was unchallenged." Taylor (*ibid.*) continues this point with the observation that this naive faith in "the religious 'invisibility' of the cross" in which France is depicted "as a 'post-Christian' society, following centuries of Christian culture" stems from an equally naive belief in the neutrality of the decision that is "guaranteed by its emerging from some principle or procedure."

The question at issue here once again boils down to what constitutes society, and how different parts of it are managed by the state. The salient conflict in the headscarf debate in effect reflects another tension between French Muslims, who constitute a subnational community, and French Christians as atomistic individuals who make up the very essence of French nation in the eyes of the state (Bowen, 2008). Therefore, the real tension is between management of individual citizens that make up the French "community of equals" and of the handling subnational communities which are perceived by the state as not sharing the common culture of the French nation.[3]

Overall, the analytical framework explicated here suggests the necessity of deconstructing democratization as two separate yet related realms of action: discourse and practice. Differentiating these realms is essential to understanding the continual tensions between inclusionary and exclusionary tendencies within democratization. These tendencies are managed differently in different contexts due to the hybrid forms of state recognition that form the historical matrix of state–society relations. Therefore, making sense of democracy discourse and practice at a particular time requires understanding the historical peculiarities of these relations.

## DISCOURSE, PRACTICE, AND ETHNOGRAPHY

This chapter is a historical and ethnographic account of the political effects of the increasingly salient democracy discourse adopted by the AKP government during its first two administrations, from 2002 through 2011 in relation to Istanbul's Rum Orthodox community, which currently includes both Greek and Arabic speakers. Ethnographic method is useful for two reasons. First, it enables the researcher to locate and comprehend the gap between democracy discourse and practice. "Logic of discourse" (Wedeen, 2009, p. 90) can only be understood by situating it in relation to what it speaks for and against, and for whom. Such placement is only possible through an analysis of the historical matrix of state–society relations. This is because the audience that the discourse appeals to, and the one that it challenges, is in a historically constituted contingent relationship.

A second way in which ethnography helps the researcher is in understanding the political effects of the democracy discourse on marginalized populations. In fact, the tension between against and for whom/what the democracy discourse speaks shapes the everyday politics of marginalized populations. Through close observation of these everyday politics, ethnographic inquiry helps to make sense of the ambiguous ways in which the democracy discourse infuses, alters, and/or perpetuates practices. These ambiguities appear paradoxical to the bare eye, whereas they are inevitable to the ethnographer because the long-term participatory observation, coupled with historical research, enable the researcher to map them.

This ethnography combines (i) participatory observation within the Rum Orthodox community in Istanbul during the course of the period 2008 through 2011, obtained by attending community events in addition to conducting 25 interviews with community leaders, (ii) review of newspapers (i.e., *Zaman, Radikal, Milliyet, Hürriyet, Birgün*) and policy documents from national and international NGOs and the EU from 2002 till 2011, and (iii) historical analysis of the relations between the state and non-Muslim minority communities through parliamentary repositories, newspaper reviews, and personal stories.

## BECOMING A "MINORITY" AT THE MARGINS:
## HISTORICAL CONTEXT

The rise of Christian nationalisms[4] in the Balkans during the nineteenth century, together with the rise of the Wilsonian principle of self-determination during the early twentieth century, marked the birth of the Turkish nationalism in the early 1900s. The founding republican ethic of Turkey was based on two elements: its ethnic character, which associates being a Turk with being a Sunni Muslim, and its secular character, which is defined as the strict separation of religious and state affairs,[5] and the subsequent privatization of religion while yielding it to state control. Both of these elements were ruptures to the categories of belonging that were prevalent in Ottoman society, and the ways in which they were managed under Ottoman governance.

Ethnic and religious diversity in the empire was managed around the *millet*[6] system that was formally implemented during the *Tanzimat* (reorganization) era. The *Tanzimat* reforms were introduced in the nineteenth century with the aim of modernizing the empire and establishing unity among diverse ethnic and religious groups, especially at a time when Christian nationalisms in the Balkans were on the rise (Braude, 1982; Karpat, 1982). The Ottoman reformists attempted to integrate non-Muslims in particular ways by removing preexisting hierarchies within the system. To this end, private property, security, universal taxation,[7] and a universal citizenship identity, under the rubric of Ottomanism, were introduced into the matrix of state–society relations.

This movement toward what could be identified as the rudimentary beginnings of a modern, universal, atomistic citizenship regime simulta- neously coexisted with institutionalization of the *millet* system which classified the population around religious confessional lines. During the *Tanzimat* era, Jewish and Christian communities that were considered as the "people of the book" were consolidated into three main *millet*s besides the ruling Muslim *millet* (*millet-i hakime*): the Rum Orthodox *millet* which included Orthodox Christians who were linguistically clustered, e.g., Greek speakers, Arabic speakers, Albanian speakers, Romanian speakers, Russian speakers, Bulgarian speakers; the Armenian *millet*; and the Jewish *millet*. Each of these *millet*s was responsible for the self-administration of matters of law having to do with personal status, such as marriage, divorce, and inheritance, in addition to the governance of communal institutions such as hospitals and schools which were established by the edict of the Ottoman Sultan. Moreover, religious leaders of each *millet* assumed the role to represent their communities in front of the Sultan.

The transformation from religious *millet* to ethnic *millet* or from a religious-based community to a secular nation-state (Mardin, 1997, pp. 14–15) is central to the gradual transition from the Ottoman Empire to the Republic of Turkey. During this transition, the ruling *millet* of the empire, Sunni Muslims, was considered by the state elites to be the core of the Turkish nation (Altınay, 2004; Yeğen, 2004). These changes in the connotations and perceptions of the *millet* also gradually changed the categories of belonging, and thus the ways different religious and ethnic groups within the society related to each other. In this context non-Muslims were gradually excluded from the "community of equals" that constituted the nation.

In the realm of formal procedural rights, things unfolded slightly differently. The rights of the remaining non-Muslims were also regulated by the Lausanne Treaty, which founded the Republic of Turkey.[8] Articles 39 and 40 guaranteed equal citizenship rights to the remaining non-Muslims who were reclassified in the Treaty as "minorities." The importance of Lausanne was, however, not limited to its impact on individual non-Muslim citizens of the Republic. Articles 40 through 42 also acknowledged and protected their communal rights along the lines of the *millet* classification system.

For instance, Article 42 granted non-Muslim communities the right to apply their own canonical laws, in continuation of the *millet* system, in personal status matters as listed earlier. Immediately after the establishment of the republic, the single party government of the time, in 1925, assumed the task of negotiating with the Rum Orthodox, Armenian, and Jewish communities the possibility of renouncing their rights granted by the Article.[9] From a legal viewpoint, this can be interpreted as an attempt by state elites to avoid a potential legal pluralism, which was a prominent characteristic of the way population(s) was managed under Ottoman governance.[10] It was also part of the secularization reforms of the period that included the unification of education in 1924, the introduction of a European style family law in 1926, and the abolishment of the Caliphate in 1924 (Zürcher, 2010, p. 145). All these reforms targeting at secularizing and unifying the legal system contributed to the privatization of religion.[11] As a result, non-Muslims were formally integrated into the homogenous, unified legal system of the republic under the social contract that managed relations between the state and its individual citizens.

Legal integration of non-Muslim citizens, however, did not necessarily translate into their social integration as a result of the state's assimilation policies of the first two decades of the republic. For example, nationwide language campaigns, "Citizen, speak Turkish!" (*"Vatandaş Türkçe Konuş!"*), organized by the state in the 1920s and 1930s forced non-Muslim citizens not to speak any language other than Turkish in public. Moreover, series of employment laws legislated during the same time also aimed at Turkification of the economy, significantly harming non-Muslim businesses and their

employment in foreign companies (Bali, 1999, pp. 206–225). Dispropor-
tionate application of the Wealth Tax in 1942 on non-Muslims is another
example of such economic policies (Akgönül, 2007, pp. 119–120).

These assimilationist policies of the early republic occasioned accelerated
popular nationalist adaptation within society during the multiparty era.[12]
Later, during the 1950s and 1960s, for instance, language campaigns were
once again a source of tension for non-Muslims. This time, however,
ordinary citizens instead of the state organized these campaigns hanging
fliers on the streets to be later removed by the police (Bali, 2009, p. 67). The
pogrom and looting of shops and houses owned and occupied by non-
Muslims in Istanbul on September 6 and 7, 1955, which was later on proven
to be plotted by the state, is another example of the diminishing social
integration of non-Muslims (Akgönül, 2007; Bali, 1999, 2009; Güven, 2005;
Kuyucu, 2005; Oran, 2004; Vryonis, 2005).

Non-Muslims in Turkey were therefore left in a liminal zone between
inclusion as legally recognized citizens and exclusion from the nation as
foreigners. Hybrid forms of state recognition of non-Muslims as individual
citizens and members of their communities filled this liminality between
their inclusion and exclusion, especially in the multiparty era. For example,
adamant state denial during the early republic of religious leaders as the
representatives of the communities (Akgönül, 2007, p. 71; Miroğlu, 2009,
p. 36) was reversed during the multiparty era, especially under the Democrat
Party (DP) rule between 1950 and 1960, as was evident through the
increasing salience in the newspapers of encounters between the religious
leaders of the communities and the state.

Deployment of religion by political actors under electoral pressures in
multiparty era also brought about populist practices of secularism (Akan,
2005, 2011; Azak, 2010).[13] Significant concessions were granted to the
communities especially during the 1950s. For example, Rum Orthodox
Patriarch Athenagoras, who was based in the United States and did not
hold Turkish citizenship, was enthroned in 1949. Soon after his arrival, the
Patriarch Athenagoras renounced his American citizenship and adopted
the Turkish nationality (Bali, 2009, p. 247). Moreover, for the first time since
the establishment of the republic, the state allowed a patriarch to visit the
community schools and to publicly involve in the community matters (*ibid.*).
Similarly, the Rum Orthodox Patriarchate "was allowed to reestablish its
own press bureau and a second weekly theological journal began to be
printed in 1951" (*ibid.*).

Patriarch Karekin Haçaduryan was also enthroned as the Armenian
Patriarch around the same time in 1951 and he remained in office until 1961.

14                                                           SINEM ADAR

Bebiroğlu (2009) notes that the Armenian Patriarchate received much
attention from the state during this time period, more than it received
anytime before during the history of the republic. Similar to the Rum
Patriarch Athenagoras, Haçaduryan was also allowed to publish a periodical
named as Şoğagat in 1952. A stark example of the concessions given by
the state to the Armenian community was the opening of an Armenian
theological high school, Surp Haç Tıbrevank,[14] in 1953 with the purpose of
bringing Armenian children from Anatolia to Istanbul and training some as
clergy.[15]

The opening of Surp Haç Tıbrevank is particularly important considering
that it was not possible to establish community institutions, especially *vakıfs*,
after 1926 in accordance with the new regulations over associational life. The
school was therefore opened under the administration of an independent
*vakıf*. As a gesture, state officials even visited the school after its opening.
For instance, the mayor of Istanbul Fahrettin Kerim Gökay's visit in
March 1954 was welcomed with great zeal by the community.[16]

Besides these seemingly positive developments toward non-Muslim
communities during the 1950s, the early phase of multiparty politics,
however, a substantive discussion of expanding democratic freedoms and
rights to individual non-Muslim citizens was lacking. Moreover, state
policies and practices continued to contribute to the fragmentation of the
communal realm in the 1970s. Co-optation of community elites by the state
and state confiscation of communal property especially after 1974 are two
such examples. Non-Muslim community institutions were given the legal
status of *vakıf*[17] by the Law of *Vakıfs* that was legislated in 1936. Following
the legislation of this law, the Turkish state made a request asking for the
whole list of property owned by *vakıfs*, with the primary aim of designing
policies to keep the wealth, especially that which was administered by
Muslims, under control (Oran, 2004, p. 84). Non-Muslim *vakıfs* were
however different from their Muslim counterparts, which were established
with a written legal document called *vakfiye*, i.e., a code of rules and
regulations outlining the organizational structure and the aims of *vakıfs*, as
stated by their founder.

Non-Muslim *vakıfs*, on the other hand, were mostly founded during the
Ottoman era upon the edict of the Sultan. The absence of a *vakfiye* therefore
prepared the grounds for justifying state confiscation of non-Muslim
communal property especially since 1974. During the peak of the Greco-
Turkish conflict over Cyprus in 1974, the General Directorate of *Vakıfs*
(GDV), the main government institution responsible from controlling *vakıf*
activities, asked for the *vakfiye* of each non-Muslim *vakıf*. Not only that

*vakıf*s did not have such a written document as previously explained, but also that it was not possible to found new *vakıf*s, as Article 101[18] of Turkish civil law prohibited the establishment of any association or institution by any ethnic or religious community. Under these legal limitations, GDV, based on the 1936 declaration of non-Muslim *vakıf*s, began confiscating properties acquired between 1936 and 1974.[19] As a result, state's systematic measures to confiscate communal properties since 1974 till recently significantly deprived communities from resources.

These challenges brought non-Muslim citizens of Turkey to the realization of their exclusion from the "community of equals," while at the same time they were also deprived from their own communal safety nets. In other words, the "secular" nature of the republican ethic meant that the state was able to deprive non-Muslims of their communities while at the same time never fully integrating them as equal members of the nation. Unsurprisingly, the non-Muslim population in Istanbul has been declining dramatically, especially after 1964, when the conflict between the Turkish and Greek governments over Cyprus was highly heated. The government at the time asked Greek citizens living in Turkey, according the provisions of an agreement signed between Turkey and Greece in 1930, to leave (Akgönül, 2007, p. 262). At the time, many Greek-speaking Rum Orthodox citizens of Turkey were married to Greek citizens residing in Turkey under the provisions of this agreement. Therefore, with those Greek citizens who left, many Greek-speaking Rum Orthodox citizens of Turkey also left.

There are no reliable statistical data on the demographic trends within the Rum Orthodox community. However, school records at an aggregate level show that the number of students at Rum schools decreased from 6757 to 2469 within the period of 1964–1974 when emigration, mostly to Greece, was at its peak.[20] This decrease intensified after 1974, due to the intense political and social turmoil within the country during the period of 1970 through the mid-1980s, and consequently the demographic tilt toward an aging Rum Orthodox community. The total number of students in Rum schools in Istanbul, in the academic year of 2006–2007, was 212. The total population of the community today is estimated to be around 2500 to 3000 people living mainly in Istanbul, the Princess Islands, and on two islands in the Aegean Sea, in addition to the recent Arabic-speaking Rum Orthodox migrants from the southern city of Antakya (Antioch) and its surroundings.[21] *Kurtuluş* (*Tatavla* in Greek) and *Beyoğlu* (*Pera* in Greek) are currently the two main districts in which the Rum Orthodox population is concentrated, compared to its relative dispersion in other parts of Istanbul.

# DEMOCRACY DISCOURSE WITHIN THE STATE

The new law on *vakıf*s which was legislated in 2008 came as a relief in this contested environment of partial entitlements and marginalization. When Prime Minister Erdoğan accepted the *iftar*[22] invitation of the non-Muslim communities in August 2011, the communities were "once more assured of the goodwill of the AKP government," as expressed on different occasions by community members. When Erdoğan was invited to the stage during the dinner, he started his talk by stressing the uniqueness of Istanbul's multicultural history – a city where the three monotheistic religions coexisted for centuries; where mosques, churches, and synagogues stood side-by-side in the same street. According to Erdoğan, the AKP government's efforts "to solve the problems of non-Muslim communities" were inspired by this shared culture of historical coexistence.[23]

It is against this background that he announced at the *iftar* meal that the government would return back all the community properties confiscated since 1974 on the condition that an official application was to be filed within a period of 12 months:

> In the meantime, we are continuing with the repairs to various churches and synagogues around the country. In addition, we are also determined to solve enduring problems concerning the non-Muslim minority communities. [...] We extended the period for filing applications to reclaim ownership of immovable property. Moreover, the Press Association (*Basın İlan Kurumu*) decided to provide monetary aid, until the completion of regulatory legal changes, to six community newspapers that have been facing difficulties to maintain business. We are still working on changes that will allow these newspapers to make use of public announcements. I gave the necessary instructions to undertake these changes. I believe that you are aware of the fact that a new sociopolitical atmosphere has been created in the country as a result of all these steps taken. I strongly believe that the coming stage of drafting a *civil* constitution with the *participation* of different sectors and groups within the society, as opposed to the *top-down* nature of the 1982 Constitution that was drafted following the 1980 *coup d'état*, will be a turning point in the history of our country (emphasis added).[24]

Erdoğan's comparison between the 1982 Constitution, drafted by the military, and the one that is currently in preparation through the participation of different groups within society is central to understanding the context in which AKP's democracy discourse emerged. This discourse was diligently sewn up and legitimized through continual revocation of the military-civilian duality. This dualism symbolized the clash of the "old" regime – the Kemalist regime – that was "non-civilian," and therefore, "undemocratic," and a new "civilian" and "democratic" regime under the leadership of the AKP government. The political conjuncture of accession negotiations with the European Union that officially started on October 3, 2005, also facilitated the common public use of this binary discourse by the AKP government. The AKP party program is demonstrative of this inclusive and multicultural pro-democracy discourse:

> Our Party sees and embraces all citizens of the Republic of Turkey as first class citizens, regardless of differences in religion, language, sect, regional origin, ethnic origin or gender. In our democratic understanding there is no obligation for differences to be converted to one another. This is the *culture of differences* living together in peace, filtered through *our experience in history*. Protecting the oppressed from the oppressor is one of our crucial principles. Thus, our program targets the peace and happiness of everyone, rather than the peace and happiness of just a group or a particular section within society (emphasis added).[25]

In fact, the AKP's systematic adoption of these binary categories, such as oppressor versus oppressed, military versus civilian, sameness versus difference, and undemocratic versus democratic, was a legitimizing source for its claims on political power and the democratization of state–society relations. It is in this context that the AKP's claims to political inclusivity, to market reform policies, in addition to social policies such as the transformation of the health system, gained the party increasing support in all consecutive elections from 2002 through 2011, among a broad section of society, ranging from liberal businessmen to intellectuals who had a skeptical view of the Kemalist republican ethic; from an increasingly strong, pious urban middle and upper-middle classes, especially in Anatolia, to radical Islamists who were economically marginalized since the implementation of neoliberal economic policies during the 1980s (Tuğal, 2009).

Given the long suppressive and contentious history of the republican ethic, not only with respect to Islamists in Turkey (Azak, 2010; Tuğal, 2009; Zürcher, 1993), but also with respect to any dissident that poses a challenge to the hegemonic power of the republican ethic, the AKP's successive electoral victories in 2002, 2007, and 2011 were largely an outcome of the party's success in publicly challenging the terms of the debate by positioning itself in opposition to the military, one of the most prominent guardian institutions of the republican ethic besides the bureaucracy and the judiciary (Öktem, 2011a). As such, the party was able to emerge as a political actor that embraced and was willing to represent formerly excluded sectors within society. In a way, the party's democracy discourse created a space that made a critical public discussion of the long-standing state suppression toward dissidents possible.[26] An evaluation of to what extent this claim and the accompanying democracy discourse that the AKP government adopted to assert this claim are in harmony with its policies and practices requires a glance at the historical context within which the AKP came to power.

Although the AKP as a political party came out of the previously excluded Islamist movements and political parties of the 1990s, its ideological orientation both converges toward and diverges from the Kemalist republican ethic. The AKP shares its ethnoreligious understanding of national identity that associates Turkishness with Sunni Muslim identity. Among the manifestations of its adherence to the ethnoreligious character of nationalism are its policies toward Kurds and Alevis during the time period under scrutiny here, and its ambivalent position and reluctance in thoroughly pursuing justice in the trial for the murder of Armenian journalist Hrant Dink[27] in 2007 by manipulating evidence and solely focusing on the assassination itself without taking the events prior to it that turned Dink into a target (Akan, 2012).[28] Erdoğan's spontaneous remarks in a recent TV interview aired before the general elections in June 2011 about the government's increasing suppression of freedoms of speech and expression imply the cognitive internalization of the ethnoreligious character of national identity:

> There are severe insults in the media that are directed to me. There are also many books written about President Abdullah Gül and myself. These books refer to us as Jews, Armenians, and – I beg your pardon (*çok affedersiniz!*[29]) – even Rums. Can you imagine? They are writing these books. What can you do to these people? The only way is to use the judiciary system. Is there any other choice?[30]

On the other hand, the AKP departs from the republican ethic in its approach to religion, which increasingly became a matter of political contention in the multiparty era.[31] The aim here is not to oversimplify this contentiousness by reducing it to a tension between secularists and anti-secularists (or even Islamists). Such duality only partially represents the reality because of the multiplicity of actors and varying perceptions as to what constitutes "secularism" (Akan, 2005, 2011; Azak, 2010; Turam, 2004). Nevertheless, one notable point is that this contentiousness became salient in the midst of the electoral concerns contained in the reality of multiparty politics in a society where a significant portion of voters were still living in rural Anatolia by the mid-1940s/early 1950s, for whom the gap between religion as a cultural practice and secularism as a state ideology was still significant (Keyman, 2007, p. 223).

While a detailed account of this conflict is beyond the scope of this chapter, the parallel between the DP, which was in power between 1950 and 1960, and the AKP, in terms of their approach to religion and its role in politics, is important.[32] Understanding this parallel also contributes to unraveling the transformation of the relationship between the state and non-Muslim communities under the AKP government. The "alternative secularism" (Azak, 2010) of the DP was cautious about the Kemalist project of the first two decades of the republic, whose aim was de-Islamization of the public realm. Mainly driven by electoral concerns that were manifest in "populist and paternalistic policies for the rural poor" (Öktem, 2011b, p. 41), the DP's attitude toward religion symbolized a shift toward "a discourse promoting religious piety and social conservatism" (*ibid.*) or the "sacraliza-tion and de-privatization of religion" (Keyman, 2007).[33]

This shift aimed to change the perception of religion and its relationship in and to public life. Readoption of Arabic as the language of *ezan* (the call to prayer) by DP in 1950 and the incorporation of voluntary religious classes in 1947 by *Cumhuriyet Halk Partisi* (the Republican People's Party, "CHP" hereafter) under electoral pressures by the DP are two prominent examples of this shift. Moreover, as mentioned earlier, it was during this time that non-Muslim communities were granted state concessions and their religious leaders engaged in encounters with the state officials, as the primary repre-sentatives of their respective communities. This stands in stark contrast to the strict opposition during the first two decades of the republic to any form of interaction with religious leaders of non-Muslim communities.[34]

Unsurprisingly, policies of the AKP were consciously legitimized and contextualized within the same democracy discourse that explicitly challenges the hegemonic rule of the republican ethic. Indeed, the party program of the AKP shows many similarities to the "alternative secularism" of the DP throughout the 1950s. In this context the AKP government gained support from the Rum Orthodox community, just as the DP did during the 1950s. Rum Orthodox community members often attributed this support to the strong position the AKP government took against the marginalizing effects of the Kemalist republican ethic on non-Muslim communities. Moreover, on the basis of this "alternative secularism," the AKP government undertook positive measures in the relationship between the state and non-Muslim communities. The effects of these measures on the Rum Orthodox community are explored in the next section, before they are considered within the larger picture of the persisting gap between the AKP's democracy discourse and its practices.

## DEMOCRACY DISCOURSE WITHIN THE RUM ORTHODOX COMMUNITY

Democracy discourse within the Rum Orthodox community emerged in the midst of this changing discursive space and the contradictory practices of the state. Rum Orthodox community leaders emphasized during our conversations a shift in their interactions with the state from being "scared and on guard all the time" to "being able to communicate much more easily." Reflections of this changing perception seem also to appear in everyday encounters of community members with their fellow citizens, especially regarding the use of *vakıf* land and property. In one such incident, non-Rum residents of the neighborhood came to discuss the future of a *vakıf* property that a friend of theirs had been using without paying rent for years. They came to complain about the newly elected *vakıf* administration because it started to demand rent. Listening to them, the *vakıf* president responded by saying:

> It is okay to live on that land for years without even thinking that he needed to compensate us for using our land. The rules changed now. It is now time for transparency and accountability.

Many members of the community interpret *vakıf* elections as a movement toward transparency, accountability, and, ultimately, toward more democracy within the community. It is not surprising that the photos of election day(s) cover the walls of *vakıf* buildings as symbols of the hope for a real shift toward democratization, as the president of one of the *vakıf*s expressed:

> I hung this photo [a photo of himself taken while voting] that was taken on the day we ran elections in our *vakıf* because my friends and I see the elections as the beginning of a new era which would bring democracy, and therefore, rejuvenate the community spirit.

The post-elections era was perceived to have two interrelated implications for the community within the context of changing state–society relations in Turkey. First, many community leaders saw it an opportunity to combat corruption within the community. Second, the rise of attempts at reforms within the community embodied the hopes of the community for the demarginalization of non-Muslim communities alongside transformation of existing citizenship practices. As one community leader suggested:

> To overcome corruption within the community, we should struggle through the *language of rights*. I am a citizen of this country and I want my rights. I don't want just tolerance. I don't want anyone to come to me with the language of tolerance. Just give me my rights. We recently ran elections in our *vakıf*s, and there is a new wave of fresh air within the community, which would open up space for the language of rights (emphasis added).

"Keeping the community spirit alive" was often the metaphor for increasing transparency and accountability within the community, not only in its relations with state officials but also in daily encounters with fellow citizens. One strategy adopted by community leaders to this end was to attract the attention of non-Rums in Turkey as well as Rums originally from Istanbul who left the city beginning in the mid-1960s either for Greece or somewhere else. To this end, one of the community associations set up an email group to facilitate communication networks between Rums living in Istanbul and those who had emigrated to Greece.[35] This email group was influential in getting Greek youth to visit Istanbul. The association also provided services to assist travelers, including accommodations in *vakıf*-owned properties, volunteering opportunities, and training in the Turkish language. As noted by the president of the association, young and open-minded people, both Greek and non-Greek, were seen as a force for change within the community as well as within the country:

> [The] young population is open to living together. They don't think within the same limited circles. Therefore, I think, there is hope for the country.

For the same purpose of "showing Rums living in Greece that there is still a vibrant Rum Orthodox community in the *City*,"[36] the members of this community association organized a three-day conference in 2006 entitled "Meeting in Istanbul: The Past and the Present," where 300 people, including Rums, both in Istanbul and from the diaspora, and Turks, attended the conference. Community leaders often referred to the conference as the second turning point, elections being the first, in the democratization of the community. One member of the association who participated in the conference described it in the following words:

> I find the conference very useful not because it attracted the attention of Rums of Istanbul who are not living here anymore but also we had the opportunity to discuss our own problems. There has been chaos in the community for a while due to the lack of unity and structure. The conference at least enabled us to coherently put our problems in perspective.

Its main goals, as carefully defined by its organizers, were to portray the demographic structure of the community, as well as to discuss the problems it faced especially within the context of *vakıfs*. One of its organizers cautiously noted the lengthy meetings with state officials to get the required permissions for the conference:

> I worked very hard to get the *confidence* of the state officials. It was very difficult especially because of the preceding conferences on Armenian and Kurdish problems. I met with state officials many times and convinced them that our conference would not be the third step of these preceding two conferences. The aim of our conference was to make the voice of the community audible, and therefore, to make the community visible, especially to Rums of Istanbul currently living in Greece and to Greeks.

Despite the emerging, vocal commitments to democracy within the community, its members are still extremely cautious regarding their relationship with the state. This is reflected in the quote above, which shows the persistence of the historically constituted suspicions and fears that stem from the existing categories of belonging. This is evident in the hesitations of a community member about the possibility of applying to a special EU fund[37] targeted to improve democratic practices and human rights in Turkey:

> I will research this. The only thing that I did not like is the title of the program. I feel like any activity organized under the title of democracy and human rights might create an image of complaining and enforcement. Of course, I have not read the full content of the program. Nevertheless, as you already know very well, our extreme sensitivity to interpretation and perception of things is a natural outcome of the long-lasting sensitivities.

The emphasis here on the long-lasting sensitivities was in a way to recall the long history of exclusion of non-Muslims from the nation as foreigners who had to continuously prove their loyalty to the state. Unwanted citizens of the republic, non-Muslims in Turkey, were in a continuous state of anxiety as the above-mentioned quote clearly demonstrates. In this light, President Abdullah Gül's, who was a former AKP member, comments in January 2012 about the fairness of the legal system during the trials of Dink's assassination reflects AKP's adherence to ethnoreligious national identity. Gül noted that "the justice system treats everyone as equal in Turkey, including foreign companies and individuals of foreign origin (*yabancı uyruklu insanlar*),"[38] referring to non-Muslim citizens of Turkey.

Such gap between the AKP's democracy discourse and its practice therefore continued to incite anxieties of the members of Rum Orthodox community despite the increasing euphoria about democratization of the community institutions. Discursive aspirations within the community toward further democratization were certainly made possible through the democracy discourse and practices adopted by the AKP toward non-Muslim communities. Nevertheless, the mismatch between the universalism of discourse and the AKP's adherence to republican ethic's ethnoreligious interpretation of national identity limited the AKP's democratization attempts to the communal realm. It significantly failed to transform the existing exclusionary notions of national identity, and thus failed to reform the relationship between the state and its non-Muslim citizens. The fears and hesitations in contacts between non-Muslim citizens and the state, as expressed above, emerged in the context of this cognitive dissonance.

# THE SIMULTANEITY OF DÉ JÀ VU AND NEW FORMS OF HIERARCHY

Old and new claims for representation within the Rum Orthodox community emerged in this environment where the AKP's democratization attempts toward non-Muslims were limited to the communal realm without initiating a substantive debate about the ethnoreligious understanding of national identity that rendered non-Muslim citizens foreigners throughout the history of the republic. As a result, intra-communal hierarchies stemming from the historical legacies of co-optation of community elites by the state remained intact. While at the same time, they also contributed to new hierarchies within the community on the basis of historically embedded ethnolinguistic divisions within it, between its Greek- and Arabic-speaking members. These claims became salient during the *vakıf* elections that put the question of representation within the community at stake.

The Rum Orthodox community was known to be part of the bourgeois class during the Ottoman Empire (Keyder, 1987), and thus it had significant communal wealth, mostly in the form of land and property. The community continued to administer this wealth through the *vakıf*s during the republic. This arrangement, however, was subject to extensive state regulation to an accelerating degree, especially since 1974, as mentioned earlier. For instance, "Not having a regularly functioning administrative board" was a technical legal designation often used by the state to appropriate *vakıf* properties. Moreover, the intervals between elections in Rum *vakıf*s were extremely variable and dependent on the whims of the state. For instance, the granting of the state's permission to hold elections in 2006 within the proceeding 4 years came after a lapse of 15 years, during which there was no change in the leadership of Rum *vakıf*s.[39]

In this context the state's discretionary control over *vakıf* elections, together with the aging demographics of the community,[40] led to the concentration of large amounts of wealth under the control of few *vakıf*s, which encouraged *vakıf* administrations, especially the wealthy ones, to consider community institutions as their personal fiefdoms. This sense of entitlement was also perpetuated through the co-optation of some community leaders by the state. In this way, arbitrary and bureaucratic state regulation was fragmenting the Rum Orthodox community in such a way as to ensure the reproduction of state regulation over the *vakıf*s. It was also preventing the community from developing a safety net for their members, as mentioned above.

Although elections were perceived by many in the community as an opportunity to change the existing structure, they also perpetuated the already existing divisions and hierarchies. In fact, not all community leaders welcomed elections with the same eagerness, and not every *vakıf* ran elections. This situation created controversies within the community itself. In the midst of such contestations, an interview with a *vakıf* president criticizing another *vakıf*'s appeal to the European Human Rights Court (EHRC) for the state's seizure of its orphanage was published in *Hürriyet* newspaper. The following excerpt from the interview is demonstrative of the fragmentation and divisions within the community:

> If I am in need, I will go to the government and ask for money from the state budget. Of course, I cannot decide on another *vakıf*'s actions. But, I consider its application to EHRC a *disloyal act to the nation*. Our *vakıf*s are Turkish. I cannot complain to foreigners about the acts of my state. I have faith in the legal system of the state, the Supreme Court and the government. I, as a citizen of the Republic of Turkey, will not beg anyone. We will solve our problem within ourselves, there is no need to go and ask for help from foreigners (emphasis added).[41]

This interview, titled "Citizen Dimitri,"[42] was interpreted within the community as a political move by the president of the *vakıf* who gave the interview to push back against pressures to run elections. He employed the rhetoric of loyalty to the state, reinforcing the historically established fear and suspicion of the state toward the community and vice versa. This example demonstrates that old hierarchical forms within the community were provoked during the elections. It also demonstrates the impact of these hierarchies in perpetuating state regulation over the community.

Alongside these old hierarchies, elections also provoked new divisions within the community, especially along ethnolinguistic lines, due primarily to the challenges posed by the changing demographics of the community. The opening ceremony of summer camp for the poor or disadvantaged children of the community at the Rum monastery at *Kınalıada*, one of the Princess islands of Istanbul, is emblematic of these divisions.

The administration of the monastery had been transferred to the GDV in 1968, as the monastery's *vakıf* did not have a regularly functioning administrative board. However, the Rum Orthodox Patriarchate continued to organize its annual summer camp for the poor and disadvantaged children of the community as it had done since 1938. In 2005, the GDV asked the patriarchate for a written statement that would confirm that they had taken over the place from the state only for the period during which the summer camp operated. The patriarchate demurred, arguing that the monastery belonged to the community. As a result, the camp was not allowed to operate in the following year. Finally, in the summer of 2008, the community got permission to resume organizing its summer camp on that site.

Following this decision, community leaders had decided to organize a colorful opening with traditional Greek music and dance, mostly from mainland Greece and the Greek islands, to celebrate the resumption of summer camp following this long struggle with the state. Community members including prominent religious and political figures were all present at the celebrations. Children were running all around the garden with joy and excitement. As I was watching them play, I heard one of the community members sitting next to me saying:

> Without them [pointing to a group of children whom I later on learned that were from Antakya], our community would by now be miserable. They saved us!

The Arabic-speaking Rum Orthodox began migrating to Istanbul from the southern city of Antakya (Antioch)[43] during the 1980s. The Greek-speaking community in Istanbul, under the leadership of the Patriarchate, strongly encouraged their immigration to the city by providing welfare benefits such as employment in the churches, accommodation, and health care at Rum hospitals. To further aid their passage, their legal status as members of the Rum Orthodox community enabled them to register their children at community schools.

The relatively young demographic and high reproductive rates of the Antakya Rum community were strong motivations for the Greek-speaking Rums of Istanbul to encourage their migration. Yet after their initial welcome, the continuing presence of Arabic-speaking Rums from Antakya gradually became a contested issue within the community, especially in the everyday encounters between the Greek and Arabic speakers. During the fieldwork period of this research, from 2008 till 2011, there was a noticeable shift in the attitude of community leaders toward Arabic-speaking Rums. They became increasingly critical of the cultural differences between Greek- and Arabic-speaking Rums. As perceived by Greek-speakers, these cultural differences were mainly of between urban Istanbul and rural Anatolia, often referred to in ordinary parlance as *taşra*.

As the sensitivity to these differences became more acute, language became a critical barrier in everyday encounters. Not speaking Greek, the Rums of Antakya have faced prejudice from within the community. For example, there was the rumor that the declining performance of Rum schools was due to the increasing numbers of students of Arab origin.

The "Citizen, speak Turkish!" campaigns of the 1920s were echoed by the Greek-speaking Rums in their attempts to promote the speaking of Greek. The following incident exemplifies this shift. On Sunday mornings, community members got together in the church garden following the liturgy to have tea and pastries. On the Sunday in question, both Greek and Arabic speakers were present at the church since it was an important feast day. Antakya children were running and playing with each other in the garden. At some point, one of them called her mother, in Turkish ("Anne"[44]). An old Greek-speaking lady immediately interfered, addressing the mother: "My Friend, Speak Greek! Do not say Anne, but Mama!" Moreover, the Greek-speaking Rums were also quite adamant in keeping the language of liturgy in Greek despite the increasing demand by the Arabic-speakers for performing the liturgy in Arabic. An Arabic-speaking Rum noted the following:

> We cannot ask to do liturgy in Arabic, we get accused of wanting to divide the community. We do not want them to pay for it, we can arrange to get a priest from our village and we pay for him.

Greek-speaking Rums' image of the community as a homogenous entity gave Arabic-speaking Rums a political identity (Laclau, 1994). The politicization of this ethnolinguistic division became even fiercer in the context of elections. The question of representation, culture, and recognition became conflated with the singular problem of communal identity. As Arabic-speaking Rums of Antakya, especially the young ones, started showing interest in joining *vakıf* administrations, tensions between the Greek-speaking and Arabic-speaking segments of the community emerged. Exemplifying this tension was the election fraud complaint to the police by Greek-speaking Rums that Arabic-speaking Rums brought their relatives and friends from Antakya to vote in the elections of one of the *vakıfs*. According to the Law on *Vakıfs*, only community members who reside in Istanbul can vote in the elections. Although narrated to me by one of the community leaders as a rumor, on the morning of the elections Rums from Antakya had arrived at the *vakıf* garden in large numbers:

> Seeing them all dressed in *şalvar*s,[45] some of our community members thought that they brought people from Antakya just to make sure that their own candidate was elected. Acting on this suspicion, they applied to the police to cancel the elections due to potential fraud undertaken by Rums of Antakya. Upon this, the police checked the status of residency of all who voted in the elections. They found that those with *şalvar*s were all Rums of Antakya who were residing in Istanbul.

AKP's policies toward non-Muslims, primarily targeting the communal realm, contributed to politicization of ethnolinguistic division within the community that was attributed an imagined homogeneity by its Greek-speaking members. At first glance, these policies appear to relax the enduring limitations imposed by the state on non-Muslims. However, they failed to transform the relationship between the state and non-Muslim citizens. Instead, democratization attempts by the AKP toward non-Muslims were confined to the communal realm. This gap between the universally inclusive democratic discourse of the AKP and its selective democracy practice left the hierarchies within the community untouched. In other words, the AKP's strong adherence to the ethnic element of the nationalist ideology left categories of belonging intact. On the other hand, the AKP's emphasis on religious piety and social conservatism revoked historical legacies of management under Ottoman governance that confined the relationship between the state and its non-Muslim citizens to the communal realm along religious confessional lines.

## CONCLUSION

Democratization is a complicated, messy process, especially in places where hybrid forms of state recognition mark state–society relations. Unmasking the seemingly paradoxical democratization efforts by the AKP government and their ambiguous implications for the Rum Orthodox community in Istanbul, this chapter emphasized the importance of deconstructing democratization as an analytical exercise into the categorization of population, on the one hand, and the management of society, on the other. It argued that such a separation is important because, first, it allows the researcher to distinguish democracy discourse from practice. Second, it contributes to the ability to contextualize democratization in space and time.

Putting the political effects of AKP's democratization attempts on the Rum Orthodox community in Istanbul in comparison with other religious and ethnic groups further demonstrates the applicability of the theoretical framework developed in this chapter. The AKP's adamant adherence to the ethnoreligious interpretations of national identity, while at the same time its revoking of the *millet* forms of managing society are manifest in its reluctance to grant communal rights to Alevis and Kurds who historically, as part of the Muslim *millet*, fell into the national boundaries. In the case of Armenians and Jews, the AKP's attempts to return confiscated properties extend to these communities as well. However, as the examples of Dink's assassination and trial process demonstrated, the gap between the AKP's democracy discourse and its practice remains in tact.

Overall, the findings in the chapter imply that politics lies within the gap between discourse and practice, where inclusion and exclusion simultaneously happen, leading to selective inclusion. Such a gap however is not unique to Turkey but exists in other places, from France, in the case of the veil, as discussed above in this chapter, to the United States, in the context of the marginalization of racial groups. The management of selective inclusion by political forces, however, differs significantly.

In France, this management takes a social contractual form, confining subnational communities to a continuous limbo between their existence as individual citizens and their membership in the community. At the other extreme is Canada where the social contractual relationship is central to the state's management of society, allowing for and codifying under the law the fact that cultural differences exist as part of the national identity. In contrast, the state's management of society in India mostly happens through communal lines of communication and authority. In spite of the existence of the social contract between the state and its individual citizens, the bulk of everyday life revolves around communal lines of communication as a result of state policies regarding the management of society.

Analysis of these different forms of societal management and how they came into being is important for better understanding the process of democratization. Democratization and its relation to the categorization of population, and the management of society are crucial questions with implications for what constitutes society and what knits it together. At a time when social and political cleavages within different societies are dangerously on the rise, these questions are especially important. Learning from different national contexts about forms of societal management sharpens the imagination for improving solidarity and peaceful coexistence.

# NOTES

1. "Beyond the Veil," *The Economist*, June 12, 2008.
2. The Rums (pronounced as "Rooms") are the adherents of the Rum Orthodox Church, which is the direct descendant of the state church of the Eastern Roman (or Byzantine) Empire. Following the conquest of Constantinople (Istanbul) by the Ottomans in 1453, the Orthodox subjects of the Roman Empire continued to live in the city as subjects of the Sultan, forming a distinct community of their own. Under the *millet* system that was institutionalized during the modernization efforts of the 1800s, non-Muslim communities were divided into three main *millet*s: Rum,

Armenian, and Jewish. The Rum *millet* historically included Orthodox Christians who were linguistically clustered, e.g., Greek speakers, Albanian speakers, Bulgarian speakers, and Arabic speakers. Among these, Greek speakers were the most powerful both in economic and political terms because of the essential role played by the Constantinople Patriarchate. Increasing linguistic awareness of different communities during the eighteenth century, as well as efforts to centralize the Ottoman administrative system during the eighteenth and nineteenth centuries, triggered national uprisings, mainly in the Balkans. Within this context, being Rum had come to be associated with "Greek-ness."

3. See Kastoryano (2002), Mandel (2003), and Al-Rustom (2013) for a discussion of state recognition of population in France in the context of some communities such as Jews, Algerians, and Armenians.

4. These nationalisms were premised on the strong association of religion, ethnicity/nationality, and language. For example, Greek-ness was closely tied to the membership in the Eastern Orthodox religion.

5. Akan (2005) demonstrates that the relationship between religion and state was defined and institutionalized differently throughout Turkish history. He argues that despite the separation discourse and the accompanying institutional arrangement during the first two decades of the republic, there has been a growing tendency especially in the multi-party era toward a civil religion tradition where religion was deployed under the control of the state as a tool of nurturing public morality.

6. The word *millet* comes from the Arabic word *millah* that means nation. Although there is still an ongoing unresolved debate among Ottoman historians concerning when the *millet* system was formally in operation during the empire, this debate is beyond the purposes of this chapter. What is at stake for my purposes here are the implications of such a system for managing diversity and coexistence (Barkey, 2008). Non-Muslim communities were organized during the empire as semiautonomous socio-political groups called *millet*s in which the religious leader of each millet community (i.e., Rum Orthodox, Armenian, or Jewish) represented the community before the sultan. The *millet*s also administered marriage, divorce, inheritance, and other social institutions including hospitals and schools.

7. Non-Muslims were subject to capitation – *jizya* – tax in the pre-*Tanzimat* era.

8. Under the Lausanne Treaty, the Turkish and Greek governments initiated a huge population exchange based on religious affiliations for the first time in modern history. For a comprehensive study of this exchange, see Yıldırım (2006) and Clark (2006). Under Lausanne, close to half a million Greek Muslims were forced to go to Turkey as "Turks" (because they were Muslims) and around 1.3 million Rum Orthodox were returned to Greece as "Greeks" (because they were Orthodox Christians). Arabic-speaking Rum Orthodox who were mainly living in Antakya (Antioch) were exempt from the population exchange due to Antakya's late inclusion in the Turkish Republic in 1939. The period from the Greek War of Independence in 1921 and the signing of the Lausanne Treaty in 1923 was one of wars. Continuous movement of people during this period significantly contributed to emptying Anatolia (Asiatic Turkey) from non-Muslims, while at the same time the Balkans were de-Islamicized (Öktem, 2011a; Zürcher, 2010). For instance, the 1911–1912 Balkan Wars and the ensuing "forced migration" of the Aegean Rum in 1913; the 1922–23 emigration of Rum Orthodox during the Independence Struggle in the aftermath of the 1919 Greek invasion of Smyrna. In addition, the Armenian population living in

30                                                                SINEM ADAR

the Ottoman Empire was exposed to systematic massacres throughout 1914–1915, and as a result, out of approximately 2 million Ottoman Armenians in 1914, between 65,000 and 75,000 remained as Turkish citizens (Al-Rustom, 2013, p. 3; Zürcher, 1993, p. 172). Today approximately 0.1% of the population of Turkey is non-Muslim. Rum Orthodox, Armenian, and the Jewish *millets* of the empire were accepted as the official minority communities of the Republic. The full text of the Lausanne Treaty can be found at http://www.mfa.gov.tr/lausanne-peace-treaty.en.mfa.

9. The author's interview with Bebiroğlu in August 2011. Also see Bebiroğlu (2009) at http://www.hyetert.com/yazi3.asp?s=1&Id=442&DilId=1. Also see Akgönül (2007, pp. 70, 71) and Alexandris (1992, pp. 135–139).

10. Such legal pluralism continued to exist in other post-Ottoman territories such as Syria, Lebanon, and Egypt, as well as in other postcolonial contexts such as India (Hansen, 1999).

11. Alexandris (1992, pp. 135–139) notes the reactions within the religious community from the religious leaders of the Greek-speaking Rum community in Istanbul to these secularization policies, especially the denouncement of Article 42.

12. I emphasize elsewhere the importance of not limiting politics merely to the interactions between state and its citizens, and treating everyday interactions among people, especially of different religious and ethnic identities, as a manifestation of politics that reflects categories of belonging (cf. Brubaker, Feischmidt, Fox, & Grancea, 2006; Hansen, 1999; Navaro-Yashin, 2002; Wedeen, 1999).

13. There is contention in the literature over whether the commitment of Kemalism was to secularism or laicism (Berkes, 1964, Parla & Davison, 2004). I choose to stick to the term secularism in this chapter mainly because I do not think that the issue is limited solely to the separation of religious affairs from state affairs. It is more complex and comprehensive than being an institutional problem, but is also a continual cognitive issue that covers all aspects of life (cf. Azak, 2010, p. 8).

14. See footnote number 9. Also, "Ermeni Ruhban Okulu Açılmıştır." *Milliyet*, January 25, 1964.

15. See Al-Rustom (2013) for a detailed discussion of the conditions under which the surviving Armenians continued to live in Anatolia after the establishment of the Republic of Turkey in 1923.

16. "Gökay Ermeni Ruhban Mektebini Ziyaret Etti." *Milliyet*, March 6, 1954.

17. See Bakar (2002) for further information on the historical and legal transformation of non-Muslim *vakıf*s during the transition from empire to republic. Currently, there are 161 non-Muslim *vakıf*s in existence in Turkey, most of which are located in Istanbul, Antakya, and Mardin.

18. "No community based on a particular ethnicity or religious affiliation can establish civil institutions to support its own community."

19. For example, 75% of the property owned by *Balıklı Rum Hospital Vakıf*, a Rum Orthodox community hospital, was confiscated since 1974. Moreover, the fiscal deficits of the hospital have not been compensated by the state since 1972. The hospital is still exempt from value added tax in its purchases according to the Law 2762. As such, the only source of income for the hospital is the income obtained from the remaining communal property and the donations made. This information is based on an interview with the president of the *vakıf* published at *Akşam* on September 22, 2003.

20. The statistical information was taken from the largest Rum Orthodox School, Zografyon Rum High School.

21. Arabic-speaking Rum Orthodox in Antakya (Antioch) survived the transition from empire to republic relatively better than Greek-speaking Rum Orthodox in Istanbul mainly because Antioch was under French mandate until it became a part of Turkey in 1939. According to the 1935 census, 58% of the population was Sunni Muslims, 25.5% Alevis, and 14.5% Christian Arabs (mainly Rum Orthodox). The city is in the Eastern Mediterranean area bordering Syria. Following its inclusion into the Republic of Turkey, its name was officially changed to Hatay after 1939. Local inhabitants still speak in Arabic in their everyday lives up until today.

22. Ramadan meal to break the fast.

23. AKP's policies and position in international relations were recently been described as neo-Ottomanism. For a detailed discussion see Göçek (2011) and Öktem (2011b).

24. Translated from Turkish by the author.

25. http://eng.akparti.org.tr/english/partyprogramme.html#2.5

26. Since the early to mid-2000s there has been an increase in popular culture products such as movies, soap operas, and fiction writings, as well as academic publications that are centered on the diverse history of the Ottoman Empire and the continuous state violence and suppression of ethnic and religious communities.

27. For more detailed information on the trial process see the annual trial reports published on the website of Hrant Dink Foundation, http://www.hrantdink.org/?HrantDink = 16&Lang = en. One striking feature of the trial process has been the reluctance of the AKP to push for a more comprehensive investigation of Dink turning into an open target that he himself mentioned in an article he published at Agos on January 12, 2007 – a week before he was shot dead. For more information see http://www.hrantdink.org/img/Hrant_Dink_Murder_Case-Four_Years_After.pdf.

28. Although I agree with Akan's (2012) criticism of the AKP with respect to its position toward Kurds, Alevis, and Armenians, I do not completely agree with his claim that there is a parallel between the AKP government and the early decades of the Republic with respect to religion and secularism. Although both might see religion as "the cement of society," which thus needs to be under the control of the state, there is a significant difference between the perception and political imaginary of the AKP government and that of the Kemalist regime, in terms of the relationship between religion and citizenry. In other words, even though they might have institutional and administrative similarities with respect to control of religion, they differ significantly in terms of the cultural and cognitive values they attribute to religious practice.

29. This is used in Turkish to express apology for an inappropriate and sometimes even insulting act or statement.

30. Translated from Turkish by the author.

31. Therefore, the argument here diverges from those that trace the AKP to the rise of radical Islamist movements and political parties which were strongly supported by an emerging provincial Anatolian bourgeoisie in the post-1980 period (cf., Yavuz, 2009). Although I do share the importance of a newly emerging bourgeoisie in the transformation of Islamist parties and their increasing acceptance by larger segments of the society, I argue that the ideological path toward countering

the Kemalist republican ethic which had been the hegemonic rule in Turkey was paved much earlier than the 1980s (Keyman, 2007).
32. Also see Öktem (2011b).
33. I thank the anonymous reviewer for emphasizing that this shift in perception of religion also emerged in a time of a significant generational shift in elite composition as many deputies of the former reigning Republican People's Party (RPP) retire to be replaced by the new, often younger DP deputies who do not promote republican secularism as it pertains to the non-Muslim communities as strictly as the earlier generations. It is also important to note the difficulty of a complete separation between DP and the RPP since the founding elites of the DP were ex-RPP members.
34. See Miroğlu (2009) for a discussion of the disputes between the state and Armenian community during the 1930s concerning the ownership of the land of an Armenian cemetery in Istanbul.
35. See Theodorelis-Rigas (2013) for a discussion of the role of cyberspace in Greek–Turkish encounters.
36. City starts with a capital letter because this is a direct translation from Greek *i Poli* meaning "the City" as Istanbul is usually referred to in Greek, indicating its political and cultural importance.
37. European Instrument for Democracy and Human Rights (EIDHR), accessible at http://www.avrupa.info.tr/EUCSD,D.hag.html.
38. http://www.sabah.com.tr/Gundem/2012/01/19/bu-dava-ayri-bir-hassasiyet-tasi yordu. Retrieved by the author from the address above on August 7, 2012.
39. The 1991 election was carried out under close police control. Some respondents believe that the lack of elections is evidence of the state punishing the community because of tensions between Turkey and Greece over Cyprus.
40. The disproportional relationship between the relatively high number of Rum *vakıf*s and the tiny size of the community has made administrating *vakıf*s extremely challenging. The previous Law on *Vakıf*s allowed the transfer of the *vakıf*s, which do not have a regularly functioning administrative board for 10 years to the GDV or the Treasury.
41. *Hürriyet*, January 13, 2007. Translated from Turkish by the author.
42. It is important to note there that the interview also created a controversy in the media. The newspaper in which the interview was published was criticized for the choice of the interview's title. Some within the media argued that the title of the interview represented in the persona of the *vakıf* president "loyalty to the state" as a prominent citizenship trait.
43. See footnote number 21.
44. "Mother" in Greek.
45. Loose pants that are mostly worn by locals in the countryside across Anatolia.

# ACKNOWLEDGMENTS

I would like to thank the anonymous reviewers, Gianpaolo Baiocchi, Nitsan Chorev, Jose Itzigshon, Karen Barkey, Hakem Al-Rustom, Brian T. Connor, and Dikshya Thapa for their valuable feedback on previous drafts. I would also like to thank audiences at 2008 meetings of Middle Eastern Studies Association, at a 2008 Graduate Program in Development workshop at Watson Institute, Brown University, and at 2010 Annual Mediterranean Research Meetings at the European University Institute.

# REFERENCES

Akan, M. (2005). *The politics of secularization in Turkey and France: Beyond Orientalism and Occidentalism.* PhD Dissertation, Department of Political Science, Columbia University, New York, NY.

Akan, M. (2011). The infrastructural politics of Laiklik in the writing of the 1961 Turkish constitution. *Interventions: International Journal of Postcolonial Studies, 13*(2), 190–211.

Akan, M. (2012). Twin tolerations or Siamese twins: Kemalist laicism and political Islam in Turkey. In D. Chalmers & S. Mainwaring (Eds.), *Institutions and democracy: Essays in honor of alfred stepan.* University of Notre Dame Press. Retrieved from http://www.pols.boun.edu.tr/faculty.aspx?iid=2#. Accessed on July 10, 2012.

Akgönül, S. (2007). *Turkiye Rumlari: Ulus-Devlet Cagindan Kuresellesme Cagina Bir Azinligin Yok Olus Sureci.* Istanbul: Iletisim Yayinlari.

Al-Rustom, H. (2013). *Anatolian fragments: Armenians between Turkey and France.* PhD Dissertation, Department of Anthropology, The London School of Economics, London.

Al-Rustom, H. (2013). Diaspora activism and the politics of locality: The Armenians in France. In A. Quayson & G. Daswani (Eds.), *A companion to diaspora and transnationalism* (pp. 473–494). West Sussex, UK: Blackwell.

Alexander, J. (2006). *The civil sphere.* Oxford: Oxford University Press.

Alexandris, A. (1992). *The Greek minority of Istanbul and Greek-Turkish Relations, 1918–1974.* Athens, Greece: Center for Asia Minor Studies.

Altınay, F. (2004). *The myth of the military-nation, militarism, gender, and education in Turkey.* New York, NY: Palgrave Macmillan.

Anderson, B. (1983). *Imagined communities: Reflections on the origin and spread of nationalism.* London: Verso.

Azak, U. (2010). *Islam and secularism in Turkey: Kemalism, religion and the nation state.* London: I.B. Tauris.

Baiocchi, G. (2005). *Militants and citizens: The politics of participatory democracy in Porto Alegre.* Stanford, CA: Stanford University Press.

Baiocchi, G. (2012). Cultural sociology and civil society in a world of flows: Recapturing ambiguity, hybridity, and the political. In J. Alexander, R. Jacobs & P. Smith (Eds.), *Handbook of cultural sociology.* Oxford: Oxford University Press.

Baiocchi, G., Heller, P., & Silva, M. K. (2011). *Bootstrapping democracy: Transforming local governance and civil society in Brazil.* Stanford, CA: Stanford University Press.

Bakar, D. (2002). *Ulusal, Ulusalüstü ve Uluslararasi Hukukta Azınlık Haklari.* Istanbul: Istanbul Barosu, Insan Haklar Merkezi.

Bali, R. (1999). *Cumhuriyet Yıllarında Türkiye Yahudileri: Bir Türkleştirme Serüveni, 1923–1945.* Istanbul: Iletişim Yayınları.

Bali, R. (2009). *Devlet'in Örnek Yurttaşları; Cumhuriyet Yıllarında Türkiye Yahudileri*. Istanbul: İletişim Yayınları.

Barkey, K. (2008). *Empire of difference: The Ottomans in comparative perspective*. Cambridge: Cambridge University Press.

Bebiroğlu, M. (2009). *Cumhuriyet Döneminde Patrikler ve Önemli Olaylar*. Retrieved from http://www.hyetert.com/yazi3.asp?s=1&Id=442&DilId=1. Accessed on July 10, 2012.

Benhabib, S. (Ed.). (1996). *Democracy and difference: Contesting the boundaries of the political*. Princeton, NJ: Princeton University Press.

Berkes, N. (1964). *The development of secularism in Turkey*. New York, NY: Routledge.

Bourdieu, P. (1985). The social space and the genesis of groups. *Theory and Society, 14*(6), 723–744.

Bowen, J. R. (2008). *Why the French don't like headscarves: Islam, the state, and public space*. Princeton, NJ: Princeton University Press.

Braude, B. (1982). Foundation myths of the millet system. In B. Braude & B. Lewis. (Eds.), *Christians and Jews in the Ottoman Empire* (pp. 69–87). New York, NY: Holmes and Meier.

Brubaker, R. (1992). *Citizenship and nationhood in France and Germany*. Cambridge, MA: Harvard University Press.

Brubaker, R., Feischmidt, M., Fox, J., & Grancea, L. (2006). *Nationalist politics and everyday ethnicity in a Transylvanian town*. Princeton, NJ: Princeton University Press.

Clark, B. (2006). *Twice a stranger: Greece, Turkey and the minorities they expelled*. London: Granta Books.

Dahl, R. (1989). *Democracy and its critiques*. New Haven, CT: Yale University Press.

Göçek, F. M. (2011). *The transformation of Turkey: Redefining state and society from the Ottoman Empire to the modern era*. London: I.B. Tauris.

Güven, D. (2005). *Cumhuriyet Dönemi Azınlık Politikaları Bağlamında 6-7 Eylül Olayları*. Istanbul: Tarih Vakfı.

Habermas, J. (1991). *The structural transformation of the public sphere: An inquiry into a category of bourgeois society*. Cambridge, MA: The MIT Press.

Habermas, J. (2001). *The postnational constellation: Political essays*. Cambridge, MA: The MIT Press.

Hansen, T. B. (1999). *Saffron wave: Democracy and Hindu nationalism in modern India*. Princeton, NJ: Princeton University Press.

Heller, P. (2001). Moving the state: The politics of democratic decentralization in Kerala, South Africa, and Porto Alegre. *Politics and Society, 29*(1), 131–163.

Houtzager, P. P., & Acharya, A. K. (2011). Associations, active citizenship, and the quality of democracy in Brazil and Mexico. *Theory and Society, 40*(1), 1–36.

Huber, E., Rueschemeyer, D., & Stephens, J. D. (1997). The paradoxes of contemporary democracy: Formal, participatory, and social dimensions. *Comparative Politics, 29*(3), 323–342.

Karpat, K. (1982). The roots of the incongruity of nation and state in the post-Ottoman Era. In B. Braude & B. Lewis (Eds.), *Christians and Jews in the Ottoman Empire* (pp. 141–170). New York, NY: Holmes and Meier.

Kastoryano, R. (2002). *Negotiating identities: States and immigrants in France and Germany*. Princeton, NJ: Princeton University Press.

Keyder, C. (1987). *State and class in Turkey: A study in capitalist development*. London: Verso.

Keyman, F. (2007). Modernity, secularism and Islam: The case of Turkey. *Theory, Culture and Society, 24*(2), 215–234.

Kuyucu, A. T. (2005). Ethno-religious 'Unmixing' of 'Turkey': 6–7 September riots as a case in Turkish nationalism. *Nations and Nationalism, 11*(3), 361–380.

Laclau, E. (Ed.). (1994). *Making of political identities.* London: Verso.

Laclau, E., & Mouffe, C. (1985). *Hegemony and socialist strategy: Towards a more radical democratic politics.* London: Verso.

Mandel, M. S. (2003). *In the aftermath of genocide: Armenians and Jews in twentieth-century France.* Durham, NC: Duke University Press.

Mann, M. (2005). *Dark side of democracy: Explaining ethnic cleansing.* New York, NY: Cambridge University Press.

Mardin, Ş. (1997). *Religion, society and modernity in Turkey.* Syracuse, NY: Syracuse University Press.

Mills, C. W. (1997). *The racial contract.* Cornell, NY: Cornell University Press.

Miroğlu, A. (2009). Tarihi 16.yy'a Uzanan Pangaltı Ermeni Mezarlığı (Surp Hagop Mezarlığı). *Toplumsal Tarih, 187,* 34–38.

Navaro-Yashin, Y. (2002). *Faces of the state: Secularism and public life in Turkey.* Princeton, NJ: Princeton University Press.

Öktem, K. (2011a). Between emigration, de-Islamization, and the nation-state: Muslim communities in the Balkans today. *Southeast European and Black Sea Studies, 11*(2), 155–171.

Öktem, K. (2011b). *Angry nation: Turkey since 1989.* London: Zed Books.

Oran, B. (2004). *Turkiye'de Azinliklar: Kavramlar, Lozan, Ic Mevzuat, Ictihat, Uygulama.* Istanbul: TESEV Yayinlari.

Parla, T., & Davison, A. (2004). *Corporatist ideology in Kemalist Turkey: Progress or order.* Syracuse, NY: Syracuse University Press.

Putnam, R. (2001). *Making democracy work: Civic traditions in modern Italy.* Princeton, NJ: Princeton University Press.

Rancière, J. (2004). *Disagreement: Politics and philosophy.* Minneapolis, MN: University of Minnesota Press.

Rao, V., & Woolcock, M. (2007). The disciplinary monopoly in development research at the World Bank. *Global Governance, 13,* 479–484.

Stephens, J. D. (1989). Democratic transition and breakdown in Western Europe, 1870–1939: A test of the Moore thesis. *American Journal of Sociology, 94,* 1019–1077.

Taylor, C. (1998). The dynamics of democratic exclusion. *Journal of Democracy, 9*(4), 143–156.

Taylor, C. (2002). Democratic exclusion (and its remedies?). *Eurozine.* Retrieved from http://www.eurozine.com/articles/2002-02-21-taylor-en.html. Accessed on July 15, 2012.

Theodorelis-Rigas, H. (2013). From imagined to virtual communities: Greek-Turkish encounters in cyberspace. *Studies in Ethnicity and Nationalism, 13*(1), 2–19.

Tilly, C. (2007). *Democracy.* Cambridge: Cambridge University Press.

Tuğal, C. (2009). *Passive revolution: Absorbing the Islamist challenge to capitalism.* Stanford, CA: Stanford University Press.

Turam, B. (2004). *Between Islam and the state: The politics of engagement.* Stanford, CA: Stanford University Press.

Vryonis, S. (2005). *The mechanism of catastrophe: The Turkish pogrom of September 6–7, 1955 and the destruction of the Greek community of Istanbul.* Greekworks.Com Inc., Athens, Greece.

Wacquant, L. (1997). For an analytic of racial domination. *Political Power and Social Theory*, *11*, 221–234.

Wedeen, L. (1999). *Ambiguities of domination: Politics, rhetoric and symbols in contemporary Syria*. Chicago, IL: The University of Chicago Press.

Wedeen, L. (2009). Ethnography as interpretive enterprise. In E. Schatz (Ed.), *Political ethnography: What immersion contributes to study of power* (pp. 75–94). Chicago, IL: The University of Chicago Press.

Wimmer, A. (2008). The making and unmaking of ethnic boundaries. A multi-level process theory. *American Journal of Sociology*, *113*(4), 970–1022.

Yavuz, M. H. (2009). *Secularism and Muslim democracy in Turkey*. Cambridge: Cambridge University Press.

Yeğen, M. (2004). Citizenship and ethnicity in Turkey. *Middle Eastern Studies*, *40*(6), 51–66.

Yıldırım, O. (2006). *Diplomacy and displacement: Reconsidering the Turco-Greek exchange of populations, 1922–1934*. New York, NY: Routledge.

Young, I. M. (1989). Polity and group difference: A critique of the ideal of universal citizenship. *Ethics*, *99*, 250–274.

Young, I. M. (1997). *Intersecting voices: Dilemmas of gender, political philosophy, and policy*. Princeton, NJ: Princeton University Press.

Young, I. M. (2000). *Inclusion and democracy*. Oxford: Oxford University Press.

Zürcher, E. (1993). *Turkey: A modern history*. London: I.B. Tauris.

Zürcher, E. (2010). *Young Turk legacy and nation building: From the Ottoman Empire to Ataturk's Turkey*. London: I.B. Tauris.

# BINDING INSTITUTIONS: PEASANTS AND NATION-STATE RULE IN THE ALBANIAN HIGHLANDS, 1919–1939

Besnik Pula

## ABSTRACT

*The seminal literature on state formation proposes a model of "co-opt and expand" to explain the rise of centralized nation-states in modern and early modern Europe. Building on this literature's distinction between direct and indirect rule, other analysts have expanded the scope of this model to explain patterns of state building in the non-Western world, particularly in the construction of centralized authority in postcolonial and postimperial contexts. According to this literature, the failure of central rulers to co-opt local elites has frequently produced weak states lacking capacities of rule in their peripheries. Using archival materials to examine the Albanian state's relatively successful penetration of the country's highland communities during its early decades of national independence, this article suggests that state building can proceed along an alternative path called "co-opt and bind," in which state builders "bind" peasant communal institutions to the institutional idea of*

Decentering Social Theory
Political Power and Social Theory, Volume 25, 37–70
Copyright © 2013 by Emerald Group Publishing Limited
All rights of reproduction in any form reserved
ISSN: 0198-8719/doi:10.1108/S0198-8719(2013)0000025008

*the nation-state to legitimize and implement state building goals. The
article identifies three mechanisms used by early Albanian state builders
to generate legitimacy and institute political order in its remote communities, including disarmament, the institution of new forms of economic
dependency, and the invocation of peasant cultural codes of honor.*

It is now commonly accepted that the path of state formation proceeded
through "jagged peaks and profound valleys," as Tilly (1990, p. 28) put it
metaphorically. Yet, while much comparative historical work has gone into
explaining the causes behind the rise of the centralized nation state in
western Europe, much less work has been done in understanding the
historical trajectories of nation states whose paths of development have
taken routes very different from that in the early modern West. Policies that
do not get implemented, governments that must negotiate with constituents,
and citizens who flout the authority of states seem like prevailing features of
many states around the world, in a vision that is very much at odds with the
solid Weberian conception of the state as a robust coercive and extractive
mechanism. Does the history of west European state formation provide any
lessons at all in explaining the trajectories of such states?

     There is a general consensus among a number of scholars that one of the
distinguishing marks of success of the centralizing states of western Europe
was the extension of the administrative authority of the central ruler
through the defeat and cooptation of regional centers of power in the early
phases of state centralization (Anderson, 1974; Ertman, 1997; Levi, 1981;
Mann, 1984; Tilly, 1975, 1985). It is also commonly accepted that the
techniques rulers employed in processes of cooptation included the exchange
of loyalty of regional powerholders for offices, titles, and other privileges
(Fischer & Lundgreen, 1975; Schneider, 1984), including the sale of offices
and titles of nobility, as occurred in France. In more recent work, Gould
(1996) stresses the role of co-optation through patronage, as opposed to the
wholesale co-optation of dominant or ascending classes into the service of
the state, as an important alternative tool state builders used in their efforts
to expand the state's administrative capacity and political authority
(Adams, 2005; Padgett & Ansell, 1993). In all these cases, state building is
described as a process proceeding through the exchange of loyalty for
official titles or positions in the state-created hierarchy, as that hierarchy
itself expands and is, in most cases, integrated into the state's formal
organization. What this emphasis leaves out is consideration of a significant

realm of informal practices and non-state institutions that state builders may mobilize in their efforts to expand state power.

Most recent theories of state formation recognize that modern states, while creating new forms of authority, were not created ex nihilo but emerged out of the mobilization and reconfiguration of existing institutional patterns (Adams, 2005; Ertman, 1997; Gorski, 2003; Mamdani, 1996; Mann, 1993).[1] The dominant model of state building in the prevailing literature on state formation draws on what can be termed the *co-opt and expand model*, in which central rulers co-opt regional elites, or rivals of existing local elites, with the result being a significant expansion of the formal administrative apparatus of the state and an overall increase in the concentration of power in the state, and with long-term effects in the structuring of state power. This model includes both formal bureaucratic centralization, such as occurred in postrevolutionary France (Tilly, 1990, pp. 103–117), as well as forms of indirect rule through intermediaries who may enjoy autonomy of action, but who are nonetheless ordained as members with some definitive status within the formal state hierarchy. Similar cases of indirect rule include the *caciques* in Spanish America, *mafia* in southern Italy, and the Native Authorities of African colonial states (Blok, 1974; Mamdani, 1996; Scott, 1976; Young, 1994). The distinction comes from Tilly's (1990) seminal work, which distinguishes between direct rule, where central rulers exercise authority directly through centralized mechanisms, and indirect rule, where political power is exercised by intermediaries between primary rulers and ruled populations. The distinction also informs the literature on colonial state formation, which argues that European colonial powers, while relying on a mixture of strategies, typically employed indirect rule to govern remote rural populations in colonial states, especially in Africa (Mamdani, 1996; Young, 1994), while others suggest that *caciques*, *mafia*, and a panoply of other politically powerful figures emerged in regions requiring the coercive mobilization of agrarian labor (Arrighi & Piselli, 1987; Blok, 1974; Brenner, 1985; Paige, 1975; Scott, 1976; Wallerstein, 1995). For Tilly, the path of European (and, by extension, most other cases) of state formation almost necessarily involved the passage from indirect to direct rule, with outcomes depending primarily upon the dominant mechanisms used to secure compliance by the governed (Tilly, 2005, pp. 30–38).[2] This dualistic scheme leaves little room for explaining patterns of state formation where state authority expands without the implementation of indirect rule (and where attempts to do so fail), but where state authority nonetheless is capable of penetrating the local social order.

This alternative path of state building involves what I am terming *co-opt and bind*. In this path, co-optation does not focus primarily on securing the loyalty of local elites or intermediaries, but of creating mechanisms that collectively bind, through a combination of administrative and extra-administrative means, peripheral social groups to the state. In this form of co-optation, the legitimacy of the state building project is constructed through the implicit and informal subordination of existing "traditional" social institutions by the formal administrative apparatus of the state. As a result, states create situations of institutional "bifurcation" (Mamdani, 1996) where the legitimacy of the exercise of bureaucratic authority becomes partly reliant upon the continuing assent and effectiveness of local institutions and their own internal logics. *Binding* implies that the expansion of state power does succeed at destroying the autonomy of nonhierarchical, "stateless" communities, making them increasingly dependent on the state for economic and security needs. But as a consequence of such an oblique, partial, and unmediated penetration of social life, administrative authority remains continually vulnerable to challenge and, in the long run, weak. The process of administrative rule is never fully regularized and seems like a constant negotiation between ruler and ruled.

I suggest that this form of co-optation is most likely to take place in nationalizing states with recalcitrant peripheries that share long traditions of political autonomy from external authorities. In these contexts, local elites may prove unable or unreliable to employ in indirect rule by central authorities. At the same time, nationalizing elites may attach cultural stigmas to "traditional" institutions of rural society. Because of inherent cultural assumptions that have informed projects of national modernization, unlike colonial state builders, nationalizing bureaucratic elites may be hesitant in taking the step of granting formal recognition and authority to preliterate, agrarian institutions such as village councils and chieftainships, clan-based authorities, and systems of unwritten customary law, all the while reliant on their cooperation to attain state goals.[3] This paper uses the case of state building in the Albanian highlands during the immediate postindependence period to demonstrate this alternative path of state building and their resulting mechanisms of governance. In this case, the state's attempt to institute indirect rule failed, yet state elites found other means of penetrating local social life and securing the legitimacy of national rule. Based on an analysis of archival documents and other historical sources, this paper traces the development of state power in the highlands to identify the chief mechanisms that served the central authorities to extend and exercise state power in a remote and historically politically autonomous region.

The paper argues that modernizing national states with limited administrative capacities and recalcitrant peripheral territories rely less on forms of indirect rule that co-opt local elites and more heavily on the co-optation and binding of informal social institutions in ways that blur the state–society divide.[4]

## STATE FORMATION AND STATE WEAKNESS IN THE NON-WESTERN WORLD: A THEORETICAL DISCUSSION

Though non-Western postindependence states were once seen as highly autonomous from classes and other social forces (Alavi, 1972), and for many a promise of emancipation and rapid development, more recent interest has cast many of them in the role of feeble and incompetent actors on the historical stage. Beyond the extreme cases in which a state's authority is under serious threat by armed domestic challengers, even those with relative control over the means of violence may be incapable of effectively carrying out policy and implementing decisions, or may be fraught with internal corruption and largely ineffective in governing society (Bayart, 1993; Boone, 2003; Callaghy, 1987; Cohen, Brown, & Organski, 1981; Evans, 1989; Migdal, 1988, 2001). One of the distinguishing features of weak states is the lack of "infrastructural power" (Mann, 1984), that is, bureaucratic elites do not possess effective administrative and coercive means to implement decisions and carry out policy throughout the territorial realm and within the entire population of the state. Examples of such states abound in the contemporary world, and much research and theorizing has gone into explaining the causes of such condition.

By its very definition, state weakness is about state power in the official sense, exercised through the state's formal administrative infrastructure. Like analyses of state building discussed previously, their locus of analysis is the formal organizational aspect of the state. In his influential study of the causes of state weakness in the Third World, Migdal (1988; see also Migdal, Kohli, & Shue, 1994) argues that state weakness is a consequence of "pathological" relationships between rulers and subordinates within bureaucratic apparatuses in the centralizing states of the postcolonial/ postimperial world. As rulers make efforts to guard from challengers that arise from within the state apparatus, they weaken and pulverize the very means through which they rule. This pathological development in the construction of administrative apparatuses initially resulted from the disruption of traditional patterns of authority by colonialism and forceful integration into the world capitalist economy, creating situations in which rulemaking authority becomes fragmented and decentralized. Alternative sources of authoritative rulemaking in exceptionally "strong" societies and bureaucratic weakness combine to produce the reality of state weakness, given that weak states become reliant for their legitimacy on the very strongmen who jeopardize the state's monopoly over binding rulemaking. By contrast, one could argue along the same lines that, the main reason why states in the West are marked by "strong" bureaucratic apparatuses and societies that are largely subordinate to their rule is that in the West, domestic challengers and competing bases of authority were defeated or co-opted successfully in the process of early modern state building, and prior to or in tandem with the spread of capitalism. In Migdal's account, the impact of colonialism and inclusion into the world market disrupted traditional systems of authority in Third World societies, but nascent centralizing states failed to effectively concentrate the means of social control within the expanding administrative apparatus (cf. Huntington, 1968). In Migdal's words, "in many cases [of Third World nation-state building], weblike societies have survived with social control dispersed among various social organizations having their own rules rather than centralized in the state or organizations authorized by the state" (1988, p. 40).

Migdal's analysis has three merits. First, its focus on the state reintroduced and reframed the problem of "stateness" (Nettl, 1968) for postindependence states, which had been largely neglected by prior class-centered analyses of non-Western political development (Alavi, 1972; Frank, 1966; Moore, 1966; Paige, 1978; Wallerstein, 1979). Second, it illuminates part of the political and social dynamics of state weakness by emphasizing the diffuse nature of institutions exercising social control and the ways in which the national state may in fact fail to subordinate alternative sources of binding rulemaking. And third, it shows that understanding these dynamics requires an analysis of the ways in which state power expands and incorporates peripheral, and typically rural, regions within the authority of the central state, rather than the traditional focus on the politics in the national capital.[5] However, the explanation also has three weaknesses. First, it does not adequately account for weak state apparatuses that are nonetheless still capable of pursuing particular state goals. Contra to the imagery, weak states are not frail, feeble, and benign. Even weak states get things done – the question is, what things and why those and not others.[6] Second, in spite of Migdal's attempt to escape from a state-centered perspective, his state-in-society alternative fails to reconceptualize the state along lines that can account for social mechanisms that breach the presumed state–society divide. As Migdal notes, states deeply affect the societies in which they rise, but his framework is limited to an analysis of political dynamics in formal institutional settings, rather than how the construction of apparatuses of governance reconfigure existing institutional patterns and social relations *within* civil society. And finally, Migdal's macro approach to what are for the most part meso- and even micro-dynamics leaves many questions unanswered about the ways in which expanding states intervene and penetrate into a presumably "stateless" society. I suggest that this problem for the most part stems from Migdal's reliance on a static theoretical definition of the state to organize his analysis, and that analysis ought to examine the historical emergence of a new mode of governance and the social mechanisms mobilized in rule (Bourdieu, 1999, 2004; Elster, 2007; Steinmetz, 2008; Stinchcombe, 1991; Tilly, 2001, 2005).

In line with the Weberian inclination of the cohort of theorists who implored social scientists to "bring the state back in" (Evans, Rueschemeyer, & Skocpol, 1985), Migdal defines the state as an organization that is autonomous in its actions, has centralized control over its various administrative bodies, and enjoys, at least in the normative sense, monopoly over the means of violence.[7] State capacity therefore relates to the ability of incumbents to effectively use the state's autonomy and administrative and coercive infrastructure to implement policy decisions throughout the territory of the state, for programmatic goals declared by the state elite. State strength is thus positively correlated with greater state capacities for social control, while state weakness implies a situation in which the state is either incapable of achieving its ends or is compelled to compromise its legal authority by negotiating with non-state actors and institutions.

There are two problems in using such a definition to analyze state power in societies undergoing transitions toward centralized state rule. First, by starting off with a synchronic, ideal-typical definition of the state (itself derived from a particular understanding of the state in Western political development), the analysis may assume a "normal," mostly normatively based outcome, and then attempt to explain its lack in the particular case. This includes the risk that the analysis expects an outcome which was, in the case of West European development, the end result a unique historical process (Abrams, 1988). And yet, while organizational templates of the modern national state of the West served as a model for many modernizing states in the postcolonial/postimperial world (Meyer, Boli, Thomas, & Ramirez, 1997), part of the challenge of the comparative historical sociology of state formation is the examination of processes of struggle and how those produced particular institutional configurations of power, including struggles surrounding the ability of states to successfully claim jurisdiction over specific domains of social life (Loveman, 2005). In contrast, Migdal's measure of state capacities is based on a normative theoretical definition. To treat state capacities as a single measurement has its problems, as Weiss (1998) argues, even for the "strong" states of the West, who suggests that analytic focus must shift to the structural features and institutional fields of states, rather than relying on a generalized and abstract notion of state capacity.[8] Second, and as a consequence, Migdal's definition of state capacity may obscure cases in which states are limited in their general administrative capacities, but are nonetheless capable of exercising a significant degree of social control within their civil societies. As many cases of state building, including the one analyzed here, show, an administratively weak state does not entail the lack of efficacy. An alternative analysis examines the ways in which states elites enlist *all* forms of power available to them – ranging from proper administrative and legally derived authority to various non-state actors and institutions – in the service of state goals.[9]

In his critique of prevailing conceptions of state power, Gorski (1999) points to a failure of prevailing theories to make the important distinction between *extensive* and *intensive* state power. The former includes the state's administrative capacities of coercion (monopoly over the means of violence, binding rulemaking, and the ability to impose decisions upon populations) and extraction (of resources, such as taxes and soldiers, necessary for state survival). These definitions, as Gorski emphasizes, have been the theme of existing studies of state formation, which conceive of the state as a formal organization and understand its capacities to be an internal property of the state apparatus. According to Gorski, what these discussions have neglected is an analysis of the role of *intensive* state power, that is, the institutional and ideological means available to states that permit them to engage in processes of what Gorski terms "social disciplining." Social disciplining involves the effective employment by the state of non-state actors and institutions to produce predictable order in society, create citizenries who agree to be bound by laws and other formal rules, and punish offenders for acts the state defines as criminal. States have either entered in alliances with such institutions, or their own logics enhanced the control capabilities of the state (see also Gorski, 2003). In his own analysis, Gorski argues the decisive role of the sixteenth century Calvinist "disciplinary revolution" in enabling the formation of highly centralized states in northwestern Europe. In Gorski's view, through the production of discipline, the spiritually driven intensive power of hierocratic institutions served the politically more intentional goals of rulers to expand the extensive powers of the state. I suggest that maintaining and developing this important distinction between the two forms of state power helps explain the apparent anomalies of state building in the case of the Albanian highlands during the early phase of postindependence state building – and perhaps other similar cases as well. That is because while the nascent state scored poorly in the highlands in measures of extensive power – collecting taxes, conscripting soldiers, and enforcing the law – as the historical record shows, it did not lack the means, either direct or indirect, of exercising disciplinary and punitive measures against challengers and those who threatened the political order. I argue that the means by which, in the case of the Albanian highlands, the state accomplished this was through the mobilization of existing forms of social organization – not by securing the loyalty of particular agents, but by instrumentalizing the collective institutions of local society. The system of what will be termed *rule by institutional binding* did not proceed chiefly through a strategy of co-optation through the distribution of official positions in the state hierarchy, or through the alternative system of formal indirect rule through the formalization and legal codification of "native authorities" as in colonial state building, but by establishing ties between state and society within a growing sphere of extra-administrative, extra-legal action, produced by the state to ensure compliance of local institutions with overarching state goals.

The remainder of this paper discusses the dynamics of binding by examining two key episodes of state building in the Albanian highlands in the immediate postindependence period. The first discusses the origins of institutional binding as a solution to problems of national governance in the highlands after the failure of indirect rule. The second examines the elaboration of mechanisms that helped sustain institutional binding and increased the dependence of the rural highlands on the state, and which ultimately led to the weakening political autonomy of highland peasant communities vis-à-vis the state. The historical narrative is based on the author's examination of archival records, including policy documents, reports, and local correspondence, especially those of the Albanian Ministry of Interior Affairs, in elaborating and responding to problems of governance in Albania's highland region during the first decades of the state's existence.

# STATE BUILDING IN THE ALBANIAN HIGHLANDS

*Highland Rebellions and the Failure of Indirect Rule, 1919–1925*

While Albania was recognized as an independent state by the European Powers in 1913, foreign occupation during World War I prevented the nascent Albanian government from establishing administrative authority throughout the territory of the new state. Under Ottoman rule, the territory of what became modern Albania was divided between four Ottoman *vilayets* (provinces), neither of which had fully centralized authority.[10] An autonomous, internationally recognized government was reestablished in Albania with the departure of foreign militaries in 1919.

The new government was aware of the particular problem of establishing authority in the northern highlands, which had existed as politically autonomous communities for most of the prior Ottoman era. The clan-based society of the Albanian highlands inhabited the vast and rugged mountainous region covering most of northern and northeastern Albania, containing roughly a quarter of the country's population of the time. In early 1919, the prefect of the northern district of Shkodër had reported to his superiors the mood dominating the highlands. Corresponding with his superiors in the capital, he wrote, "if one is to consider the psychology of the peasants, they no doubt do not want the government because they are concerned about tithes, head taxes, and the confiscation of weapons [...]." At a meeting of village chiefs with the local government representatives, at which the prefect had been personally present, he believed that "they likely came together just to tell the leadership that they want no government."[11]

One of the early solutions to this rejection of the government was to continue the traditional Ottoman system of indirect rule in the highlands. This arrangement would permit local chieftains, known as *bajraktar*, to continue practicing authority locally, while ensuring their loyalty to the government. While straightforward in theory, the strategy would prove unviable after a series of highland rebellions diverted the government's attempts to collect taxes and confiscate weapons from highland populations.

The origins of rule by institutional binding thus began with a failed attempt to negotiate indirect rule. In 1920, the Minister of Interior Ahmet Zogu, in charge of construction of a new regional territorial administration, issued an order which stated that the system of administration in Mirdita, a region deep in the hinterlands of the northern Albanian Alps and one of the most recalcitrant toward Tirana's authority, would be exempt from the regular system of legal administration and would be based upon the local customary system of authority known as the *kanun* (from the Turkish word for "law"). The *kanun* was a system of unwritten customary norms and practices that governed questions from the proper procedures of avenging the blood of a kinsman, the resolution of property disputes, the exchange of brides between clans and the domestic roles of men, women, and children, to the most ordinary aspects of everyday life such as the proper arrangement of family and kin around the dinner table (Doll, 2003; Hasluck, 1954; Valentini, 1969; Whitaker, 1968; Young, 2000). For much of the Ottoman era, the *kanun* was tolerated and sometimes even encouraged by the Ottoman authorities based in faraway towns, who had been satisfied with the ability for the occasional collection of taxes from the Albanian highlands, or the use of Albanian highlanders as mercenaries, without attempting to extensively regulate local social life (Blumi, 2003). During the early 1800s, a local village chieftain of Mirdita had successfully challenged the Ottoman authorities and negotiated a deal with the Sultan whereby the Mirditores would be permanently exempt from taxes, in exchange for the service of Mirditore men as auxiliaries in Ottoman warring campaigns. As a result, the chieftain by the name of Bib Doda was given the formal title of *kapedan* (Doçi, 1996).[12]

The offer for indirect rule in Mirdita was extended by Albania's Ministry of Interior to Gjon Marka Gjoni, a successor of Bib Doda and the reigning *kapedan* of Mirdita. The order giving autonomy to Mirdita stated that the system rule in Mirdita will be the same "as in the times of [Ottoman] Turkey," and that all consideration will be taken for "the work of the *bajraktar*s [chieftains] and [village] elders," who would be compensated for their service by the central government in grain, much as they had been in the Ottoman period.[13] In exchange, Marka Gjoni and the regional *bajraktar*s would be responsible for maintaining order in Mirdita and pledging loyalty to the government. The fate of the Ministry's order is uncertain in the historical record, but what is certain is that less than a year after it was issued, the new Albanian government faced one of its harshest challenges ever, coming in the form of an antigovernment rebellion led by Marka Gjoni. It is unclear whether the motive behind the rebellion was dissatisfaction with the government's offer, disagreement between Marka Gjoni and the central government with regard to the closure of the Albanian-Yugoslav border (a key passage for grain supplies for Mirdita), failure of the government to hold up to its promises of payment (for instance, the government had failed to compensate Marka Gjoni for his service on a special committee set up by the government to administer the *kanun* in all of Albania's highlands), or on the spurring of the government of neighboring Yugoslavia on behalf of its own geopolitical interests, or a combination of these.[14] Whatever the motives, the rebellion soon exploded from a regional uprising into an international scandal, since the League of Nations received a note, delivered by the Yugoslav representative and on behalf of Marka Gjoni, demanding recognition of a self-ruling "Republic of Mirdita" in the heart of the Albanian highlands. In any event, the Mirdita rebellion ultimately failed as government troops and irregulars defeated the rebels and soon put Mirdita under a state of siege, proclaimed Marka Gjoni and his followers to be traitors to the nation, and punished many in the government's Political Court. Among the casualties of the conflict between the central government and Mirdita were the existing arrangements of indirect rule.

The placing of Mirdita under direct military occupation did not resolve the problem of building a local administration in Mirdita and the rest of the highlands. Moreover, military rule was expensive and difficult to sustain for the young and cash-strapped Albanian state, especially in a region difficult to access and provide with supplies and maintain communication links. Local governments had been set up fairly quickly in the lowland regions of Durrës, Tirana, Elbasan, Vlora, and Korça in central and southern Albania throughout 1913–1917, partly a legacy of the civil–military administrations built by Austrian, French, Italian, and other Western armies that had occupied Albania during World War I. But ruling the highlands remained an ongoing challenge for the government. The failure of indirect rule, the distrust created between the government and highlanders as a consequence of the Mirdita rebellion, the fact that most highlanders were armed, as well as the need to protect the northeastern border region from Yugoslav encroachments, forced the government to find new ways of establishing authority in the highlands.

The answer to this problem came in the form of a policy document drafted by the commander in charge of quelling the Mirdita uprising. The officer urged the government to use its military advantage to establish its authority in the highlands through a combination of punitive and pedagogic measures intended to reform the social and cultural way of life of the highlands.[15] Out of his wide array of suggestions, many of which the fledging government had no means of turning into reality within a short period of time (such as building schools and communication systems, or deploying doctors who, according to the officer, would prevent the spread of disease from the highlands into the cities and could be useful for teaching highland peasants modern norms of personal hygiene), two of them stand out, because these two would form the pillars of what can henceforth be termed "highland policy" in Albania: maintain mobile military detachments in nearby cities, with the authority to intervene in cases of unrest and proclaim local states of emergency; and procure the loyalty of the highland peasantry through the institution of the *besa*, evidently proposed as an alternative to dealing with local chieftains.

The *besa* represents one of the central institutions of the *kanun* and is a pledge or oath between parties, by placing one's personal, family and clan honor at stake, to uphold an agreement or suspend an ongoing blood feud while some other major event (such as a war) transpires. The *besa* could also be used collectively to form a regional alliance between rival villages and clans in cases when there is a threat of attack from the outside. The *besa* had also been used throughout Albania's war of independence and after, especially in the highlands, to strike alliances between feuding clans and regions against common enemies, such as the Ottoman military and, during the Balkan Wars of 1912–1913, the invading Serbian troops. In any event, the *besa* came to be seen as a possible instrument of policy by the state. It had already proven its effectiveness in Mirdita after the defeat of the rebels, when the population of Mirdita would be compelled to demonstrate their loyalty by pledging their *besa* to the government authorities. The *besa* could thus, in the eyes of this state official, serve to undercut all other loyalties by securing that individual highland communities are *collectively*, on a communal basis, loyal to the state. For the remainder of the 1920s and 1930s, Albania would experience a number of significant events and turning points, including rapid and major changes in government and regime in 1924 and the establishment of the monarchy in 1928. However, the use of the *besa* by the state as a tool of policy in the highlands would remain an indelible feature of the history of Albanian state building. In the following discussion I examine in greater detail the *besa* as well as the other mechanisms of state building that came to be employed in the Albanian highlands in the aftermath of the Mirdita revolt.

### *Guns, Honor, and Poor Relief: Mechanisms of State Building in the Albanian Highlands, 1926–1939*

The move toward the use of the *besa* and other piecemeal measures to secure the loyalty of highland communities became particularly prominent after a second highland rebellion threatened state authority. In early winter 1926, the heads of the clans inhabiting the Dukagjini range along Albania's northwestern border with Montenegro reacted to increased burdens of taxation by expelling the local government authorities from their region. The Dukagjini revolt experienced the fate of the Mirdita rebellion, and the Dukagjini clans were soon violently overrun by government troops and irregulars. But what this (and, as it would turn out, final) highland rebellion would prove to the government is that, in the highlands, a systematic policy was out of the question. From then on, state building in the highlands proceeded in piecemeal fashion to turn into an institutional patchwork of temporarily negotiated truces between the state and the local society. The lack of systemic and coherently articulated policy, however, does not preclude the existence of a *strategy*, in the sense of patterned, directed, and systematic efforts, in the government's attempts to establish authority in the highlands.[16] What changed between the Mirdita and Dukagjini rebellions, however, was a shift in the *goals* of state building in the highlands. While the initial period was characterized by attempts to secure the loyalty of regional strongmen and ensure that highland peasants pay tribute to the state through taxes, in the latter period the priorities shifted toward securing "order" and using local institutions to secure the collective loyalty of highland communities. Attempting to move away from exclusive reliance on local strongmen, the state would bind the highland peasantry to the state through the mechanisms of guns, honor, and poor relief. Guns – negotiating disarmament to permit loyalists to hold on to weapons; honor – through negotiating, affirming, and reaffirming through the *besa* ritualistic vows of allegiance to the government by highland communities; and poor relief – providing food aid to an increasingly impoverished highland peasantry suffering under the worsening economic conditions in the region. In the period from 1926, guns, honor, and poor relief became the chief tools of state building in the Albanian highlands and the mechanisms through which the highland peasantry became bound to the state.

*Guns: Selective Disarmament as a Tool of State Building*

The classic "fiscal-military" model of the state (Ertman, 1997) suggests that one of the key tasks of centralizing states is to disarm the population and concentrate weaponry in the hands of uniformed officials under centralized command. Success in this matter is key to ensuring the state's monopoly over the means of violence and overwhelming power of the state against potential rivals. What the fiscal-military model does not conceive, however, is a situation in which disarmament itself can turn into a matter of extra-legal bargaining between the state and local populations. This is indeed what occurred with the process of disarmament in the Albanian highlands.

As indicated above, the government had been keenly aware of the problem of weaponry in the Albanian highlands. Armaments were a legacy of the Ottoman era when Albanian highlanders were permitted to carry their own weapons, and which those recruited as auxiliaries were required to bring in fighting campaigns. While weaponry could also serve the purposes of banditry, the use and handling of weaponry in local society was regulated by the *kanun*. The relatively stateless highlands had developed an extremely elaborate system of controlling and regulating the use of weapons. At the price of loss of honor, excommunication from the village, and other forms of collective punishment, customary law required Albanian highland men to bear arms visibly when venturing outside of their village (women were generally forbidden from bearing arms), to submit them when entering the domicile of another, and to use them only for defensive action. The use of weapons for offensive purposes was permitted most prominently for drawing vengeance for kin killed by a member of another clan. However, vengeance was a cyclical matter between feuding parties and as a result, blood feuds in the Albanian highlands carried on for generations, decimating many families in the process. In the Albanian highlands, personal weapons were a constitutive component of the system of regulation based on honor, the chief social currency or form of "symbolic capital" (Bourdieu, 1977) in highland society.[17] As the principal mark of vengeance of "blood by blood" as the *kanun* prescribed, the use of weapons for blood vengeance was one of the main routes by which adult male peasants could defend, claim, and enhance their personal and their clan's stake in the currency of honor in highland society. These practices as manifested in the early twentieth century have been extensively documented especially by English travelers Edith Durham and Margaret Hasluck (Durham, 1909; Hasluck, 1954).

The government understood that the very same weapons could be turned against it. A series of events made the government especially sensitive to the availability of weaponry in the highlands. First, the antigovernment rebellions of Mirdita and Dukagjini clearly demonstrated that highland peasants were not only armed, but capable of mobilizing collectively against the authorities. Moreover, armed fighters based in the northeastern highlands along the border with Yugoslavia, such as those under the leadership of Bajram Curri, a veteran of the war for independence, were not only a regional menace, but could threaten the balance of national politics as well. In 1924, Curri aligned with a number of disgruntled officials and radical intellectuals to help overthrow the government in a coup and helped establish a radical government led by the American educated bishop Fan Noli (the revolutionary government lasted only six months, after which Zogu reclaimed power). Moreover, Zogu, who would come to rule Albania for most of its early life as an independent state, himself knew the value of armed highland men. He had made his own initial mark on Albanian politics chiefly due to his inherited position as local chieftain of the hilly Mati region in central Albania. His ability to mobilize the fighting men of Mati with personal loyalty to him, for military campaigns, proved one of his key political assets in his early political career (Tomes, 2004). In any event, disarming the highlands meant that highland peasants would no longer represent a threat to the government, a simple fact recognized by the commander of the government anti-insurgent force in Mirdita in his proposal for administering the highlands.

As early as 1922, the Albanian parliament had passed a law banning the bearing of arms. However, while the disarming of citizens by members of the military and the gendarmerie took place sporadically and only in extreme circumstances (such as armed revolt), it was only in 1930 that a new law gave government agents greater authority to confiscate weapons by force. Understanding the dynamics between the government and highland communities requires a brief discussion of the changing political context in which social order and its attainment through state centralization became an increasing priority of political elites.

In 1924, the attempts of Albania's short-lived revolutionary government to institute agrarian reform and a number of other liberal reforms failed, and Zogu, with Yugoslav political and logistical support, managed to recapture power and install himself as president. After four years of serving on that post and after gaining the political and financial backing of Italy, Zogu claimed the post of king of Albania.[18] While building an increasingly authoritarian system of rule, Zogu's period nonetheless marks an era of political stability, in that the defeat of 1924 had either killed or exiled most of Zogu's opposition. Historians agree that the establishment of the monarchy in 1928 marks the period when Albania entered a phase of intense centralization (Fischer, 1984; Vickers, 1999). Propounding a platform of rapid Westernization, part of the regime's efforts were directed toward reforming the remnants of the Ottoman system of administration in favor of a European-type, professional civil bureaucracy. For example, a centralized police system was instituted in 1925. French-style Penal and Civil Codes were adopted in 1927 to replace the Ottoman-era justice system based on Islamic sharia law and locally based systems for administering justice.

With the assistance of British advisors, the military and gendarmerie were reorganized along professional lines beginning in 1928, and by the 1930s over 400 gendarmerie posts had been set up throughout the country, including the once authority-free highlands (Fischer, 1984, pp. 101–104; Tomes, 2004). A clear political advantage against rivals and international political and financial support put the Zogu regime in place to advance centralizing reforms at a rapid pace, in alliance with some of the more conservative landowning elites of Albanian society. As for the highlands, Zogu had as early as 1923, when he was Prime Minister, indicated in a conversation with a British diplomat the uselessness of appointing educated but uninfluential southerners as heads of local Sub-Prefectures, and need to rule through the use of the traditional authorities of the *bajraktars* (Tomes, 2004, p. 59).[19] Zogu and the regime grew particularly concerned over banditry in the highlands, which Zogu sought to end. As unchallenged ruler, Zogu now was in a better position to push for his policies without the resistance of the defeated and exiled intellectual elite that had pressed for liberalization and reform. Zogu instead preferred "exemplary order and discipline throughout the country" (quoted in Tomes, 2004, p. 152), to be achieved by the most expedient means. In fact, Zogu's move to restore the Albanian monarchy was ideologically justified as the best means to secure an orderly society.[20]

One of the reported motives behind the Dukagjini revolt was to resist the effort by the local authorities – Sub-Prefects appointed by the regional Prefect based in the nearest town – to seize weapons from highland peasants.[21] Weapons were eventually seized, but only after government troops and volunteers had violently repressed the revolt and laid siege to the region. What had been apparent became fully evident, which is that highland peasants would not voluntarily disarm, and that attempts at confiscating weapons by force could provoke resistance. Instead of embarking on a systematic campaign of disarming the highlands, however, the authorities would use the confiscation of weapons as a punishment against those individuals and groups deemed criminally or politically dangerous. Exact numbers are unavailable, but one source estimates that by the early 1930s, the government confiscated some 180,000 weapons throughout the country. But the policy of disarming "continued in an intermittent and selective fashion" (Tomes, 2004, p. 152). In the highlands, it was primarily resistance by peasants that made confiscating weapons a selective measure. While the revolts of Mirdita and Dukagjin had failed militarily, their lasting mark on the state was that the highland peasantry needed to be handled with particular care – or with particular ruthlessness.

The state could not arrive, demand taxes, issue legal edicts, and change the way of life of the highland peasantry by decree. Instead, the state had to expand its authority while at the same time appearing to protect the customary way of life in the highlands. It partly did this by tolerating – even though this plainly contradicted the word of the law – the possession and use of weapons by highland peasants that continued well into the beginning of World War II.

### Honor: "Primitive Society" in Service of the Modern State

As described earlier, weapons served highland peasants not only for the practical purposes of defense, but were also instrumental in the customary system of the highlands' honor-based society. The institution of the *besa* was also linked to the question of individual and clan honor and, as described earlier, came to serve the government as a tool for undercutting the authority of local chieftains. Hypothetically speaking, the government could have pursued a more effective measure of gaining the *besa* of the local chieftain alone, and allow him to govern on behalf of the state. Such an attempt was made by the Zogu regime, but it evidently did not prove to be effective. One year after he had returned to power, Zogu ordered his administration to draw up lists of names of regional chieftains in the highlands and soon after summoned all, some 350 of them, to the capital to participate in a historically unprecedented "Congress of *Bajraktars*." The meeting, which consisted more of pomp and ceremony than any effective bargaining, required all chieftains to pledge their personal *besas* to Zogu. Believing that local chieftains could be pacified by simply tolerating their traditional authority, Zogu promised that the state would allow the *kanun* to continue to be practiced in the highlands, and assigned all of them as pensioned officers in the army's reserve corps. What Zogu had attempted to do and failed in Mirdita in 1920, when he was Minister of Interior, he was now trying to do on a larger scale involving the entire northern highlands. But what was evidently not clear to Zogu was that rule through the *bajraktars* was a practical impossibility, given the limitations of *bajraktar* authority in their communities, as described extensively through first-hand observation by anthropologist Margaret Hasluck (1954). First, while some regions had hereditary *bajraktars*, in others, they were elected communally and could be changed when the community became dissatisfied with their performance. Second, many *bajraktars* wielded no real authority in their local regions. They could serve as mediators in conflict, preside over communal meetings, or even lead men into battle, but could not bind others or enforce decisions without collective assent. Few *bajraktars* actually had men under their command, and if they did, they were usually kinsmen, cronies, or clients. In principle and generally in practice, *bajraktars* were first among equals, rather than rulers of any sort. *Bajraktars* were rarely wealthier or owned more land and livestock than others.[22] Furthermore, *bajraktars* may have served as mediators between the state and the local community, but were typically not employed by the Ottoman state to perform governing duties in their region. Thus, the lack of an explicit hierarchy and form of authority in this region frustrated the government's efforts to put a system of authority in place with clear ranks and lines of command. Moreover, the sheer number of local *bajraktars*, their primary loyalty to the local community out of which they derived their status, made control over the activities of all a practical impossibility. More importantly, Zogu never attempted to regularize and formalize relations with the *bajraktars* by setting up a legal framework regulating their authority, or turning the title of *bajraktar* into an official state post. Other than the demand for personal loyalty to Zogu, no legal or administrative require-ments were placed upon the *bajraktars*. The question of loyalty to the state, represented by the person of Zogu, remained an oath of honor, but even at that level, it is unclear what honor, a currency specific to the communal and interpersonal nature of highland society, meant in transactions with an impersonal organization. For the state, however, rule through the manipulation and mobilization of honor was appropriate given what was believed to be the cultural distinctiveness of highland peasant society. For the state, honor was an asset in the pursuit of state building, and it would turn out that the honor of all highland communities was, in the eyes of Tirana's bureaucratic elites, an asset of greater value than the honor of individual *bajraktars*.

The failed route of indirect rule by the state through *bajraktars* meant that honor could serve the state in other ways. Thus, after the Congress, the authorities reverted to the more prevalent practice of communal *besas* that were demanded by the authorities to be pledged by entire villages and regions to the ruler and his agents, and which required the collective punishment of transgressors. For instance, the *besa* concluded between government representatives and the population of the Lezha region neighboring Mirdita, after the revolt of 1921, states that the local population made the following vow: "We give our word on our *besa* and our faith that from this day forward, as per the wishes of our Government and the interest of our State, we will forever be subject administratively to the [regional] Subprefecture of

Lezha." And that, "we are ready to willingly and wholeheartedly submit and to execute any command that is issued by the Government for whatever decision is taken for the *bajrak*s [customary administrative regions] of the mountains."[23] While archival documents show a number of *besa*s written in the form of contracts and signed by all parties, in customary practice *besa*s among the mostly illiterate peasants were concluded verbally with the presence of mediators in their role as facilitators and witnesses. However, there was great resistance to formalize the *besa* and accord it recognition as state law, as the *kanun* was continually stigmatized by elites in Tirana as a backward, primitive, and embarrassing system that had to be obliterated. *Besa*s were also not routinely demanded by the local authorities on any regular interval, but only on extraordinary occasions such as in the aftermath of local rebellions, during the pursuit by government officials of wanted men, or in cases when local government officials believed some kind of disorderly conduct would occur, whether politically motivated or due to banditry.

At any rate, even without formal legalization, what was deemed by bureaucrats and intellectuals in the capital as a remnant of "primitive" practice, turned out to be an effective tool for the state to ensure loyalty and, more importantly, its pursuit of order.[24] That is because *besa*s were necessary not only for ensuring loyalty to the government, but also to help alleviate blood feuds that were a defining feature of the Albanian highlands under the *kanun*. As indicated earlier, blood feuds were constitutive of the honor-based society of the highlands. Tomes also points out that blood feuds were tolerated because the lack of policing in the highlands made them necessary for protecting against banditry, that is, by allowing "honorable" men the ability for self-defense and for taking revenge for acts of transgression. The state thus, while officially opposing "primitive" forms of justice, indirectly encouraged blood feuds, and there is some evidence in the historical record suggesting that it may have on occasion even instigated them.[25] Thus, while officially proclaiming to uproot the practice of the feud, historical evidence indicates that the state may have directly and indirectly contributed to their perpetuation. Beside using blood feuds, the state appropriated other forms of customary punishment. For instance, one of the punishments in customary practice was the communal burning of homesteads and the confiscation of livestock and other property as punishment for a variety of deeds deemed by village councils to be immoral and dishonorable. The state appropriated such form of punishment in the pursuit of brigands and political enemies, by giving the gendarmerie authority to engage in such forms of punishment against wanted men. The state appropriated another similar clan-based system of collective punishment as a form of penal practice. For example, in the early 1920s, the Ministry of Interior instituted a policy whereby entire families would be detained as punishment for the deeds of one of their kin. While the extent and frequency of this form of punishment is unclear in the existing historical record, however, it was partly also a reflection of the conviction shared by Zogu and his urban-based bureaucratic elite that highland society needed to be modernized, but in order to do that, the state had to first and foremost gain the respect of highlanders. And in order to achieve the respect of the "primitive" highlanders, the most effective tool, at least in Zogu's view, was a demonstration of sheer force (Tomes, 2004, p. 96). At any rate, what is clear is that it was not the state which was transforming highland society in any desirable way; it was rather the state's efforts to penetrate highland society that were producing an especially ruthless state.

## Poor Relief: Food for Order

It would be wholly one-sided to claim that state building in the Albanian highlands proceeded only through punitive measures, without regard for the role of welfare. Welfare systems have long been recognized as components of modern state building. Pauperism and poor relief were constitutive features of the building of modern states and markets, as political and other pressures pushed states toward assuming greater responsibility over the welfare of citizens through redistributive measures, in what T. H. Marshall (1992 [1950]) famously described as an expansion of the state in the realm of social rights, and what Tilly (1990, pp. 117–121) calls the "unintended burdens" of state formation. In early modern state building, welfare systems commonly served to shore up the legitimacy of the state in societies increasingly defined by class differentiation rooted in the realm of property relations, production, and labor markets (Polanyi, 2001 [1944]), and only later did pressure from labor movements push governments to expand the array of welfare provisions available to citizens (Esping-Andersen, 1990; Rueschemeyer, Stephens, & Stephens, 1992). Initial systems of poor relief, introduced in seventeenth century England, were generally intended to protect against rural poverty, whereas later nineteenth century reform more directly addressed the problems of unemployment created by an expanding capitalist economy, including institutional innovations such as means-based testing and the workhouse, as well as more elaborate system of social insurance as developed first in nineteenth century Germany. In contrast, the Ottoman empire never developed a strong welfare component, relying instead on local and regional networks of support and charitable aid to relieve economic shocks and problems of urban and rural poverty, while policies of land reclamation and resettlement ensured that the population of landless peasants remained relatively small (Kafadar, 1995; McGowan, 1981). In addition, the largely closed agrarian economy which existed for most of the nineteenth century guarded the peasant population against the effects of external shocks from the ongoing crises of the industrializing economies of western Europe (McGowan, 1981). Finally, the late empire's decentralized taxation system, based on the *çiflik* system of land holdings, meant that sectors of the population, particularly in remote regions, could, by relying on herding and subsistence farming, evade urban-based taxation authorities altogether. This was the case in most parts of the Albanian highlands, with a long history of resistance against Ottoman efforts to tax local populations (Mile, 1984; Progni, 2000, pp. 152–165). The demise of the empire meant the dissolution of this old system of patronage-based support, while fiscal crises of the new state compounded the needs of the new administrative apparatus to seek to expand the collection of taxes, which, until the reforms of 1936, were collected in the form of tithes and on livestock heads. But while government officials complained throughout the 1930s that the highland peasantry were not paying their dues to the state, the series of economic crises that hit Albania throughout the 1920s and 1930s forced the government to push tax collection to the side and instead take measures to relieve the problem of poverty in the highlands. This was because in the highlands, where terrain and a climate inhospitable to large-scale cultivation dictated a predominantly pastoral economy, economic crises came in the form of famines, and when food was in short supply, revolt was not a distant prospect.

It is has been argued that peasantries bore the heaviest burdens for the political transformations that the Balkans were undergoing in the late nineteenth and early twentieth century (Lampe & Jackson, 1982; Palairet, 1997). But that burden was probably heaviest for those subsisting on the margins of the agrarian economy. Highland populations constituted one of these groups, given the dearth of arable land in the rocky, rugged terrains of the mountainous Balkans, and the reliance of highland populations on trade, especially with market towns in nearby lowlands, to secure basic foodstuffs, clothing, weapons, money, and other essential goods. For example, in the Albanian case, the formation of new political boundaries after national independence was a highly disruptive measure, because it cut the highlands off from market towns to the north and east.[26] The disruption of trade placed a greater burden on subsistence farming, and to the same contributed also the growing monetization of the economy, the fiscal policies of the state, and its growing openness to the importing of foreign grain and other basic staples (Fishta & Toçi, 1983). The overall disruptions, combined with occasional low annual yields, translated primarily into a rise in the price of grain, and especially of wheat, a basic staple. According to one calculation, highland peasants – whose nourishment was, as Edith Durham (1909) describes in her travels, quite meager – could under normal circumstances grow enough food to feed a household for three months (Belegu, 1978). The remainder was obtained through trade. In years with low yields, the price of grain could greatly exceed that which highland peasants could afford. Highland peasants faced a number of years in which the population was threatened by growing prices of the basic staples of wheat, grain, and bread: 1922–1923, 1927–1928, and 1935 (Buda & Frashëri, 1985). Under such emergency situations the government responded by purchasing foreign grain (mostly from Italy, and usually on credit) in order to redistribute to peasants.

It is striking that while grain crises affected all of Albania's peasantry, including, in years of bad harvest, the population in the more fertile plains of middle and southern parts of the country, food aid was initially distributed only in the highlands. No distinct welfare bureaucracy developed under the Zogu regime, and thus one cannot speak of a permanent welfare system. Instead, what was generally termed "poor aid" was sporadic and a result of immediate political pressures rather than an institutionalized system of welfare redistribution. With poor aid, the category of *vobekt* (pauper) was added to Albania's political and legal vocabulary, and it was initially used to designate primarily the poor of the highlands. Albania's first law on poor aid, passed in 1924, was intended to facilitate the importation of food aid to the Albanian highlands from a British relief organization. Subsequent laws, adopted in 1925, 1927, 1928, and 1929 were dedicated exclusively for food aid to the poor of the highlands. It is only in 1931, after the onslaught of the Great Depression, that a more general law for aiding the poor was passed, in part probably due to the rising number of protests and anti-regime movements in the south (including the growing perception among peasants in the south that grain produced by them was being used to relieve poverty in the highlands).

The introduction of poor aid by the national authorities in the highlands represented a significant shift from historical forms of patronage in the region. As indicated, the Ottoman state never developed a unitary system of welfare support, and the existing networks of poor aid (typically based on the *waqf*, or charitable organization centered upon a mosque) were based in urban areas. Highland populations had been recipients of different kinds of transfers. These were mainly support provided in the form of patronage (provided to individuals like the *kapedan* of Mirdita, or to groups or communities either directly or through local leaders), and typically as compensation for services, especially as mercenaries.[27] Rather than "aid," transfers to the highlands came in the form of "earned" material goods, regardless of the means used to procure those goods – which, as Reinkowski (2003) points out, sometimes involved duplicity, treachery, and threats of revolt in ways that often irked the Ottomans. The introduction of a needs-based system of food aid by the national authorities radically transformed the nature of these historical transfers. Aid was received on the basis of a household's belonging to a category (*vobekt*) rather than as compensation for services or as a result of individual prowess or the adroitness of locals in negotiating with outsiders. In a fundamentally changing mode of "governmentality," aid was no longer distributed through patronage networks but directly to individual recipients through the subprefecture office. We know little of how highland communities viewed poor aid, but the historical record does show that many households did accept aid when it was disbursed by local prefecture offices.[28] Repeated measures to distribute food aid to assist "the poor of the highlands" as they were explicitly defined by the central government in the 1920s, and the more general law on poor aid adopted in 1931, suggests strongly that reliance on the state for food aid became an increasingly important feature of the peasant economy of the highlands, whose populations had for centuries survived – although meagerly, but nonetheless independently – without reliance on such redistributive systems. The growth of state power inevitably meant the state would have to respond to economic crises, some of which it had itself produced, but also use those crises to reinforce its role as a central social authority, and the provision of food aid became a central mechanism to accomplish that task.

    The mechanisms of binding may suggest that the breakdown of state – society boundaries increased participatory opportunities for marginalized segments of the society, given that increasing interaction with state officials enabled peasants to press demands upon the state. The Albanian record provides little evidence that such a development took place. The capacities for autonomous political action of highland communities, it could be argued, diminished, as the state expanded its presence in the region. This is evinced not only by the decline in rebellious activity after the violent repression of highland rebellions in the early 1920s (a sure indication of political autonomy), but also by the increasing marginalization of representatives from the highlands in the formal structure of the state.

The demise of Mirdita leader Marka Gjoni is exemplary of this process. After the failure of the Mirdita rebellion, Marka Gjoni was marginalized politically and his influence in the region kept in check by national authorities (Fischer, 1984). In the 1930s, increasingly, subprefectural offices in the highlands were no longer headed by locals, but by officials dispatched from other parts of Albania. Moreover, the increasing penetration of society by the state arguably generated a culture of local distrust that increasingly crippled the potential for collective action by peasant communities. I say arguably because the historical record on the actual conditions of highland peasant communities is primarily derived from the perspectives of outsiders, though testimony by contemporary observers familiar with the region, like the Francescan priest Anton Harapi, point in that direction (Harapi, 1999, p. 126). However, the disappearance of the traditional weapon of rebellion to negotiate terms of rule with outsiders, even during disastrous famines, increasing state repression, and dramatic social and cultural dislocation, indicate the increasing political marginalization of the highlands in Albanian social and political life. Binding thus does not necessarily generate increasing opportunities for political participation in governance, and may in fact be accompanied by increasing degrees of social and political marginalization.

# CONCLUSION

While the seminal literature on state formation distinguishes direct and indirect rule as two types of modern state rule, the *co-opt and expand* model of state building underlies the understanding both. Under this model, the bureaucratic state expands its power through the co-optation of existing social authorities by incorporating them into the realm of formal officialdom and the existing legal framework of the state. The model extends into modern colonial state formation, but here, co-optation is only partial as a clear barrier is erected between the central government and the "Native Authorities" charged with the administration of peripheral populations on its behalf under laws, norms, and practices that are distinct from those of the center. As pointed out, this model also underlies explanations of the rise of "weak states" in many parts of the non-Western world, where administrative weakness arises out of the interests of rulers to cripple the capacities of social mobilization from the bottom to challenge political authority at the top.

62                                                              BESNIK PULA

The alternative model developed here is that of *co-opt and bind*. It suggests that even states with relatively weak administrative capacities can develop mechanisms of governance (understood as the capacity to mobilize and direct society toward goals defined by state elites). It argues that this path of state formation does not proceed through the co-optation of local powerholders via indirect rule, but through the direct binding of the institutions of marginal communities to the state. Existing institutions are mobilized in ways that advance state building goals, without the co-optation of local elites into the formal state apparatus, but rather through the use of state mechanisms to mobilize and reorganize the social and cultural structures of local society. In the case discussed here, state elites used three chief mechanisms to accomplish such goals, here named guns, honor, and poor relief. Each opened up realms of a negotiated co-dependence between state and society in ways that effectively obscured a clearly bounded state–society distinction, while at the same time producing what Mitchell (1999) calls a "state effect" – the formation of an administered social order without the immediate presence of the state's formal institutions or personnel to directly oversee such an order.

The mechanisms of guns and poor relief cohere neatly with processes of state building as articulated in the classical literature, since they involve the state using its organizational capacities to control the availability of a given scarce resource among a population. What is most significant about the binding process, however, are the set of social and cultural mechanisms found among marginalized populations that come to serve nation-state building goals. The successful mobilization by state elites of a local cultural resource – in the case of Albanian highland society, that of honor – to generate legitimacy for state rule is arguably the most significant feature of the binding process. Rather than imposing state codes and categories upon society (Bourdieu, 1999), state officials appropriated and manipulated existing cultural vocabularies. Mechanisms of the local social order, such as feuding, customary law, and forms of local power organization, were employed as organizations of state building. To do so the state generated an extra-legal, extra-administrative realm of political power which remained outside of the sphere of formal legal regulation. It is in this respect that binding differs from forms of indirect rule in colonial state building. While informal practices underlie any and all processes of formal organization building (DiMaggio & Powell, 1983; Jepperson & Meyer, 1991), the distinction here is that the effects of hierarchical authority are attained by members operating outside of formally regulated relations – in this case, that of the law. In the Albanian highlands, compacts achieved with local society had no legally binding effect for the state, and local customary laws, while explicitly or implicitly acknowledged by state elites, were never formally recognized by state law. By contrast, colonial rule typically granted some kind of formal legal recognition to "Native Authorities" and native customary law, codified and incorporated within formal legal systems, as Chanock (1985) shows. Such a path may be untenable for nation-state builders not only because of the impracticability of indirect rule, the conflicting interests of rulers in the center and agents in the periphery, and the capacity of organized rural communities to act in politically autonomous ways, but also because local institutions, while proving their usefulness for the purposes of governance, may be stigmatized by elites. The contradictory nature of nation-state building, where elites selectively mobilize popular culture to define national identity, but denounce particular popular practices because of their "backward" and "primitive" character, is a familiar theme in the literature on nationalism (Anderson, 1991; Chatterjee, 1993; Hobsbawm & Ranger, 1983). However, it turns out that "backward" institutions and practices may turn out to be useful tools to nation-state builders.

# NOTES

1. As may be evident from usage, the terms *state building* and *state formation* are here used to denote two distinct phenomena. *State building* refers to policies, practices, and strategies employed by ruling elites to expand the control of the state in processes of centralization. *State formation* denotes the outcome of such activity, in terms of the distinct institutional features of states. For a clarification of the distinction see Steinmetz (1999).

2. In later work, Tilly (2005) introduces "trust networks" as mediating mechanisms between political rulers and governed populations in nonhierarchical structures. The form of such networks varies from traditional patronage systems to "brokered autonomy" and "evasive conformity," imposing upon rulers distinct costs for securing the compliance of the ruled.

3. Chirot (1986) terms this upwardly mobile, urban, educated, and typically Westernized social class that emerges in modernizing "peripheral" societies of the non-West the "new upper-middle class." It is constituted primarily by intellectuals, civil service, and other professional employees and Western-oriented merchants. Historically, the political leanings of this class have been typically radical and/or reformist. For a good individual case study on the attitudes of such a class in a modernizing society of the interwar era see Maghraoui (2006), who discusses the views of Egyptian nationalist elites toward Egypt's "traditional" Islamic past. For the Albanian case see Sulstarova (2006). These specific class dynamics are not analyzed in this paper, but they are important when considering cultural

understandings of modernity that underlie and inform state building policies in much of the non-Western world.

4. I thank an anonymous reviewer for suggesting this formulation.

5. In spite of this emphasis, Migdal's empirical analysis rarely moves beyond a macro view of political dynamics, to examine the more specific ways in which states interacted with local agents.

6. Evans (1989) for example, argues that weak states tend to act in predatorial ways toward their societies (e.g., enriching elites while crippling broad-based economic development), suggesting that weak states do not necessarily lack political and administrative capacities but that those capacities are employed toward narrower political ends of ruling elites.

7. In more recent work, Migdal (2001) attempts to reintroduce the question of state legitimacy, and thus the ideological dimension of state formation, which was excluded in his earlier work. Curiously, however, his partly revised view of the state does not lead him to any fundamental reevaluation of his argument on weak states.

8. As Weiss points out, determining state "weakness" using states as whole units is a practical impossibility. For instance, the United States is comparatively much weaker in its ability to engage in domestic policy than comparable west European states, but much stronger in its ability to pursue foreign policy goals.

9. I am intentionally using the term "state goals" to distinguish from those of rulers. While rulers may have specific political goals, the concern here is not with those, but with the ways in which the actions of rulers and other members of the state hierarchy contribute to the expansion of the state's overall capacity to govern society.

10. On the decentralized nature of Ottoman territorial governance in the late empire see Barkey (2008).

11. CSA, Fund 152, Dossier 2, pp. 11–12, 1919. Other archival documents from the government's early days also indicate its preoccupation with the problem of authority in the highlands and the need to mobilize influential individuals to ensure the loyalty of highland peasants to the government. CSA, Fund 152, Dossier 2, p. 49, 1919.

12. For a detailed history of Mirdita and its local system of self-government see Doçi (1996).

13. CSA, Fund 149, Dossier I–207, 1920.

14. Albanian historiography generally reflects a nationalist position in describing the Mirdita uprising as an act of treason by Marka Gjoni and his followers, or that he and others had been simply manipulated by the Yugoslav government, while ignoring the events that led to revolt. These denunciatory (and simplifying) explanations have failed to discover the issues and dynamics that led to the revolt. My reconstruction of the events is based on archival documents of the Albanian Ministry of Interior.

15. CSA, Fund 152, Dossier 73, 1921.

16. Authorities in the capital saw the highlands as a homogenous social and cultural unit, regardless of local regional cultural variation (such as those between Roman Catholic and Muslim populations) and the administrative division of the highland region into several prefectures. For example, government documents frequently use the terms *malci* ("highlands") to refer to highlands as a specific regional unit and *malcorë* ("highlanders") to highlanders as a particular social group,

often described as possessing a given "mentality" and "psychology" that differed from the rest of the population.

17. Bourdieu (1977) describes a similar system among the Kabyle of Algeria.

18. The recognition of Albania by the European Great Power in 1913 included the provision that these powers appoint Albania's ruler. However, Wilhelm Wied, the Austrian prince who became king of Albania, abdicated after an extremely short reign of six months. Zogu made himself monarch by laying claim to the vacant throne.

19. In regions such as Mirdita, Sub-Prefects had a difficult time gaining recognition as authorities in their local regions, and would feel compelled to express respect for the traditional authorities of the *bajraktars* whom they were sent to displace (CSA, Fund 152, Dossier 959, 1921, p. 19).

20. For instance, after Zogu's proclamation of the monarchy, the main pro-Zogu newspaper argued that a monarchy will help end "anarchy" and secure an orderly society, because the "nature" of Albanians required a strong state (Koka, 1985, pp. 15–22). Similarly, Zogu's movement was for a long time known as *Legaliteti*, that is, legality in Albanian, that is, a pro-order and pro-discipline party. The pursuit of discipline and order was not merely an idiosyncrasy of Zogu, as some historians suggest, but an ideology that resonated with a broader segment of Albania's postindependence upper class elites, as well as the increasingly authoritarian political culture of interwar Europe.

21. Constitutionally defined as a unitary state, Albania's local government was organized around a system of prefectures, subdivided into subprefectures. During Zogu's rule, the Prefects and Sub-Prefects were appointed by the Ministry of Interior.

22. See Clastres (1989) for a comparative discussion of the precarious nature of political leadership in societies without formal hierarchical institutions. The author thanks Ermal Hasimja for the suggestion.

23. CSA, Fund 152, Dossier 959, 1921. This particular *besa* did not hold up for long. A little more than a month passed and local villagers plundered the weapons and supplies of government troops.

24. Members of the bureaucratic and cultural elite in the capital held a rather contradictory view of the *besa* and other institutions deriving from the *kanun*. For instance, a government report published in 1937 scolded highland peasants for their "primitive customs," while only few pages later extolled "the mountain village, a valuable treasure that has preserved the knightly traditions and customs of our nation" (Selenica, 1937, pp. 266–269).

25. This may have been particularly true in cases when the government posted bounties for political enemies and "bandits." This would ensure that clan-based vengeance against perpetrators would follow the murder of men wanted by the government.

26. Mile (1984, p. 351), for instance, notes that among the punitive measures that the Ottoman administration employed against Albanian highlanders was to prohibit them from entering market towns in the lowlands for trade. The formation of a political boundary between Albania and Yugoslavia to the east would mean that trade would be made a permanently difficult activity, particularly for the northeastern highlands, which relied on the lowland towns of Kosovo and Macedonia for most of their trade.

27. Albanian highlanders had been favored mercenary recruits among European rulers at least since the fifteenth century. The tradition of using Albanian recruits continued after the Ottoman conquest of the Balkans. See Kiernan (1957) and Braudel (1966) for Albanian mercenaries in the pre-Ottoman period and Gawrych (2006) on the use of Albanian recruits by the Ottoman Porte.

28. Among the small surviving portion of local government archives in Mirdita are individual slips signed by heads of households acknowledging receipt of packets of grain from the subprefecture office (CFA, Fund 377, Dossier 2). These indicate the individualizing nature of bureaucratically managed poor aid.

## ACKNOWLEDGMENTS

In the writing and revision of this paper the author has benefited from valuable feedback from George Steinmetz, Howard Kimeldorf, Margaret Somers, Michael Kennedy, Ronald Suny, Philip Gorski, Richard Lachmann, Hiro Saito, Shinasi Rama, Nathalie Clayer, and two anonymous reviewers. The author bears sole responsibility for any and all shortcomings. The author would also like to thank the staff of the Central State Archives of Albania for their valuable assistance.

Research for this paper was supported in part by a Fulbright-Hays Fellowship and a grant from International Research & Exchanges Board with funds provided by the United States Department of State through the Title VIII Program and the IREX Scholar Support Fund. None of these organizations is responsible for the views expressed.

## REFERENCES

Abrams, P. (1988). Notes on the difficulty of studying the state. *Journal of Historical Sociology*, *1*, 58–89.

Adams, J. (2005). *The familial state: Ruling families and merchant capitalism in early modern Europe*. Ithaca, NY: Cornell University Press.

Alavi, H. (1972). The state in postcolonial societies: Pakistan and Bangladesh. *New Left Review*, *74*, 59–81.

Anderson, B. (1991). *Imagined communities: Reflections on the origin and spread of nationalism*. London: Verso.

Anderson, P. (1974). *Lineages of the absolutist state*. London: New Left Books.

Arrighi, G., & Piselli, F. (1987). Capitalist development in hostile environments: Feuds, class struggles, and migrations in a peripheral region of southern Italy. *Review: A Journal of the Fernand Braudel Center*, *X*, 649–751.

Barkey, K. (2008). *Empire of difference: The Ottomans in comparative perspective*. New York, NY: Cambridge University Press.

Bayart, J.-F. (1993). *The state in Africa: The politics of the belly*. London: Longman.

Belegu, M. (1978). E ashtuquajtura reformë agrare e A. Zogut dhe dështimi i saj. *Studime historike, 32*, 199–227.

Blok, A. (1974). *The mafia of a Sicilian village, 1860–1960: A study of violent peasant entrepreneurs*. Prospect Heights, IL: Waveland Press.

Blumi, I. (2003). Contesting the edges of the Ottoman Empire: Rethinking ethnic and sectarian boundaries in the Malësorë, 1878–1912. *International Journal of Middle Eastern Studies, 35*, 237–256.

Boone, C. (2003). *Political topographies of the African State: Territorial authority and institutional choice*. Cambridge: Cambridge University Press.

Bourdieu, P. (1977). *Outline of a theory of practice*. Cambridge: Cambridge University Press.

Bourdieu, P. (1999). Rethinking the state: Genesis and structure of the bureaucratic field. In G. Steinmetz (Ed.), *State/culture: State-formation after the cultural turn* (pp. 53–75). Ithaca, NY: Cornell University Press.

Bourdieu, P. (2004). From the king's house to the reason of state: A model of the genesis of the bureaucratic field. *Constellations, 11*, 16–36.

Braudel, F. (1966). *The Mediterranean and the Mediterranean World of Philip II* (Vol. 1). New York, NY: Harper Torchbook.

Brenner, R. (1985). Agrarian class structure and economic development in pre-industrial Europe. In T. H. Aston & C. H. E. Philpin (Eds.), *The Brenner debate: Agrarian class structure and economic development in pre-industrial Europe*. Cambridge: Cambridge University Press.

Buda, A., & Frashëri, K. (1985). *Historia e Shqipërisë*. Tirana: Instituti i Historisë.

Callaghy, T. (1987). The state as Lame Leviathan: The patrimonial-administrative state in Africa. In Z. Ergas (Ed.), *African state in transition*. London: Macmillan.

Chanock, M. (1985). *Law, custom and social order: The colonial experience in Malawi and Zambia*. Portsmouth, NH: Heinemann.

Chatterjee, P. (1993). *The nation and its fragments: Colonial and postcolonial histories*. Princeton, NJ: Princeton University Press.

Chirot, D. (1986). *Social change in the modern era*. San Diego, CA: Harcourt Brace Jovanovich.

Clastres, P. (1989). *Society against the state*. New York, NY: Zone Books.

Cohen, Y., Brown, B. R., & Organski, A. F. K. (1981). The paradoxical nature of state making: The violent creation of order. *American Political Science Review, 75*, 901–910.

DiMaggio, P. J., & Powell, W. W. (1983). The iron cage revisited: Institutional isomorphism and collective rationality in organizational fields. *American Sociological Review, 48*, 147–160.

Doçi, P. (1996). *Vetëqeverisja e Mirditës: vështrim etnologjik e historik*. Tirana: Shtëpia botuese enciklopedike.

Doll, B. (2003). The relationship between the clan system and other institutions in Albania. *Southeast European and Black Sea Studies, 3*, 147–162.

Durham, E. (1909). Anonymous (Ed.). *High Albania*. London: Edward Arnold.

Elster, J. (2007). *Explaining social behavior: More nuts and bolts for the social sciences*. New York, NY: Cambridge University Press.

Ertman, T. (1997). *Birth of the leviathan: Building states and regimes in medieval and early modern Europe*. Cambridge: Cambridge University Press.

Esping-Andersen, G. (1990). *The three worlds of welfare capitalism*. Princeton, NJ: Princeton University Press.

Evans, P. (1989). Predatory, developmental, and other apparatuses: A comparative political economy perspective on the third world state. *Sociological Forum, 4*, 561–587.

Evans, P., Rueschemeyer, D., & Skocpol, T. (1985). *Bringing the state back in.* Cambridge: Cambridge University Press.

Fischer, B. J. (1984). *King Zog and the struggle for stability in Albania.* Boulder, CO: East European Monographs.

Fischer, W., & Lundgreen, P. (1975). The recruitment and training of administrative and technical personnel. In C. Tilly (Ed.), *The formation of national states in Western Europe.* Princeton, NJ: Princeton University Press.

Fishta, I., & Toçi, V. (1983). Gjendja ekonomike e Shqipërisë në vitet 1912–1944, prapambetja e saj, shkaqet dhe pasojat. Tirana: 8 Nëntori.

Frank, A. G. (1966). *The development of underdevelopment.* Boston, MA: New England Free Press.

Gawrych, G. W. (2006). *The crescent and the eagle: Ottoman rule, Islam and the Albanians, 1874-1913.* London: I.B. Taurus.

Gorski, P. (1999). Calvinism and state-formation in early modern Europe. In G. Steinmetz (Ed.), *State/culture: State formation after the cultural turn.* Ithaca, NY: Cornell University Press.

Gorski, P. (2003). *The disciplinary revolution: Calvinism and the rise of the state in early modern Europe.* Chicago, IL: University of Chicago Press.

Gould, R. V. (1996). Patron-client ties, state centralization, and the whiskey rebellion. *American Journal of Sociology, 102,* 400–429.

Harapi, A. (1999). *Kulla e Babelit.* Tirana: Phoenix.

Hasluck, M. M. H. (1954). *The unwritten law in Albania.* Cambridge: Cambridge University Press.

Hobsbawm, E., & Ranger, T. (1983). *The invention of tradition.* Cambridge: Cambridge University Press.

Huntington, S. P. (1968). *Political order in changing societies.* New Haven, CT: Yale University Press.

Jepperson, R. L., & Meyer, J. W. (1991). The public order and the construction of formal organizations. In W. W. Powell & P. J. DiMaggio (Eds.), *The new institutionalism in organizational analysis.* Chicago, IL: University of Chicago Press.

Kafadar, C. (1995). *Between two worlds: The construction of the ottoman state.* Berkeley, CA: University of California Press.

Kiernan, V. G. (1957). Foreign mercenaries and absolute monarchies. *Past and Present, 11,* 66–86.

Koka, V. (1985). *Rrymat e mendimit politiko-shoqëror në Shqipëri në vitet 30 të shekullit XX.* Tirana: Instituti i Historisë.

Lampe, J. R., & Jackson, M. (1982). *Balkan economic history, 1550–1950: From imperial borderlands to developing nations.* Bloomington, IN: Indiana University Press.

Levi, M. (1981). The predatory theory of rule. *Politics and Society, 10,* 431–465.

Loveman, M. (2005). The modern state and the primitive accumulation of symbolic power. *American Journal of Sociology, 110,* 1651–1683.

Maghraoui, A. M. (2006). *Liberalism without democracy: Nationhood and citizenship in Egypt, 1922-1936.* Durham, NC: Duke University Press.

Mamdani, M. (1996). *Citizen and Subject: Contemporary Africa and the legacy of late colonialism.* Princeton, NJ: Princeton University Press.

Mann, M. (1984). The autonomous powers of the state: Its origins, mechanisms and results. *European Journal of Sociology, 25,* 185–213.

Mann, M. (1993). *The sources of social power: The rise of classes and nation-states, 1760–1914* (Vol. 2). Cambridge: Cambridge University Press.

Marshall, T. H. (1992 [1950]). T. Bottomore (Ed.), *Citizenship and social class*. London: Pluto Press.

McGowan, B. (1981). *Economic life in Ottoman Europe: Taxation, trade and the struggle for land, 1600–1800*. Cambridge: Cambridge University Press.

Meyer, J. W., Boli, J., Thomas, G. M., & Ramirez, F. O. (1997). World society and the nation-state. *American Journal of Sociology, 103*, 144–181.

Migdal, J. (1988). *Strong societies and weak states: State-society relations and state capabilities in the Third World*. Princeton, NJ: Princeton University Press.

Migdal, J. (2001). *State in society: Studying how states and societies transform and constitute one another*. New York, NY: Cambridge University Press.

Migdal, J., Kohli, A., & Shue, V. (1994). *State power and social forces: Domination and transformation in the Third World*. New York, NY: Cambridge University Press.

Mile, L. K. (1984). *Çështje të historisë agrare shqiptare*. Tirana: Instituti i Historisë.

Mitchell, T. (1999). Society, economy, and the state effect. In G. Steinmetz (Ed.), *State/culture: State-formation after the cultural turn* (pp. 76–97). Ithaca, NY: Cornell University Press.

Moore, B. (1966). *Social origins of dictatorship and democracy: Lord and peasant in the making of the modern world*. Boston, MA: Beacon Press.

Nettl, J. P. (1968). The state as conceptual variable. *World Politics, 20*, 559–592.

Padgett, J. F., & Ansell, C. K. (1993). Robust action and the rise of the Medici, 1400–1434. *American Journal of Sociology, 98*, 1259–1319.

Paige, J. (1975). *Agrarian revolution*. New York, NY: Free Press.

Paige, J. (1978). *Agrarian revolution*. New York, NY: Free Press.

Palairet, M. (1997). *The Balkan economies, c. 1800–1914: Evolution without Development*. Cambridge: Cambridge University Press.

Polanyi, K. (2001 [1944]). *The great transformation: The political and economic origins of our time*. Boston, MA: Beacon Press.

Progni, K. (2000). *Malësia e Kelmendit*. Shkodër, Albania: Camaj-Pipa.

Reinkowski, M. (2003). Double struggle, no income: Ottoman borderlands in northern Albania. In K. H. Karpat & R. T. Zens (Eds.), *Ottoman borderlands: Issues, personalities and political changes*. Madison, WI: University of Wisconsin Press.

Rueschemeyer, D., Stephens, E. H., & Stephens, J. (1992). *Capitalist development and democracy*. Chicago, IL: University of Chicago Press.

Schneider, R. (1984). Swordplay and statemaking: Aspects of the campaign against the duel in early modern France. In C. Bright & S. Harding (Eds.), *Statemaking and social movements: Essays in history and theory*. Ann Arbor, MI: University of Michigan Press.

Scott, J. C. (1976). *The moral economy of the peasant: Rebellion and subsistence in Southeast Asia*. New Haven, CT: Yale University Press.

Selenica, T. (1937). *Shqipënija më 1937: Veprimi shtetnor gjat njëzet e pesë vjeteve të parë të vetqeverrimit*. Tirana: Komisjoni i kremtimeve të 25 vjetorit të vet-qeverrimit, 1912–1937.

Steinmetz, G. (1999). *State/culture: State-formation after the cultural turn*. Ithaca, NY: Cornell University Press.

Steinmetz, G. (2008). The colonial state as a social field: Ethnographic capital and the German overseas empire before 1914. *American Sociological Review, 73*, 589–612.

Stinchcombe, A. L. (1991). The conditions of fruitfulness of theorizing about mechanisms in social science. *Philosophy of the Social Sciences, 21*, 367–388.

Sulstarova, E. (2006). *Arratisje nga lindja: orientalizmi shqiptar nga Naimi te Kadareja.* Tirana: Dudaj.

Tilly, C. (1975). *The formation of national states in western Europe.* Princeton, NJ: Princeton University Press.

Tilly, C. (1985). War making and state making as organized crime. In P. Evans, D. Rueschemeyer & T. Skocpol (Eds.), *Bringing the state back in.* Cambridge: Cambridge University Press.

Tilly, C. (1990). *Coercion, capital, and European states, AD 990–1990.* Cambridge, MA: Blackwell.

Tilly, C. (2001). Mechanisms in political processes. *Annual Review of Political Science, 4*, 21–41.

Tilly, C. (2005). *Trust and rule.* New York, NY: Cambridge University Press.

Tomes, J. (2004). *King Zog of Albania: Europe's self-made Muslim king.* New York, NY: New York University Press.

Valentini, G. (1969). La Legge delle montagne albanesi nelle relazioni della missione volante. 1880–1932. In *Studi albanesi. Studi e testi* (Vol. 3). Firenze: L. S. Olschki.

Vickers, M. (1999). *The Albanians: A modern history.* London: I.B. Tauris.

Wallerstein, I. (1979). Dependence in an interdependent world: The limited possibilities of transformation within the capitalist world-economy. In I. Wallerstein (Ed.), *The capitalist world economy.* Cambridge: Cambridge University Press.

Wallerstein, I. (1995). *Historical capitalism and capitalist civilizations.* London: Verso.

Weiss, L. (1998). *The myth of the powerless state.* Ithaca, NY: Cornell University Press.

Whitaker, I. (1968). Tribal structure and national politics in Albania, 1910–1950. In I. M. Lewis (Ed.), *History and social anthropology.* London: Tavistock Publications.

Young, A. (2000). *Women who become men: Albanian sworn virgins.* New York, NY: Berg.

Young, C. (1994). *The African colonial state in comparative perspective.* New Haven, CT: Yale University Press.

# PART II
# DECOLONIZING SOCIOLOGY

# PARAMETERS OF A POSTCOLONIAL SOCIOLOGY OF THE OTTOMAN EMPIRE

Fatma Müge Göçek

## ABSTRACT

*The traditional postcolonial focus on the modern and the European, and pre-modern and non-European empires has marginalized the study of empires like the Ottoman Empire whose temporal reign traversed the modern and pre-modern eras, and its geographical land mass covered parts of Eastern Europe, the Balkans, Asia Minor, the Arabian Peninsula, and North Africa. Here, I first place the three postcolonial corollaries of the prioritization of contemporary inequality, the determination of its historical origins, and the target of its eventual elimination in conversation with the Ottoman Empire. I then discuss and articulate the two ensuing criticisms concerning the role of Islam and the fluidity of identities in states and societies. I argue that epistemologically, postcolonial studies criticize the European representations of Islam, but do not take the next step of generating alternate knowledge by engaging in empirical studies of Islamic empires like the Ottoman Empire. Ontologically, postcolonial studies draw strict official and unofficial lines between the European colonizer and the non-European colonized, yet such*

Decentering Social Theory
Political Power and Social Theory, Volume 25, 73–104
Copyright © 2013 by Emerald Group Publishing Limited
All rights of reproduction in any form reserved
ISSN: 0198-8719/doi:10.1108/S0198-8719(2013)0000025009

74                                                  FATMA MÜGE GÖÇEK

*a clear-cut divide does not hold in the case of the Ottoman Empire where
the lines were much more nuanced and identities much more fluid. Still, I
argue that contemporary studies on the Ottoman Empire productively
intersect with the postcolonial approach in three research areas: the
exploration of the agency of imperial subjects; the deconstruction of the
imperial center; and the articulation of bases of imperial domination other
than the conventional European "rule of colonial difference" strictly
predicated on race. I conclude with a call for an analysis of Ottoman
postcoloniality in comparison to others such as the German, Austro-
Hungarian, Russian, Persian, Chinese, Mughal, and Japanese that
negotiated modernity in a similar manner with the explicit intent to
generate knowledge not influenced by the Western European historical
experience.*

Due to the traditional postcolonial focus on the modern and the European,
pre-modern and non-European empires have been much less studied. And
the Ottoman Empire is one such empire: its temporal reign traversed the
modern and pre-modern eras, and its geographical land mass covered parts
of Eastern Europe, the Balkans, Asia Minor, the Arabian Peninsula, and
North Africa. In this article, I approach the Ottoman Empire through the
vantage point of postcolonial studies. I first place the three corollaries of
postcolonial studies, namely the prioritization of contemporary inequality,
the determination of its historical origins, and the target of its eventual
elimination in conversation with the Ottoman Empire. I then discuss and
articulate the two criticisms that ensue from taking a postcolonial
sociological approach to the Ottoman Empire; these concern the role of
Islam and the fluidity of identities in states and societies. I argue that
epistemologically, postcolonial studies criticize the European representations of Islam, but do not take the next step of generating alternate
knowledge by engaging in empirical studies of Islamic empires like the
Ottoman Empire. Ontologically, postcolonial studies draw strict official and
unofficial lines between the European colonizer and the non-European
colonized, yet such a clear-cut divide does not hold in the case of the
Ottoman Empire where the lines were much more nuanced and identities
much more fluid. Still, I argue that contemporary studies on the Ottoman
Empire productively intersect with the postcolonial approach in three
research areas, namely, the exploration of the agency of imperial subjects;
the deconstruction of the imperial center; and the articulation of bases of

imperial domination other than the conventional European "rule of colonial difference" strictly predicated on race. I conclude with a call for undertaking the postcolonial analysis of the Ottoman Empire in comparison to others such as the German, Austro-Hungarian, Russian, Persian, Chinese, Mughal, and Japanese that negotiated modernity in a similar manner; such a comparison, I contend, would generate knowledge not influenced by the Western European historical experience.

## THREE COROLLARIES OF POSTCOLONIAL STUDIES AND THE OTTOMAN EMPIRE

Scholars who cannot often agree on the theoretical lineage of postcolonial studies nevertheless concur on how it is practiced. A postcolonial researcher takes an interdisciplinary approach to critically analyze the connection between power and knowledge, focuses primarily on the adverse impact of eighteenth- and nineteenth-century Western European transformation on the rest of the world, and employs often a cultural lens to destabilize the power-knowledge connection with the political intent to establish a more just and equitable world. As such, I think that the approach of the postcolonial scholar as well as those following in their footsteps reveal what can be termed "the three corollaries of postcolonial studies." These are specifically the following: (i) the prioritization of contemporary inequality: the research focus is on the intersection of power with knowledge that empowers the subject while enfeebling the object; (ii) the determination of its historical origins: the roots of such contemporary empowerment are often traced spatially to Western Europe, temporally to the seventeenth and eighteenth centuries, and culturally to the Enlightenment; and (iii) the elimination of contemporary inequality: the persisting empowerment needs to be eliminated in order to create a common humanity predicated on equality, justice, and world peace. The ensuing discussion of these three corollaries in relation to the Ottoman Empire provides three novel insights. First, the Ottoman Empire has been marginalized due to its demise during the rise of the West; second, the Ottoman Empire's temporal and spatial location traversing the Enlightenment period and the geographical boundaries of Europe provides the perfect vantage point from which to productively question the often unbearable weight of Western domination. And third, the empirical analysis of the Ottoman Empire would help promote the postcolonial vision of eliminating contemporary inequality by destabilizing the Western colonization of knowledge on the one side and the production of an alternate approach on the other.

*Prioritization of Contemporary Inequality*

The specific focus of postcolonial scholars in approaching contemporary inequality varies significantly. Some deconstruct the subject/scholar in order to destabilize its hegemony over power, others instead concentrate on the object/the studied with the intent to empower the silenced object (Nandy, 1983), while still others undertake both endeavors simultaneously (Magubane, 2004). What unites all postcolonial scholars is their subjectivity: all have either lived in or worked on more than one culture, or have been marginalized in one cultural context due to their religion, ethnicity, race, sexuality, or research topic. Their experiences therefore facilitate the acquisition of a certain critical reflexivity that in turn enables them to better identify, articulate, and analyze the relationship between power and knowledge.

Temporally, many focus on contemporary inequality, but eventually step back into history in tracing its origins to the early modern period and spatially to states and societies that do not starkly signal the connection of power to knowledge on the one side and to the critical analysis of variations within Western European Enlightenment on the other (Mehta, 1999; Muthu, 2003; Washbrook, 2009). As such, recent postcolonial analyses of the early modern Iberian empires of Spain and Portugal, Italian city-states, as well as contemporaneous settlements, colonies, and states in the Americas, Africa, and South-East Asia have all helped alleviate the epistemological stronghold especially Great Britain and India had over the field (Ballantyne, 2003; Pagden, 1995; Subrahmanyam, 2006).

Yet the analysis of the Ottoman Empire still remains in the margins of the field. In discussing the contemporaneous inequality embedded within the Empire, scholars often focus not on internal processes but instead on the empire's escalating interaction with the Western world. The temporal intersection of the loss of Ottoman imperial power with the rise of Western European empires turns into an explanation in and of itself, thereby escaping thorough empirical analysis. And the same faulty logic applies to the German, Austro-Hungarian, Persian, Mughal, Russian, Chinese, and Japanese empires and others that also "lost" during the escalating Western world domination. I would contend, however, that one needs to analyze such "marginalized" cases in order to recover the nature of their resistance to or negotiation with the West on the one side and the dynamics of the local processes independent of the West on the other.

### Determination of the Historical Origins of Contemporary Inequality

The European Enlightenment privileged science, rationality, and progress to eventually establish and legitimate Western hegemony over the rest of the world. Such hegemony started to be critically examined initially in the aftermath of World War II, and in earnest at the end of the Cold War. Significant in this examination was the analysis of the intersection of power and knowledge in the construction and practice of the social sciences that came into being during the Enlightenment (Dubois, 2006; Eze, 1997; Linebaugh & Rediker, 2000; Muthu, 2003; Swanson, 2004). Such criticism also entailed a re-examination of the concept of difference through which the Enlightenment marginalized the rest of the world; the nature of the origins and use of the categories of race, ethnicity, tradition, and religion were re-assessed as a consequence (Dubois, 2005; Stoler, 1992). Yet, such an orientation had inherently privileged the eighteenth to the twentieth century temporally and the histories of Western European societies over the rest of humankind epistemologically; some scholars therefore questioned the application of the postcolonial framework to earlier centuries (Seidman, 2005). Others wondered if such an application did not end up reproducing the Western hegemony that postcolonial studies aimed to destabilize and deconstruct (Cooper, 2005b; Dirlik, 2002), or serving as a mere excuse to keep bashing the West (Bayart, 2011).

Spatially, some scholars analyzed the empowered, namely world empires and nation-states with imperial ambitions (Burton, 2003), while others focused on the enfeebled and the colonized (Nandy, 1983). It was in this context that the mission, content, and boundaries of postcolonial studies generated the most debate.[1] While some argued against connecting the disparate strands of postcolonial studies into a single entity lest it turned into a hegemonic tool (Dutton, Gandhi, & Seth, 1999), others defined it as "the academic, intellectual, ideological and ideational scaffolding of the condition of decolonization, [that is], the period following political independence for nations and cultures in Africa, Asia and South America (Nayar, 2010, p. 1)."[2] Such spatial orientation in turn dichotomously privileged past and present states and societies that either wielded visible power or were subjugated by such power. The imperial colonizing Western European states (especially Great Britain and France) and the United States on the one side, and the colonized India and South America on the other emerged as the prominent political actors of postcolonial analysis.

Studying the Ottoman Empire would positively contribute to settling such debates over the temporal, spatial, and epistemological boundaries of postcolonial studies. The Ottoman Empire's temporal and spatial existence destabilizes the inherent privileging of Western hegemony. Temporally, the Ottoman Empire existed from the thirteenth to the twentieth century thereby covering the pre-Enlightenment, Enlightenment, and post-Enlightenment periods. Spatially, Ottoman rule extended from the Middle East to the Balkans and Eastern Europe in the West, to the Caucasus in the East, to the Crimea in the North and the Arabian Peninsula and North Africa in the South. Such temporal and spatial location thus provides the perfect counterpoint to productively question the often unbearable weight of Western domination in postcolonial studies.

*Elimination of Contemporary Inequality*

Postcolonial analysis has a political mission in that it endeavors to establish a future where all humans exist on equal terms, where everyone respects difference instead of employing and exploiting it with the intent to establish dominance over others. Hence, such an orientation ethically moves the liberation of all humankind to the forefront (Bayly, 2006; Hasseler & Krebs, 2003, p. 96). Yet, how to proceed in actualizing such a project remains unclear: should one first deconstruct the current Western hegemony or focus on constructing an entirely new approach instead from scratch, one not 'tainted' by the West?

Analyses of empires such as the Chinese, Japanese, Russian, and Ottoman ones that do not fully fit the standard object of postcolonial studies become significant in this context because they enable scholars to engage in both endeavors simultaneously. The non-Western context challenges the inherent Western hegemony over knowledge, and empirical research of local processes enables the construction of a novel approach (Brower & Lazzerini, 1997; Makdisi, 2002c). Of these two endeavors, however, the former is much easier to undertake. It is therefore not surprising that not many scholars have engaged in such activity in the context of postcolonial studies, let alone the Ottoman Empire. The most significant recent work in this context is Raewyn Connell's ambitious book entitled *Southern Theory* (2007).[3] After acknowledging the existing power of the global "Northern theory" constructed by the colonizing West, Connell turns to the colonized local south – specifically to Australia, Africa, Iran, India, and Latin America – with the intent to generate a "Southern theory" out of local texts negotiating Western colonization. Connell specifically attempts to overcome the Western colonization of knowledge by focusing on the works of southern scholars like Ali Shariati of the Middle East, Raul Prebisch of Latin America, Paulin Hountondji of Africa, and Ranajit Guha of India. Connell provides a productive start, yet one that needs to be built upon for decades if not centuries to come. Another significant venue for expanding the boundaries of knowledge beyond its Western colonization is advocated by Walter Mignolo (2009a, 2009b, 2010) who calls for "epistemic disobedience" to generate a de-colonial cosmopolitanism of multiple trajectories. Mignolo engages in such activities with the explicit intent to imagine and build democratic, just, and non-imperial/colonial societies.[4] As such, the empirical analysis of the Ottoman Empire could help challenge the Western colonization of knowledge on the one side and the construction of an alternate approach on the other, thereby promoting the postcolonial project of ultimately eliminating contemporary inequality.

Given the advantages of empirically analyzing the Ottoman Empire in order to advance the three corollaries of postcolonial studies, it is necessary to map out the framework of a postcolonial sociology of the Ottoman Empire. Drawing such a framework provides two insights: first, contemporary practices of postcolonial studies do not adequately take into account the role of religion or the fluidity of identities. Second, contemporary work of scholars in the field of Ottoman studies actually promotes a postcolonial approach in relation to exploring the agency of imperial subjects, deconstructing the hegemony of the imperial center, and articulating the ethnic, religious, and cultural bases of imperial domination and thereby destabilizing the conventional European "rule of colonial difference" strictly predicated on race.

## TOWARD A POSTCOLONIAL SOCIOLOGY OF THE OTTOMAN EMPIRE

Like the Russian Empire, the Ottoman Empire was geographically contiguous but never fully a part of what was culturally considered to be the boundaries of Europe; the relations of either empire with the spatially adjacent regions they conquered were not easily definable as colonial. Like the Iberian empires of Spain and Portugal, the temporal span of the Ottoman Empire traversed both the early modern and modern eras, but unlike the former, it did not acquire overseas colonies at any time. What differentiated the Ottoman Empire from all empires of European origin and akin to the Mughal, Chinese, and Japanese empires was that Ottoman rule was predicated on a non-Christian religion, specifically – like the Mughal – on Islam. The Ottoman Empire ruled for more than 600 years (1299–1922) over significant parts of Eastern Europe, the Balkans, Asia Minor, the Arabian Peninsula, and North Africa only to fragment into a multiplicity of nation-states during the course of the twentieth and twenty-first centuries. As such, the Ottoman Empire presents an ideal case not only to test the Eurocentrism of existing sociological theory and practice, but also to provide additional insight into the parameters of postcolonial sociology.

## *Two Emerging Criticisms*

Recent analyses of the Ottoman Empire focusing specifically on inequalities across time and space are much more widespread within the field of history than sociology. Temporally, they tend to gravitate toward two periods in Ottoman history, the early modern period up to the end of the seventeenth century, and the late modern period from the nineteenth to early twentieth century. Spatially, those working on the central Anatolian lands of the empire tend to naturalize the connection between power and knowledge while those concentrating on the peripheral provinces in the Balkans, Arabian Peninsula, and North Africa polarize the same connection instead. While the specific vantage point of scholars thus impacts the nature of their analysis, they do not yet critically reflect upon their particular interpretations. This limitation is further compounded by the scholars' subjectivities: younger generations of scholars are more willing to challenge and replace existing analyses at all costs, while older generations continue to practice history without at all taking the postcolonial approach into account. Still, I concur with Steven Seidman (2005) that the Ottoman Empire continues to provide a significant empirical context for the development of postcolonial studies.[5] The review of recent works on the Ottoman Empire generates two insightful criticisms of postcolonial studies that concern the role of Islam on the one side and the fluidity of imperial identities on the other.

### *The Role of Islam*
The most significant dimension that emerges in the scholarly discussion of any non-Western empire is inadvertently that of difference, that centers

around not race, but culture in general and religion in particular. In the case of Islam, this emphasis on religion is often approached critically due to Edward Said's influential works on the Orientalism (1978) and cultural imperialism of Europe (1993). Utilizing Foucault's insight into the colonization of knowledge, Said articulated the manner in which Europe epistemologically colonized the Middle East by defining the parameters of local meaning production (Englund, 2008). Scholars did indeed initially start to address this criticism in their research, only to be sidelined by two recent events that once again typecast Islam. The first event in 1989 comprised Ayatollah Khomeini's issuance of a religious edict calling for the death of novelist Salman Rushdie for the latter's discussion of the prophet Muhammad in his novel *The Satanic Verses* (1988). This religious attack on a work of fiction combined with the unexpected success of the Iranian Revolution led to the regeneration of a predominantly anti-Islamic discourse in the West for infringing on an author's freedom of expression and thought. And the second event took place about a decade later in 2001 when the Twin Towers in New York and parts of the Pentagon were destroyed by a terrorist attack allegedly carried out in the name of Islam. These negative depictions of Islam were further fueled by a third event, namely the cartoon controversy in 2005 when a Danish newspaper printed editorial cartoons on the prophet Muhammad that led to protests by Muslim communities throughout the world.

The ensuing postcolonial criticisms of Rushdie and the fervent reaction of Muslim communities drew attention to political visions that were embedded not only in Islam, but also in the postcolonial rhetoric (Bilgrami, 1990; Brennan, 1992). Even though many postcolonial scholars agreed that cultural hegemonies inherent in religions needed to be destabilized for the liberation of all humanity, it became evident that how this was going to be actualized in the case of Islam was much more ambiguous. Since Islam had not been reformed and secularized like Christianity, the question posed in Western media was whether Islam should go through a similar seculariza- tion and, if so, under whose leadership. Posing the question in this manner once again highlighted the existing power inequality between countries with significant Christian and Muslim populations, where the former especially dominated the latter culturally. The scholarly discussion in the West then turned onto the divides within this initially monolithic representation of Islam, highlighting the divide between the reformist and fundamentalist interpretations (Benedict et al., 2007; Dubois, 2005; Erickson, 1998; Majid, 2000). While the moderate forces within Islam were not as well organized or as prone to engage in violent action as the fundamentalist ones, the Western coverage of Islam nevertheless continued to highlight Islamic fundament-alism at the expense of Islamic reformism. The discussion of religion, specifically Islam, thus intersected not only with power, but also knowledge. Soon Western discourse moved to temporally and spatially contextualize Islam as an ideology.

The initial attempt spearheaded by Shmuel Eisenstadt (2003) and Said Arjomand (2011) to comparatively depict Islam as an "axial civilization," and the local changes within the civilization as instances of "multiple modernity" did indeed bring the Islamic world into sociological analysis, but did so under terms that were once again inherently set by the Western European experience of modernity. This traditional sociological approach has been recently challenged by the works of two postcolonial scholars, Walter Mignolo and Madina Tlostanova (Mignolo, 2006; Mignolo & Tlostanova, 2006; Tlostanova, 2006, 2007, 2008, 2011). They approach Islam from the South American (Mignolo) and Russian periphery (Tlostanova), highlighting the racial "other"ing that Islam as a religion and Muslims as believers had been subjected to as a consequence of the historical develop-ment and ensuing hegemony of the West since the Renaissance. The initial marginalization of Islam by Christian theology during the Renaissance, Mignolo argues, was reactivated and maintained by secular philosophy during and after the Enlightenment. Racially, especially the emergence and sustenance of the Black Legend by Great Britain excluded the Muslims, Jews, and the Russian Orthodox as well as the Spanish, Portuguese, and Africans as impure. In the ensuing centuries, this exclusion then legitimated the violence of capitalism and imperialism upon these "impure" peoples (Mignolo, 2006).[6] The ensuing epistemic privilege of five countries – France, England, Germany, Italy, and the United States – in defining social theory normalized this inherent exclusion up to the present (Grosfoguel, 2010). As such, knowledge from the borders was inscribed by the three imperial languages of French, German, and English of the second Western modernity,[7] making non-Western knowledge totally irrelevant to the social sciences except as an object of study. Hence in approaching Islam, postcolonial scholars first demonstrate how it had been "other"ed by the West through the centuries. Since such "other"ing of Islam provided insights into the production and reproduction of Western hegemony, the same scholars then started to focus on specific empirical contexts that had been able to withstand and often successfully negotiate Western hegemony.

It is in this context that postcolonial scholars turn to a detailed analysis of the Russian and Ottoman Empires[8] in particular. Mignolo and Tlostanova depict these two empires as "subaltern, Janus-faced, empire-colonies" that were juxtaposed between the dominant Western capitalist empires on the one side and their own colonies on the other. The Russian and Ottoman empires were infected with "secondary Eurocentrism" and with the double consciousness such Eurocentrism induced. This unique synthesis made it ontologically and empirically difficult to conceptualize them within the dominant Western hegemonic discourse. Mignolo and Tlostanova interpret this inherent difficulty with optimism, however, arguing that further postcolonial analysis of such thinking from the "borders of Europe" may generate an alternate to northern theory. Madina Tolstanova specifically locates the Caucasus within the Russian/Soviet ex-colony; by doing so, she is able to develop the parameters of border thinking not only from the periphery in Baku, but also from the standpoint of Islam (Tlostanova, 2006, 2007, 2008, 2011). Tlostanova posits the in-betweenness of the Russian and Ottoman empires with Europe and Asia on the one side and Western modernity and Islam on the other. These empires were indirectly colonized by Western modernity in multiple – epistemic, political, and economic – ways. And the power relations they developed with their subjects were unlike those Western European empires: the colonizers and the colonized had a much more equal relationship in that they were not fully overpowered by the modernized colonizer.[9]

Such postcolonial analyses of Islam and the Russian and Ottoman empires do indeed highlight and nuance the past and present inequalities in the world. Yet they fail to address criticisms especially regarding their employment of history in their analyses (Cooper, 2005a, 2005b). Frederick Cooper states that postcolonial scholars doubly occlude history: they iron out differences within European history while articulating such differences in the histories of those colonized by Europe. He notes in particular that postcolonial scholars "pluck stories" that fit their argument without taking into account the larger historical context, "leapfrog legacies" to build causal arguments without fully articulating the historical process of colonization, and "flatten time" by treating European history only in terms of the negative dimensions of the Enlightenment, thereby not analyzing Europe within its own historical complexity.[10] Perhaps the one postcolonial scholar that attempts to alleviate this criticism is sociologist Syed Hussain Farid Alatas (1981, 2007). Alatas draws on the works of Ibn Khaldun (1332–1406) to generate an alternate historical sociology of Muslim societies, a sociology that does not focus, like Eurocentric analyses do, on what does not work, but instead employs Khaldun's locally generated sociological tools to survey what actually transpires on the ground. Even though Alatas is thus able to demonstrate the inadequacy of Eurocentric analyses, he still has not fully developed an alternate explanation of how Muslim societies form and transform throughout history. Still, the insights relating to the role of Islam in states and societies lead one to query the role religion played in the Western world: specifically, how did variations in the practice of Christianity structure states and societies across time and place?

In all, then, focusing on the role of Islam in shaping states and societies did initially enable postcolonial scholars to criticize the Eurocentrism of existing theories. Yet, the same scholars have not yet been able to fully formulate an alternate approach because they have not yet adequately approached either Muslim empires or the Western empires that eventually dominated them empirically within their own historical complexity. So the first step in developing such an alternate approach is to analyze non-Christian empires in general and Islamic empires in particular through their own archives and processes of local knowledge production such as songs, poetry, literature, and oral traditions.

*The Fluidity of Imperial Identities*

Postcolonial studies distinctly separate the early modern and modern periods in terms of the emergence of a clear racial difference between the Western colonizer and the non-Western colonized. Such a depiction highlights the modern emergence of inequality with very broad brush-strokes, overlooking in the process those empires that fell in-between for long stretches of time, ones that were neither the colonizer nor the colonized as experienced in Western European history. The Ottoman Empire is one such case in point. Scholars of the Ottoman Empire carefully distinguish the "early modern period" that approximately covers the time span from the successful siege of Constantinople in 1453 to the unsuccessful siege of Vienna in 1683, from the "transition" period encompassing 1683 to the 1839 end of the reign of the reformist sultan Mahmud II, and the "modern" period from 1839 to the dissolution of the empire in 1922. Their analyses reveal that the Ottoman imperial identity remained much more fluid throughout and was often premised on categories like ethnicity, religion, and tribal affiliation.

The intersection of religion, politics, and knowledge emerge as the central focus of scholars focusing on the early modern period (Baer, Makdisi, & Shryock, 2009; Barkey, 2005; Doumanis, 2006; Ginio, 2004; Grillo, 1998; Kunt, 1974, 2003). Two Ottoman institutions are highlighted in the analyses: *devşirme*, that is the levy of mostly Christian children of the subjects as the sultan's slaves, and *millet*, that is the corporate communal organization of mostly Christian subjects within the empire. Metin Kunt demonstrates that even though such a levy was executed with the intent to produce officials loyal to the sultan, the slaves often remembered and retain their ethnic, regional origin, native languages, and customs; they also remained in contact with other members of their biological families. Eventually, two prominent factions of solidarity developed among the Ottoman administrative elites, those of the Balkan origin on the one side and the Caucasian origin on the other. Still, their loyalty to the sultan preceded all other forms of social identity. The communal organizations of non-Muslim subjects of the empire were also loosely defined, enabling all subjects regardless of religion to interact with each other on a daily basis. Marc Baer, Karen Barkey, R.D. Grillo, and Nicholas Doumanis all highlight this social accommodation and tolerance between religion and politics, principles that were not at all present in the contemporaneous European imperial counterparts.[11] Such fluidity in identity and flexibility in social boundaries contrasts with the previous Eurocentric binary, the strict postcolonial power divide between the rulers and the ruled. It leads one to surmise that the rigid, invariable, and inviolable Western European depictions probably varied across time and place as well, and often did not distinguish rhetoric from praxis.

This fluidity of identity is indeed the major contribution of scholars employing a critical, if not a postcolonial, approach to the early modern period (Baer, 2008; Dursteler, 2006; Elouafi, 2010; Hathaway, 2003; Philliou, 2011). At the imperial capital during the seventeenth century, Marc David Baer (2008, p. 31) argues that Christians, Jews, and Muslims "interacted on a daily basis, in the tavern, on the street, during public festivals and imperial celebrations, in the Shariah court and other institutions." Likewise, Eric Dursteler (2006, p. 20) studying the Venetians in Constantinople takes a stand against the Orientalist stand of a binary, oppositional, and conflictual relationship between Muslims and Christians, arguing instead that early modern identity was "multilayered, multivalent and composite." Identity construction entailed a socially constructed, contingent, and relational process where even the political and religious identity boundaries of non-Muslims residing at the imperial often shifted depending on the pressures of the particular local context. Even though the idea of a nation existed, it was "notoriously imprecise," referring to "people born in the same city or region" (2006, p. 13); as such, the primary identity among the communities of merchants and diplomats living in the Ottoman Empire was regional, spatial, and geographical. Christine Philliou (2011, p. xix) reiterates the same argument for the eighteenth century in the context of the Ottoman Balkans, stating that "family and patronage relationships helped forge projects across formal institutions and confessional divides."

Such was the case in Ottoman North Africa as well. In studying Tunisia, Amy Aisen Elouafi (2010) notes that a combination of factors including "religion, ethno-national origin, trade or descent from a prominent family" determined elite status; African slaves were a visible component of elite society as they were incorporated into the households of the wealthy. Race and rank comprised the two components of social identity alongside kinship, occupation, and religion; as such, these differences were recognized, but not politicized. They eventually transformed into a binary relationship under European occupation. In analyzing Ottoman Egypt and Yemen, Jane Hathaway (2003, p. 5) concurs that households, that is conglomerations of patron–client ties under one person in charge, provided the main political organization in these contexts; a broad range of people of various ethnic, geographical, and occupational backgrounds including "Balkan and Anatolian mercenaries, Circassian and Georgian slaves, Bedouin or Turcoman tribesmen, peasants and artisans" coexisted within the political culture of the household where the primary factional alliance provided all household members with an overarching identity. Such depictions of fluidity of identity in early modern Ottoman Empire successfully challenge the Eurocentric, Orientalist formulations that instead reified differences and divides, anachronically mapping onto the empire binarisms introduced much later by European colonial rule.[12]

This epistemological reformulation of early modern Ottoman Empire is also accompanied by a spatial one whereby the empire is not solely analyzed in relation to its connection to Europe, but instead located within the global world, especially including its connections with the Islamic world and Asia through trade and conquest. Linda Darling (1998) challenges the conception of the Ottoman Empire as stagnant and declining, revealing that such terms of difference only became universalized during the age of imperialism with the spread of Western hegemony. It was not the decay of the east in general and the Ottoman, Mughal, and Safavid empires in particular that allowed the European to emerge into global predominance, Darling contends, but instead the development of capitalism through political violence and economic exploitation of the rest of the world. Andrew C. Hess (1970), Affan Seljuq (1980), Abbas Hamdani (1981), Thomas D. Goodrich (1987), and Salih Özbaran (1990) restore the agency of the Ottoman Empire during the early modern era by articulating the empire's extensive trade and political relations with the Orient in general and the Malay-Indonesian Archipelago in particular. They point out the communication of the Ottoman sultan with the Portuguese king in an attempt to stay active not only in the western Mediterranean and the Indian Ocean, but also to contend for a while in the discovery of the New World. On their maps, the Ottoman officials clearly marked the New World as their administrative province of "Antilia." The Sa'dian regime of Morocco prevented Ottoman access to the Atlantic Ocean, however, and the Ottoman engagement in wars on the European continent thwarted the Ottoman activities against the Portuguese on the Indian Ocean. As a consequence, the Ottoman Empire remained contained within its contiguous territories. This early modern Ottoman narrative recounts the age of discovery not solely from the hegemonic vantage point of Europe, but highlights and brings in the activities of non-Western empires on their own terms, thereby relativizing and provincializing the Western narrative.

In terms of the "transition" period encompassing 1683 to the 1839 end of the reign of the reformist sultan Mahmud II, scholars often debate the nature of the transformation the Ottoman Empire started to undergo mostly in reaction to the rise of Western military and economic pressure. The majority interpret the military, fiscal, and administrative reforms in and of themselves, rather than as harbingers of an inevitable decline. By doing so, they have once again taken the first step in successfully challenging the act of reading history back from the present through a unilinear, predetermined trajectory of decline. Yet the development of a more contextually careful narrative still need to work on the differentiation of form from content: during this time period, even though the Ottoman state and society increasingly appear Westernized in form, how much this change in form also translated to the transformation of content remains unclear. Hence, the issue of how similar and different Ottoman imperial practices were from their Western European counterparts brings back the Saidian anxiety regarding the use of Western categories to explain the rest of the world. In this context, Salzmann and Tracy provide significant nuanced insights. Ariel Salzmann (1993) notes specifically that the modern Ottoman state structure was ushered in the early nineteenth century through two practices, fiscal privatization and administrative decentralization. James Tracy (1994) points out that Mughal and Ottoman trade continued strong during the eighteenth century, thereby putting to rest the previous argument that European powers came to dominate regional commerce right away.

The process of Ottoman imperial change during this transition period is now being carefully analyzed in its own terms, without falling into the historical determinism of escalating Western European hegemony and ensuing inevitable Ottoman decline. Virginia Aksan reflects on this process the most (2005/2006, 2007, 2008); she demonstrates that Ottoman fiscal and military reform impoverished state control over the path of change and

polarized society along religious lines. Gradually, the sense of belonging to
the empire by sharing in its resources became increasingly constricted to
Sunni Muslims – and later to ethnic Turks; this constriction was most
evident in the composition of the reformed military. Reforming the empire
along Western European lines thus started to adversely impact the fluidity of
Ottoman imperial identity. It is therefore no accident that Ussama Makdisi
(2000) discusses the significance of sectarianism in eighteenth century
Lebanon since this period did indeed mark the polarization of boundaries
across communal groups of the empire. Such boundaries had been closely
monitored by the Ottoman state through the legal system and by the
communal leaders who monitored daily practice. Yet as social groups
started to increasingly fight over the distribution of resources, state and
communal leaders could no longer contain the escalating violence. In the
process, the social actors of modernity multiplied, with the actors ranging
from Ottoman reformists officials, to non-Muslims and foreigners engaged
in trade, to missionaries introducing their particular vision through the
schools they founded (Makdisi, 1997, 2002b).

   In all then, during the transition period, Ottoman state reforms undertaken after the Western European practices and institutions adversely
impacted the fluidity of Ottoman identity. Initially, many imperial subjects
located in the Ottoman social structure had belonged to intersecting
communities with varying degrees of clout making their identities fluid.
With the Westernizing reforms, identities became more solid and stratified,
introducing publicly visible inequality and enmity among social groups. This
Ottoman analysis generates a novel insight: How can one narrate the
Western European transformation through the vantage point of fluid
identities? Specifically, was there a process through which identities became
solidified in a similar manner or had they been differently constructed all
along?

# INTERSECTIONS OF OTTOMAN STUDIES AND
# POSTCOLONIAL ANALYSIS: THE MODERN PERIOD

Scholarly work on the Ottoman Empire during its "modern" period from
the end of the reign of the reformist sultan Mahmud II in 1839 to the
dissolution of the empire in 1922 has been most influenced by postcolonial
analysis because of the temporal intersection of European and Ottoman
modernities. In this context, the debate among scholars once again revolves

around interpreting the nature and degree of separation of form from content: adopting Western practices brings the Ottoman Empire much closer to its European counterparts *in form*, thereby enabling many scholars to identify similarities to European colonial rule. Yet the spatial and temporal boundaries of this impact *in content* remain understudied and unclear. How practices predating Westernized ones may have stayed in play in spite of the adoption of new forms needs to be further studied in depth. Still, many scholars of the Ottoman Empire have started to converse with postcolonial studies, bringing the analysis of power inequality to front stage. The predominant scholarly focus on Ottoman formal political power certainly highlights escalating power inequalities within the Ottoman Empire. Once again, however, how these inequalities exist across time and space, that is, how they are negotiated by different imperial communities like the non-Muslims, Kurdish tribes or Chechen, and Circassian immigrants, and how this negotiation differs during the autocratic rule of sultan Abdülhamid II as opposed to the ensuing proto-nationalist rule of the Young Turks are not yet apparent.

The discussion of late Ottoman history in the context of the postcolonial debate has to commence with the scholarly intervention of Selim Deringil (2003). In a seminal article, Deringil argued that during the course of the nineteenth century, the Ottoman administrative elite gradually adopted the mindset of Western imperialism in interpreting their periphery, thereby inadvertently conflating the Western ideas of modernity and colonialism. This "borrowed colonialism" led Ottoman officials to depict the provincial subjects as living in "a state of nomadism and savagery." After identifying the tension within Ottoman modernity through such "borrowed" scale of difference, Deringil extends this argument to the Ottoman state's treatment of nomads in general and those in Tripoli, Hijaz, and Yemen in particular. His intervention builds upon Ussama Makdisi's introduction (2002a, p. 768) of the concept of Ottoman Orientalism, that is, the emergent Ottoman mode of administration of its own Arab periphery "based on a hierarchical system of subordination along religious, class, and ethnic lines." Through the works of Makdisi and Deringil, the postcolonial approach to the late Ottoman Empire thus starts to become articulated.

Most of the recent work employing the postcolonial approach literally focuses on the Ottoman Empire's last three decades from the 1880s to the 1910s. This was the period of rapid land contraction during which the empire literally lost 95% of its land mass (Paker, 2007, pp. 137–140). Given this extremely high rate of social change, it is no accident that identities became increasingly polarized internally and power inequalities in the empire escalated as a consequence. Postcolonial scholars approach this polarization in a manner that constructively overcomes the traditional emphasis on the naturalized power of the imperial center at the expense of the periphery, and on the political rhetoric of the Ottoman state instead of local empirical realities on the ground. They do so through conducting in-depth empirical analyses of especially the periphery with the intent to reveal how imperial power was negotiated across the center-periphery divide. As such, they not only reveal that power binarism did not exist in the Ottoman Empire in a manner similar to Europe, but that people at the periphery had much more agency than previously thought. Yet I would argue that the causal leap postcolonial scholars make from such polarized identities to escalating power inequalities needs to be further questioned. It is still unclear as to whether this renegotiation of power was due to the impact of Ottoman modernity espousing to adopt and apply a Western mode of imperial administration, or the simply empirical consequence of a rapidly shrinking empire, one that would have occurred regardless of the onset of modernity. Nevertheless, postcolonial scholars working on the Ottoman Empire have generated three significant insights in the analysis of inequality in Ottoman history regarding the agency of imperial subjects, the hegemony of the imperial center, and the alternate bases of imperial domination.

*Exploring the Agency of Imperial Subjects*

Scholars who focus on Ottoman modernity trace its particular character-istics through the travel accounts and memoirs of the officials of Turkish descent serving solely in the Arab and North African provinces. Their studies reveal an increasing divide between the educated, "civilized" officials of the imperial center who attempt to study, discipline, and improve the "colonial" subjects in the periphery (Herzog & Motika, 2000; Provence, 2011). Scholars analyzing the Ottoman provinces of the Transjordan (Carroll, 2011), Yemen (Kühn, 2007), Algeria (Shuval, 2000), and the Balkans (Spiridon, 2006) also empirically substantiate this new polarization between the Ottoman-Turkish officials and their colonial subjects.[13] All agree that the Ottoman "colonial" relationship was much more nuanced than its Western European counterpart: the local was not summarily "other"ed, denigrated, and exploited; instead, it retained its agency and negotiated relations with the Ottoman capital, Western Europeans, and their local counterparts. Yet these postcolonial scholars naturally assume that the origin of this increased inequality was embedded in Ottoman modernity. None critically analyze and deconstruct the imperial center, especially in terms of contextualizing who these Ottoman officials appointed to the provinces were, and how, where, and why they adopted their colonial attitudes. Also lacking are comparative studies of Ottoman officials adopting a colonial attitude with those serving the empire in less peripheral parts of the empire or in capacities other than as governors. After all, the Ottoman "colonial" attitude toward the nomads or ethnic Arabs may be similar to or different from the officials' attitudes toward the Greek Rum, Assyrian, Armenian, and Jewish minorities, Alewites, Kurds, and Circassians of the empire; the nature of this possible difference needs to be analyzed in depth.

A truly postcolonial sociology of the Ottoman Empire needs to apply the critical analysis of the intersection of power and knowledge not only to purposely selected imperial social groups like nomads and Arabs, or deliberately selected imperial provinces such as some in North Africa and the Arabian Peninsula. Transformations in social relations in the currently excluded Caucasus, Anatolia, and the Balkans and among the various officials serving in different capacities at these imperial spaces need to be undertaken as well. Temporally, such transformations in power relations also have to be systematically compared to periods predating the last 30 years of the empire. Only after such spatial, temporal, and epistemological comparisons could postcolonial scholars of the Ottoman Empire conclude that what they observe is indeed a new colonial relationship between the Ottoman imperial center and its peripheries. After all, empires contain within them a spectrum of power relationships predicated on the type of formal political rule, where the imperial attitude toward a chieftainship or an emirate is often primarily shaped by historical legacy that widely differs from a province close to the imperial center. Postcolonial scholarship indeed explains the polarizing changes in some types of Ottoman formal political rule in some empirical contexts, but I do not think such explanations are not yet generalizable to the Ottoman Empire as a whole.

In particular, existing postcolonial analyses of late Ottoman imperial rule have generated an epistemological divide predicated on whether such scholars focus primarily on the subject (the colonizer state) or object (the colonized locals) of their analysis. Makdisi, for instance, prioritizes the imposition of a new reformist Ottoman state ideology in the provinces, thereby privileging the subject. He then argues that this central imperial ideology and practice in generated unequal local relations. Jens Hannsen (2002, 2005) instead focuses on the object; he privileges local relations, recovering the agency of provincial Ottoman subjects in successfully negotiating their relations with the center. In his explanation, it is unequal local relations that impact and fragment the imperial center. Whether the scholar focuses on the subject of the colonizing Ottoman state or the object of the colonized populace makes a difference in the ensuing interpretation: Makdisi traces the postcolonial origins of inequality to the imperial center while Hannsen challenges the same inequality by articulating the power located in the periphery. And it seems that the latter group of scholars is gaining the upper hand in recent academic work. Indeed, Isa Blumi (1998, 2002, 2003a, 2003b, 2011)[14] working on Yemen and Albania, and Beshara Doumani (1992) analyzing Palestine history actually employ the complexity of relations during the Ottoman era to destabilize existing dominant, naturalized, Eurocentric nationalist narratives. In doing so, they restore the power and agency of local actors, but fail to critically reflect on the two other sources of power: first, the power located at the imperial center, and second, the power embedded in the particular standpoint and ensuing empirical focus of the postcolonial scholar. While those scholars like Makdisi and Deringil gazing through the lens of the Ottoman imperial center observe and highlight the unequal relationship between the Ottoman capital and the provinces, others like Hannsen and Blumi who adopt the lens of specific provinces instead tease out the process of negotiation between the imperial capital and the province where local subjects retain their agency. In all, then, exploring the agency of the Ottoman imperial subjects articulates the significance in postcolonial studies of time, place, and meaning in interpreting existing power relations.

*Deconstructing the Hegemony of the Imperial Center*

It is next important to discuss the works of a group of scholars that has recently started to deconstruct the lens of the Ottoman imperial center (Constantinou, 2000; Gölbaşı, 2009, 2011; Riedler, 2011; Turan, 2009). Costas Constantinou initially focuses on the colonization of the Western European diplomatic imagination at the Ottoman imperial capital, demonstrating how such diplomats viewed and imposed binary interpretations onto the complex process of Ottoman administrative rule.[15] Building upon this initial critical insight, Ömer Turan ingeniously inverts the subject and the object by focusing instead on how the significant Ottoman thinker and statesman Ahmed Rıza criticized the Western civilizational project from the vantage point of its lack of universal morality. Edip Gölbaşı instead approaches possible Ottoman coloniality from the imperial capital institutionally through the practice of military conscription; he reveals that local conditions dictated the Ottoman administrative decision-making as impeiral officials often excluded certain communities like the Yezidis from being conscripted. Florian Riedler further challenges the uniformity of the Ottoman decision-making process at the imperial center by analyzing emergent forms of political opposition in general and conspiracies in particular. He argues that many conspiracies developed in cases where there initially was no space for a loyal opposition, thereby once more articulating the complexity of the imperial decision-making process. Hence, these scholars challenge the conceptual boundaries of late Ottoman coloniality from the vantage point of the center where such decisions were made.

In addition to contesting the hegemony of the imperial center through the analyses of particular officials and institutional practices, scholars of late Ottoman history have also started to question the nature of the impact of the Westernizing reforms. After all, while there has been agreement in the field that there has certainly been a transformation in the empire that could be labeled Ottoman modernity in form, debates continue over the exact content as well as the extent of the transformation. And it is in this context that some scholars have recently started to develop a novel approach to study the Ottoman Empire, one that prioritizes not individuals or institutions, but instead particular sites of modernity. Such sites not only challenge the hegemony of the imperial center, but also identify their often dialectical impact upon Ottoman imperial domination.

*Articulating Alternate Bases of Imperial Domination*

Scholars working on the Ottoman Empire (Aral, 2004; Bektaş, 2000; Brummett, 2007; Hanssen, 2011) through the standpoint of sites of modernity are able to move beyond the limitations of time and space to capture their impact on Ottoman imperial power. So far, they have employed three cultural sites, namely technology transfer, gender relations, and human rights to reveal how the negotiation of these sites within Ottoman state and society produced complex power transformations. Yakup Bektaş analyzes the 1857–1864 construction of the Istanbul-Fao overland telegraph line that traversed the full length of the Ottoman domains in Asia, thereby uniting Britain with India. Such technological modernity both empowered, but also eventually weakened Ottoman imperial rule. The sultans initially utilized the advantage of electric communication to consolidate their control over the empire, but eventually sultan Abdülhamid II was removed from power when the Young Turks in opposition employed the same communication channel to actualize their 1908 constitutional revolution. Focusing on the rearticulation of Ottoman gender roles and relations in cartoon space from 1876 to 1914, Palmira Brummett argues that women emerged as new, yet contradictory symbols during this time period: they embodied the empire or its pieces, but were also purposefully left at home. Such experienced contradictions of Ottoman modernity enabled the empire to articulate its exceptionalism vis-a-vis Western Europe, emphasizing four differentiating characteristics, namely its multiethnic, polyglot nature; a long history of cultural achievement; morality (especially female); and Islam. Hence, Ottoman modernity forced state and society to enunciate what made their imperial rule different from their Western European counterparts, thereby emphasizing disparities instead of similarities.

Berdal Aral moves beyond the binarism inherent in modernity in relation to comparing the West with the rest. He analyzes the idea of human rights not in terms of how it was conceived in the West to be then exported to the rest, but instead on how it evolved in the Ottoman Empire on the latter's own terms. The empire employed religious law to ascertain and protect the rights of all subjects, prioritized the benefits of collectivities rather than those of individuals, and emphasized justice rather than freedom. In addition, it did not initially seek to control the "public sphere" unless politics set in, as it did after mid-nineteenth century. Hence, Aral demonstrates that the Ottoman negotiation of human rights singled out particular concepts and practices at different junctures. Finally, in his most recent work, Jens Hanssen takes a different epistemological route by tracing the Ottoman transimperial networks that start to form with the advent of modernity. He studies the rise and fall of the Levantine Malhame family at the Ottoman imperial court by focusing on transimperial networks among Levantine society, late Ottoman bureaucracy, European diplomacy, and capitalist expansion. Through his focus on such networks, Hanssen approaches late Ottoman imperial actors on equal terms with other local and transimperial ones. In all then, studying specific cultural sites of modernity challenges the hegemony of the Ottoman imperial center by demonstrating how such sites both enhanced and undermined imperial power. And it also provides for a new venue through which to introduce Western European empires to the non-Western context, not as monist hegemons but instead as actors that slip in through local contradictions and crises.

# CONCLUSION

This extensive review of the intersections of Ottoman studies with postcolonial analysis points to the significance of the initial point of origin of the research: those scholars focusing on the imperial center interpret escalating power inequality within the empire differently than those approaching the empire from the periphery. Also significant is the unit of analysis of the research: scholars often move beyond the contours of formal structural analysis to concentrate on particular individuals, institutions, as well as cultural sites such as informal social networks, human rights, or telegraph technology. In mapping out the possible future direction of the postcolonial studies of the Ottoman Empire, I would propose focusing on social practices rather than the actions of specific social actors located at either the imperial center or the periphery. Such focus has three distinct advantages: it enables scholars to concentrate on the historical process where all actors negotiate with each other on equal terms; it eliminates the epistemological divide privileging either the subject or the object of analysis, and it restores the agency of all parties without prioritizing the standpoint of one over the others.

Such future scholarly emphasis on Ottoman social networks and social practices needs to also incorporate a comparative perspective placing Ottoman imperial history in conversation with other imperial practices. Exemplary is Sanjay Subrahmanyam's (1997, 2005, 2006a, 2006b) contextualization of the early modern Ottoman Empire through his framework of "connected histories" where he specifically compares the Mughal, Ottoman, and Habsburg Empires[16] with the intent to differentiate the imperial encounters from colonial ones. Even though all three empires covered vast, mostly contiguous territory, Subrahmanyam argues, none has been written into the history of modernity. That history privileged the British, Dutch, and French empires, duly dismissing the Mughal, Ottoman, and the Habsburg as "declining" empires.[17] When he analyzes the latter three empires in detail, however, it becomes evident that the Habsburg Empire, based on the dual principles of settlement and economic exploitation, was the only one that was explicitly colonial from its inception. The Mughal and Ottoman empires instead controlled contiguous territories through compromise and administrative and ideological flexibility, often maintaining the local practices of the newly incorporated territories. These two empires also did not systematically exploit and draw in resources from the outlying territories, attempt to culturally homogenize them or employ race as a cultural marker legitimating exploitation like the Habsburg Empire did; as such, they were not colonial empires. Their systematic exclusion from the history of modernity, Subrahmanyam states, silenced the global and conjunctural nature of modernity, instead giving full agency to Europe as the *sole* producer and exporter of modernity to the world at large. Such a return to the sixteenth century reveals that history was not then and still is not – and ought not be – the monopoly of the single cultural tradition of Europe.

This conception of connected histories has recently inspired many scholars to engage in theoretical and empirical comparisons of the Ottoman Empire during the modern period (Emrence, 2008; Jacoby, 2008; Khoury & Kennedy, 2007; Rogan, 1999). Dina Khoury and Dane Kennedy bring the Ottoman and British Indian empires to the same analytical space, articulating the similarities and differences between the two in relation to the global and internal crises in the nineteenth century in general and the conjunctures of global war (1780–1830), centralization (1835–1775), militant control (1875–1895), and war and nationalism (1905–1916) in particular. Tim Jacoby instead enters into a dialogue with Michael Mann's taxonomy of imperial rule predicated on compulsory cooperation,[18] arguing that the taxonomy privileging Western European empires does not fully hold in the Ottoman case. The Ottoman Empire did not only develop a more benign relationship with its peripheries, but also adopted many local practices in doing so. Cem Emrence adopts a trajectory-specific approach that further articulates the Ottoman imperial structure. During the nineteenth century, the Ottoman coast, interior and frontier, emerged spatially as distinct imperial paths with varying economic, political, and social orders. Emrence thus nuances the existing postcolonial perspective that does not properly take into account the variations of rule in the Ottoman provinces. Eugene Rogan's work further differentiates the nature of Ottoman rule in East Anatolia (Kurdistan), the Transjordan, the Hijaz, Yemen, and Libya, arguing that each region displayed different modes of incorporation into the Ottoman state. Focusing on the Ottoman Transjordan in particular, he then argues that this particular province comprised an Ottoman "frontier," specifically a contact zone between the Ottoman state and tribal society. In general then, such studies point to similarities and differences not only among, but also within empires and do so in a manner that treats each one on equal terms.

I end this article with a call for the comparative analysis of the Ottoman Empire in relation to all those empires that negotiate and adopt elements of Western modernity only to pass them onto their provinces. The German,

Austro-Hungarian, Russian, Persian, Chinese, Mughal, and Japanese empires all fall into this category for instance. Yet, to my knowledge, there have not yet been any sustained workshops or conferences that specifically place the scholars working on these empires in conversation with each other. Such imperial comparisons would undoubtedly highlight similarities and differences not only in how these empires negotiated modernity, but also how such negotiations impacted their subject populations. And in doing so, they would generate knowledge that is not overshadowed by the Western European historical experience.

# NOTES

1. For the most recent debate in the context of postcolonialism in France, see *Public Culture* 23(1) (2011), especially the criticisms of scholars calling French scholars to acknowledge their colonial heritage and its violence on the one side (Baneth-Nouailhetas, 2011; Bertaux, 2011; Gandhi, 2011; Lazreg, 2011; Mbembe, 2011; Stoler, 2011; Young, 2011) and those resisting such acknowledgement on the other (Bayart, 2011).

2. Nayar (2010, pp. 1–4) also defines *colonialism* as "the process of [actual] settlement by Europeans in Asian, African, South American, Canadian and Australian spaces ... entailing an exploitative political or economic process as well as a cultural conquest of the native," *colonial discourse* as "the construction in European narratives of the native usually in stereotypical ways ... upon which Europeans perceive, judge and act upon the non-European," *imperialism* as "the [Western] ideology legitimating remote governance and control of Asian or African [or other] nations, often entailing economic, political, military domination and exploitation ... without actual settlement in the non-European spaces," *neocolonialism* as "the actual practice of imperialism," *postcoloniality* as "the historical and material conditions of formerly colonized Asian, African and South American nations," and *decolonization* "as the process whereby non-white nations and ethnic groups in Asia, Africa and South America strive to secure economic, political and intellectual freedom from their European masters." Osterhammel (1997, pp. 4, 29–38) likewise defines *colonialism* as "a system of domination established by a society that expands beyond its original habitat" to then further articulate six colonial epochs, namely (1) 1520–1570 construction of the Spanish colonial system in Mexico, (2) 1630–1680 establishment of the Caribbean plantation economy, (3) 1760–1830 onset of European territorial rule in Asia, (4) 1880–1900 with a new wave of colony formation in the old world, especially Africa, (5) 1900–1930 heyday of colonial export economies, as especially the French and British seized former Ottoman provinces, and (6) 1945–1960 period of the "second colonial occupation" of Africa. For additional discussions of postcolonialism, see Gandhi (1998) and Loomba (2005, 2008) who articulate the new humanities, identities, feminism, and nationalism, Quayson (2000) who emphasizes literature as a politically symbolic act, Young (2001) who analyzes

practices of freedom struggles, and Hiddleston (2009) who especially focuses on postcolonial ethics.

3. See also Levander and Mignolo (2011) on the global south, Alcoff (2007) in critically analyzing Mignolo, and Rumford (2006) on theorizing borders.

4. The two other significant works are undertaken by Ann Stoler (2001) who draws on her work on Dutch colonies to then compare it with the condition of Native Americans in North American history and by Bart Moore-Gilbert (2009) who critically studies the colonial activities of his own colonial ancestors in India. Such comparisons across time and space also destabilize the connection between knowledge and power.

5. Seidman traces the origins of the dichotomy of empires and nations to the Enlightenment thinkers who imagined that the early modern era dominated by empires was followed by the modern, unilinear social progress of nations. These thinkers conveniently overlooked the fact that from the sixteenth century through at least World War II empires, no nation-states provided the dominant political framework throughout the world.

6. According to this formulation, the rhetoric of Western modernity could only be sustained through its dark and constitutive side, namely the logic of coloniality (Mignolo and Tlostanova, 2006, p. 206).

7. The first Western modernity was that introduced to the rest of the world by the Iberian empires of Spain and Portugal from the fifteenth to the seventeenth centuries. The ensuing colonization of knowledge especially after the second Western modernity was in turn silenced by the rhetoric of the globalization of culture (Mignolo and Tlostanova, 2006, p. 208).

8. Also included among these empires were that of Japan (1895–1945), but it was not analyzed in as much detail as the Ottoman and Russian empires (Mignolo and Tlostanova, 2006, p. 209).

9. The resulting ambiguity of location leads these regions to highlight their sacred geography or geopolitics in an attempt to recover their lost identity on the one hand and to form alliances with both the North and the South on the other. For another similar analysis of Russia's imperial borderlands, see Brower and Lazzerini (1997).

10. It should be noted that Sankar Muthu (2003) does indeed address the complexity of discourse regarding the non-West within the Enlightenment discourse, but does not necessarily employ the postcolonial approach in doing so.

11. Eyal Ginio (2004) additionally analyzes the place of Gypsies (*kıptî*) in Ottoman society only to reveal that they formulated an ambiguous group that was neither Muslim nor non-Muslim.

12. For additional studies, see also Brummett (1994), Goffman (1998, 2002), and Greene (2000).

13. Lynda Carroll (2011) treats the Ottoman administrative attempts to forcefully settle nomadic tribes in the Transjordan as an indication of this new colonial mentality while Thomas Kühn (2007) nuances the "exclusionary inclusiveness" of Ottoman rule in Yemen by arguing that the locals were included in local administration, but now along sectarian lines. Tal Shuval (2000) articulates the manner in which the local janissary corps sustained their exclusionary Turkishness through recruiting Turks into the militia and marrying selectively. Monica Spiridon (2006) discusses the coexistence of two sets of local elites in the Balkans, one

retaining the traditional Turkish-style hierarchy and the other embracing the social consequences of Western-style education to challenge that hierarchy.

14. Isa Blumi employs the Ottoman experience to destabilize binary nationalist narratives in Yemen and Albania. Viewing the issue of identity formation from the standpoint of the Ottoman imperial subjects, Blumi destabilizes the narratives that assume what was proposed by the Ottoman state and interpreted by Western Europeans in the context of Albanians did not at all capture the complexities on the ground as many Albanians had very disparate views and identities, ones systematically silenced by nationalist historiography.

15. For a similar study on the Enlightenment thinkers' binary images of the Turks, see also Çırakman (2001).

16. Subrahmanyam (2006, p. 69) also mentions the Persian Safavid and the Chinese Ming and Qing empires, but does not analyze these as extensively.

17. Also overlooked in the process were the world-embracing ambitions of the Ottoman and Habsburg empires in the sixteenth century; the former was dismissed as the "Sick Man of Europe" and the latter through the "Black Legend." The Black Legend demonized the Spanish Empire and the Habsburgs that ruled over it for a while in terms of the treatment of the indigenous subjects overseas and religious minorities in Europe.

18. Michael Mann's five part taxonomy of "compulsory cooperation" comprises military pacification, the military multiplier effect, the correlation of authority with economic power, labor intensification, and the coerced diffusion of cultural norms (Jacoby, 2008, p. 268).

# REFERENCES

Aksan, V. H. (2005/2006). Ottoman to Turk: Continuity and change. *International Journal*, *61*(1), 19–38.

Aksan, V. H. (2007). The Ottoman military and state transformation in a globalizing world. *Comparative Studies of South Asia, Africa and the Middle East*, *27*(2), 259–272.

Aksan, V. H. (2008). Theoretical Ottomans. *History and Theory, 47*, 109–122.

Alatas, S. F. (2007). The historical sociology of Muslim societies: Khaldunian applications. *International Sociology*, *22*(3), 267–288.

Alatas, S. H. (1981). Intellectual captivity and developing societies. In A. Abdel-Malek (Ed.), *The civilization project: The visions of the Orient* (pp. 19–62). Mexico: El Colegio de Mexico.

Aral, B. (2004). The idea of human rights as perceived in the Ottoman Empire. *Human Rights Quarterly, 26*(2), 454–482.

Arjomand, S. A. (2011). Axial civilizations, multiple modernities, and Islam. *Journal of Classical Sociology, 11*(3), 327–335.

Baer, M., Makdisi, U., & Shryock, A. (2009). CSSH discussion: Tolerance and conversion in the ottoman empire: A conversation. *CSSH, 51*(4), 927–940.

Baer, M. D. (2008). *Honored by the glory of Islam: Conversion and conquest in Ottoman Europe*. New York, NY: Oxford University Press.

Barkey, K. (2005). Islam and toleration: Studying the Ottoman imperial model. *International Journal of Politics, Culture, and Society, 19*(5), 5–19.

Ballantyne, T. (2003). Rereading the archive and opening up the nation-state: Colonial knowledge in South Asia (and Beyond). In A. Burton (Ed.), *After the imperial turn: Thinking with and through the nation* (pp. 102–124). Durham: Duke University Press.

Bayart, J.-F. (2011). Postcolonial studies: A political invention of tradition? *Public Culture, 32*(1), 55–84.

Bayly, C. (2006). Moral judgment: Empire, nation and history. *European Review, 14*(3), 385–391.

Bektaş, Y. (2000). The sultan's messenger: Cultural constructions of Ottoman telegraphy, 1847–1880. *Technology and Culture, 41*(4), 669–696.

Benedict, P., Berend, N., Ellis, S., Kaplan, J., Makdisi, U., & Miles, J. (2007). AHR conversation: Religious identities and violence. *Amarican Historical Review, 112*(5), 1433–1481.

Bilgrami, A. (1990). Rushdie, Islam and postcolonial defensiveness. *Yale Journal of Criticism, 4*(1), 301–311.

Blumi, I. (1998). The commodification of otherness and the ethnic unit in the Balkans: How to think about Albanians. *Eastern European Politics and Societies, 12*(3), 527–569.

Blumi, I. (2002). The Ottoman Empire and Yemeni politics in the Sancak of Ta'izz, 1911–18. In J. Hanssen, T. Philipp & S. Weber (Eds.), *The empire in the city: Arab provincial capitals in the late Ottoman Empire*. Beirut: Orient Institute.

Blumi, I. (2003a). Contesting the edges of the Ottoman Empire: Rethinking ethnic and sectarian boundaries in Malesore, 1878–1912. *International Journal of Mathematical Engineering and Science, 35*(2), 237–256.

Blumi, I. (2003b). *Rethinking the late Ottoman Empire: A comparative social and political history of Albania and Yemen, 1878–1918*. Istanbul: Isis Press.

Blumi, I. (2011). *Reinstating the Ottomans: Alternative Balkan modernities, 1800–1912*. London: Palgrave Macmillan.

Brennan, T. (1992). Rushdie, Islam and postcolonial criticism. *Social Text, 31/32*, 271–276.

Brower, D. R., & Lazzerini, E. J. (Eds.). (1997). *Russia's Orient: Imperial borderlands and peoples, 1700–1917*. Bloomington, IN: Indiana University Press.

Brummett, P. (1994). *Ottoman seapower and Levantine diplomacy in the age of discovery*. Albany, NY: SUNY Press.

Brummett, P. (2007). Gender and empire in late Ottoman Istanbul: Caricature, models of empire and the case for Ottoman exceptionalism. *Comparative Studies of South Asia, Africa, and the Middle East, 27*(2), 283–302.

Burton, A. (Ed.). (2003). *After the imperial turn: Thinking with and through the nation*. Durham, NC: Duke University Press.

Carroll, L. (2011). Building farmsteads in the desert: Capitalism, colonialism and the transformation of rural landscapes in late Ottoman period Transjordan. In S. K. Croucher & L. Weiss (Eds.), *The archeology of capitalism in colonial contexts: Postcolonial historical archaeologies* (pp. 115–120). New York, NY: Springer.

Çırakman, A. (2001). From tyranny to despotism: The Enlightenment's unenlightened image of the Turks. *International Journal of Mathematical Engineering and Science, 33*, 49–68.

Connell, R. (2007). *Southern theory: The global dynamics of knowledge in social science*. Cambridge: Polity.

Constantinou, C. M. (2000). Diplomacy, grotesque realism, and Ottoman historiography. *Postcolonial Studies, 3*(2), 213–226.

Cooper, F. (2005a). *Colonialism in question: Theory, knowledge, history.* Berkeley, CA: University of California Press.

Cooper, F. (2005b). Postcolonial studies and the study of history. In A. Loomba, S. Kaul, M. Bunzi, A. Burton & J. Esty (Eds.), *Postcolonial studies and beyond* (pp. 401–482). Durham, NC: Duke University Press.

Darling, L. (1998). Rethinking Europe and the Islamic world in the age of exploration. *Journal of Early Modern History, 2/3*, 221–246.

Deringil, S. (2003). They live in a state of Nomadism and savagery: The late Ottoman Empire and the postcolonial debate. *Comparative Studies in Society and History, 45*(2), 311–342.

Dirlik, A. (2002). Historical colonialism in contemporary perspective. *Public Culture, 14*(3), 611–615.

Doumani, B. (1992). Rediscovering Ottoman Palestine: Writing Palestinians into history. *Journal of Palestine Studies, 21*(1), 5–28.

Doumanis, N. (2006). Durable empire: State virtuosity and social accommodation in the Ottoman Mediterranean. *The Historical Journal, 49*(3), 953–966.

Dubois, L. (2006). An enslaved Enlightenment: Rethinking the intellectual history of the French Atlantic. *Social History, 31*(1), 1–14.

Dubois, T. D. (2005). Hegemony, imperialism and the construction of religion in East and Southeast Asia. *History and Theory, 44*, 113–131.

Dursteler, E. R. (2006). *Venetians in Constantinople: Nation, identity, and coexistence in the early modern Mediterranean.* Baltimore, MD: Johns Hopkins University Press.

Dutton, M., Gandhi, L., & Seth, S. (1999). The toolbox of postcolonialism. *Postcolonial Studies, 2*(2), 121–124.

Eisenstadt, S. N. (2003). *Comparative civilizations and multiple modernities (two volumes).* Leiden: Brill.

Elouafi, A. A. (2010). The colour of Orientalism: Race and narratives of discovery in Tunisia. *Ethnic and Racial Studies, 33*(2), 253–271.

Emrence, C. (2008). Imperial paths, big comparisons: The late Ottoman Empire. *Journal of Global History, 3*, 289–311.

Englund, S. (2008). Historiographical review: Monstre Sacre: The question of cultural imperialism and the Napoleonic empire. *The Historical Journal, 51*(1), 215–250.

Erickson, J. (1998). *Islam and postcolonial narrative.* Cambridge: Cambridge University Press.

Eze, E. C. (Ed.). (1997). *Race and the enlightenment: A reader.* New York, NY: Blackwell.

Gandhi, L. (1998). *Postcolonial theory: A critical introduction.* New York, NY: Columbia University Press.

Ginio, E. (2004). Neither Muslims nor Zimmis: The Gypsies (Roma) in the Ottoman State. *Romani Studies, 14*(2), 117–144.

Goffman, D. (2002). *The Ottoman Empire and early modern Europe.* Cambridge: Cambridge University Press.

Gölbaşı, E. (2009). "Heretik" Aşiretler ve II. Abdülhamid Rejimi: Zorunlu Askerlik Meselesi ve İhtida Siyaseti Odağında Yezidiler ve Osmanlı İdaresi (Heretical Tribes and the Regime of Sultan Abdulhamid II: Yezidis and Ottoman Administration in Relation to the Issues of Mandatory Military Service and the Politics of Conversion). *Tarih ve Toplum, 9*, 87–156.

Gölbaşı, E. (2011). *Osmanlı Kolonyalizmi Perspektiflerine dair Eleştirisel bir Değerlendirme (A critical assessment of the perspectives on Ottoman colonialism).* Working Paper.

102                                                    FATMA MÜGE GÖÇEK

Goodrich, T. D. (1987). Tarih-i Hind-i Garbi: An Ottoman book on the New World. *Journal of American Oriental Society, 107*(2), 317–319.

Greene, M. (2000). *A shared world: Christians and Muslims in the early modern Mediterranean.* Princeton, NJ: Princeton University Press.

Grillo, R. (1998). *Pluralism and the politics of difference: State, culture and ethnicity in comparative perspective.* Oxford: Oxford University Press.

Grosfoguel, R. (2010). Epistemic Islamophobia and colonial social sciences. *Human Architecture: Journal of the Sociology of Self Knowledge, 8*(2), 29–38.

Hamdani, A. (1981). Ottoman response to the discovery of America and the new route to India. *Journal of American Oriental Society, 101*(3), 323–330.

Hannsen, J. (2002). Practices of integration: Center-periphery relations in the Ottoman Empire. In J. Hannsen, T. Philipp & S. Weber (Eds.), *The empire in the city: Arab provincial capitals in the late Ottoman Empire* (pp. 49–74). Beirut: Orient Institute.

Hanssen, J. (2005). *Fin de Siecle Beirut: The making of an Ottoman provincial capital.* Oxford: Oxford University Press.

Hanssen, J. (2011). Malhame-Malfame: Levantine elites and transimperial networks on the eve of the Young Turk Revolution. *International Journal of Mathematical Engineering and Science, 43*(1), 25–48.

Hasseler, T. A., & Krebs, P. M. (2003). Losing our way after the imperial turn: Chartering academic uses of the postcolonial. In A. Burton (Ed.), *After the imperial turn: Thinking with and through the nation* (pp. 90–101). Durham: Duke University Press.

Hathaway, J. (2003). *A tale of two factions: Myth, memory, identity in Ottoman Egypt and Yemen.* Albany, NY: SUNY Press.

Herzog, C., & Motika, R. (2000). Orientalism "alla turca": Late 19th/early 20th century Ottoman voyages into the Muslim "outback". *Die Welt des Islams, 40*(2), 139–195.

Hess, A. C. (1970). The evolution of the Ottoman Seaborne Empire in the age of the oceanic discoveries, 1453–1525. *Amarican Historical Review, 75*(7), 1892–1919.

Hiddleston, J. (2009). *Understanding postcolonialism.* Stocksfield: Acumen.

Jacoby, T. (2008). The Ottoman State: A distinct form of imperial rule? *Journal of Peasant Studies, 35*(2), 268–291.

Khoury, D. R., & Kennedy, D. (2007). Comparing empires: The Ottoman domains and the British Raj in the long nineteenth century. *Comparative Studies of South Asia, Africa and the Middle East, 27*(2), 233–244.

Kühn, T. (2007). Shaping and reshaping colonial Ottomanism: Contesting boundaries of difference and integration in Ottoman Yemen, 1872–1919. *Comparative Studies of South Asia, Africa and the Middle East, 27*(2), 315–331.

Kunt, M. I. (1974). Ethnic-regional (Cins) solidarity in the seventeenth-century Ottoman establishment. *International Journal of Mathematical Engineering and Science, 5*(3), 233–239.

Kunt, M. I. (2003). Sultan, dynasty and state in the Ottoman Empire: Political institutions in the sixteenth century. *The Medieval History Journal, 6*, 217–230.

Linebaugh, P., & Rediker, M. (2000). *The many-headed hydra: Sailors, slaves, commoners, and the hidden history of the revolutionary Atlantic.* Boston, MA: Beacon.

Loomba, A. (2008). *Colonialism/postcolonialism.* London: Routledge.

Magubane, Z. (2004). *Bringing the empire back home.* Chicago, IL: University of Chicago Press.

Majid, A. (2000). *Unveiling traditions: Postcolonial Islam in a polycentric world.* Durham: Duke University Press.

Makdisi, U. (1997). Reclaiming the land of the Bible: Missionaries, secularism and Evangelical modernity. *Amarican Historical Review*, *102*(3), 680–713.

Makdisi, U. (2000). *The culture of sectarianism: Community, history and violence in nineteenth-century Ottoman Lebanon*. Berkeley, CA: University of California Press.

Makdisi, U. (2002a). Ottoman Orientalism. *Amarican Historical Review*, *107*(3), 768–796.

Makdisi, U. (2002b). Rethinking Ottoman imperialism: Modernity, violence and the cultural logic of Ottoman reform. In J. Hanssen, T. Philipp & S. Weber (Eds.), *The empire in the city: Arab provincial capitals in the late Ottoman Empire*. Beirut: Orient Institute.

Makdisi, U. (2002c). After 1860: Debating religion, reform and nationalism in the Ottoman Empire. *International Journal of Middle East Studies*, *34*, 601–617.

Mehta, U. S. (1999). *Liberalism and empire: A study in nineteenth-century European thought*. Chicago, IL: University of Chicago Press.

Mignolo, W. (2006). Islamophobia/Hispanophobia: The (re)configuration of the racial imperial/colonial matrix. *Human Architecture: Journal of the Sociology of Self Knowledge*, *5*(1), 13–28.

Mignolo, W. (2009a). Dispensable and bare lives: Coloniality and the hidden political/economic agenda of modernity. *Human Architecture: Journal of the Sociology of Self Knowledge*, *7*(2), 69–88.

Mignolo, W. (2009b). Epistemic disobedience, independent thought and decolonial freedom. *Theory, Culture and Society*, *26*(7–8), 159–181.

Mignolo, W. (2010). Cosmopolitanism and the de-colonial option. *Studies in Philosophy and Education*, *29*, 111–127.

Mignolo, W., & Tlostanova, M. (2006). Theorizing from the borders: Shifting to geo- and body-politics of knowledge. *European Journal of Social Theory*, *9*(2), 205–221.

Moore-Gilbert, B. (2009). The politics of "postcolonial" memory (extract from My father was a terrorist? A kind of a Memoir – work in progress). *Postcolonial Studies*, *12*(3), 341–357.

Muthu, S. (2003). *Enlightenment against empire*. Princeton, NJ: Princeton University Press.

Nandy, A. (1983). *The intimate enemy: Loss and recovery of self under colonialism*. Delhi: Oxford University Press.

Nayar, P. K. (2010). *Postcolonialism: A guide for the perplexed*. London: Continuum.

Özbaran, S. (1990). An imperial letter from Süleyman the magnificent to Dom Joao III concerning proposals for an Ottoman-Portuguese Armistice. *Portuguese Studies*, *6*, 24–31.

Pagden, A. (1995). *Lords of all the world: Ideologies of empire in Spain, Britain and France, c. 1500-1800*. New Haven, CT: Yale University Press.

Paker, M. (2007). Egemen Politik Kültürün Dayanılmaz Ağırlığı (The Unbearable Weight of Dominant Political Culture. In M. Paker (Ed.), *Psiko-Politik Yüzleşmeler (Psycho-political encounters)* (pp. 131–152). İstanbul: Birikim.

Philliou, C. M. (2011). *Biography of an empire: Governing Ottomans in an age of revolution*. Berkeley, CA: University of California Press.

Provence, M. (2011). Ottoman modernity, colonialism, and insurgency in the interwar Arab East. *International Journal of Middle East Studies*, *43*, 205–225.

Quayson, A. (2000). *Postcolonialism: Theory, practice or process?* Cambridge: Polity.

Riedler, F. (2011). *Opposition and legitimacy in the Ottoman Empire: Conspiracies and political cultures*. London: Routledge.

Rogan, E. L. (1999). *Frontiers of the state in late Ottoman Empire: Transjordan, 1850-1921*. Cambridge: Cambridge University Press.

104 FATMA MÜGE GÖÇEK

Rumford, C. (2006). Introduction: Theorizing borders. *European Journal of Social Theory*, 9(2), 155–169.
Rushdie, S. (1988). *The satanic verses*. New York, NY: Picador.
Said, E. (1978). *Orientalism*. New York, NY: Pantheon.
Said, E. (1993). *Culture and imperialism*. New York, NY: Knopf.
Salzmann, A. (1993). An ancient regime revisited: "Privatization" and political economy in the eighteenth-century Ottoman Empire. *Politics and Society*, 21(4), 393–423.
Seidman, S. (2005). Bringing empire back in. *Contemporary Sociology*, 34(6), 612–616.
Seljuq, A. (1980). Relations between the Ottoman Empire and the Muslim kingdoms in the Malay-Indonesian archipelago. *Islam*, 57, 301–310.
Shuval, T. (2000). The Ottoman Algerian elite and its ideology. *International Journal of Middle East Studies*, 32(3), 323–344.
Spiridon, M. (2006). Identity discourses on borders in Eastern Europe. *Comparative Literature*, 58(4), 376–386.
Stoler, A. (1992). Sexual affronts and racial frontiers: European identities and the cultural politics of exclusion in colonial Southeast Asia. *Comparative Studies in Society and History*, 34(3), 514–551.
Stoler, A. L. (2001). Tense and tender ties: The politics of comparison in North American history and (post)colonial studies. *The Journal of American History*, 88(3), 829–865.
Stoler, A. L. (2011). Colonial aphasia: Race and disabled histories in France. *Public Culture*, 23(1), 121–156.
Subrahmanyam, S. (1997). Connected histories: Notes towards a reconfiguration of early modern Asia. *Modern Asian Studies*, 31(3), 735–762.
Subrahmanyam, S. (2005). On world historians in the sixteenth century. *Representations*, 91, 26–57.
Subrahmanyam, S. (2006). A tale of three empires: Mughals, Ottomans and Habsburgs in a comparative context. *Common Knowledge*, 12(1), 66–92.
Swanson, H. (2004). Said's orientalism and the study of Christian missions. *International Bulletin of Missionary Research*, 28(3), 107–112.
Tlostanova, M. (2006). Life in Samarkand: Caucasus and Central Asia vis a vis Russia, the West and Islam. *Human Architecture: Journal of the Sociology of Self Knowledge*, 5(1), 105–116.
Tlostanova, M. (2007). The imperial-colonial chronotope. *Cultural Studies*, 21(2–3), 406–427.
Tlostanova, M. (2008). The Janus-faced empire distorting Orientalist discourses: Gender, race and religion in the Russian/(post) Soviet constructions of the "Orient." *Worlds and Knowledges Otherwise*, II(2), 1–11.
Tlostanova, M. (2011). The south of the poor north: Caucasus subjectivity and the complex of secondary "Australism." *The Global South*, 5(1), 66–84.
Tracy, J. D. (1994). Studies in eighteenth century Mughal and Ottoman trade. *Journal of the Economic and Social History of the Orient*, 37, 197–201.
Turan, Ö. (2009). Oryantalizm, sömürgecilik eleştirisi ve Ahmed Rıza Batı'nın Doğu Politikasının Ahlaken İflası'nı yeniden okumak (Orientalism, colonial critcism and Ahmed Rıza: Revisiting La Faillite Morale de la Politique Occidental en Orient). *Toplum ve Bilim*, 115, 6–45.
Washbrook, D. (2009). Intimations of modernity in South India. *South Asian History and Culture*, 1(1), 125–148.
Young, R. C. (2001). *Postcolonialism: An historical introduction*. Oxford: Blackwell.

# ORIENTALIST-EUROCENTRIC FRAMING OF SOCIOLOGY IN INDIA: A DISCUSSION ON THREE TWENTIETH-CENTURY SOCIOLOGISTS

Sujata Patel

## ABSTRACT

*This chapter shifts contemporary debates on Eurocentrism from its focus on European social theory to an analysis of its moorings in non-Atlantic sociological traditions and especially those within ex-colonial countries. It discusses the sociological/anthropological visions of two first generation sociologists/anthropologists from India, G. S. Ghurye (1893–1983) and D. P. Mukerji (1894–1961), within Orientalist-Eurocentric positions and explores how these are reinvented in the work of contemporary sociologist T. N. Madan (1933–). It suggests that colonial processes and its institutions together with "derivative" nationalist ideas have played and continue to play important mediatory role in organizing these Orientalist-Eurocentric visions.*

*The chapter presents three sets of arguments. First it suggests that in order to understand postcolonialism it is imperative to lay out the organic links between Orientalism and Eurocentrism. Eurocentrism and its mirror*

Decentering Social Theory
Political Power and Social Theory, Volume 25, 105–128
Copyright © 2013 by Emerald Group Publishing Limited
All rights of reproduction in any form reserved
ISSN: 0198-8719/doi:10.1108/S0198-8719(2013)0000025010

*Orientalism mediated to frame social science language in terms of the binaries of universal (the West) and particular (the East). The particular was represented in India through the discipline of anthropology. The latter studied "traditions" through the themes of religion, caste, and family and kinship. When sociology emerged as a discipline in India in the early twentieth century, it continued to use the language organized by anthropology to analyze the particular cultural traditions of the country. Second, I suggest that these binaries also framed nationalist thought and the latter mediated in framing the sociological ideas of G. S. Ghurye and D. P. Mukerji which were embedded in Eurocentric-Orientalist principles. Third, I analyze the ideas of the contemporary social theorist T. N. Madan to indicate how his perspective continues to derive its positions from Orientalist-Eurocentric positions and ignores an engagement with critics who have questioned Orientalist Eurocentrism. Disregarding these arguments implies the legitimation of the latter perspective derived from the disciplines of sociology/anthropology.*

*The chapter contends that a decolonized critique of colonial social science has existed in other regions of the world including India, and that this perspective needs to be retrieved by social theorists to reformulate the sociological discourse as a study of modern India. It also suggests that contemporary analysis of Eurocentrism needs to move out from within the circuits of knowledge defined by received colonial geopolitical enclaves in order to assess the way production, distribution, and consumption of Orientalist-Eurocentric perspectives have organized sociological traditions across the world including the Global South.*

The Orientalist-Eurocentric critique[1] has argued that methodological nationalism within European sociology has legitimized the organization of the world into two spatial units, the West and the East, having separate and distinct histories unrelated to each other. Thus Orientalism[2] was not only a style of thought that distinguished ontologically and epistemologically "the Orient" from "the Occident" to create knowledge on and of the Orient. It was also a discourse that constructed knowledge about the Occident that argued that the Occident was distinctive and that its history was endogenous and internal to itself. Enmeshed in the Orientalist project were two Eurocentric myths: first, the idea of the history of human civilization as a trajectory that departed from "a state of nature" and culminated in Europe. Second, it incorporated a view of the differences between Europe and non-Europeans as natural though these were based on racial differences and in turn these were regarded as a consequence of a history of power. Within Eurocentrism, the colonial experience was present in its absence. No wonder Eurocentrism has also been discussed as the episteme of colonial modernity.[3] "Both myths," according to Anibal Quijano, "can be unequivocally recognized in the foundations of evolutionism and dualism, two of the nuclear elements of Eurocentrism" (Quijano, 2000, p. 542).

Contemporary discussions on Eurocentrism has focused its critique on European social theory (Bhambra, 2007; Rodriguez, Boatca, & Costa, 2010) and there is little debate on the ways in which non-Atlantic sociological traditions and especially those within ex-colonial countries continue to carry the Eurocentric episteme. As a consequence, contemporary analysis of Eurocentrism continues to remain enclosed within the circuits of knowledge defined by received colonial geopolitical enclaves with very little assessments of the way production, distribution, and consumption of Orientalist-Eurocentric perspectives have organized sociological traditions across the world including the Global South. In this chapter, I indicate how colonial processes and its institutions together with "derivative"[4] nationalist ideas organized the growth of the disciplines of anthropology/sociology in India. In particular, I examine the moorings of the sociological vision of two first generation sociologists/anthropologists G. S Ghurye (1893–1983) and D. P. Mukerji (1894–1961) within Orientalist-Eurocentric positions and explore how these are reinvented in the work of contemporary sociologist T.N. Madan (1933–) (Patel, 2006, 2007, 2010, 2011a, 2011b).

The chapter links three sets of arguments which are presented in different sections. First, I outline the current discussions on Orientalism-Eucrocentrism that suggest that the binaries of universal and particular framed social science knowledge regarding the West as distinct from the East. Using this template, I trace how this episteme organized the discipline of anthropology in India in the late nineteenth century. As a consequence, the study of "traditions" through the themes of religion, caste, and family and kinship organized the disciplinary study of India and became the organizing structure of the discipline of sociology when it made its presence felt in the early twentieth century.[5] In the second section, the chapter discusses how Eurocentric-Orientalist principles were elaborated in the work of two contemporary Indian sociologists G. S. Ghurye and D. P. Mukerji. It suggests that this perspective was mediated through the institutionalization and internalization of the latter principles in the two strands of Indian nationalist thought – the traditional and the traditional-modern. In the third section, I examine the critic that developed against this position. Mainly expressed by historians influenced by the third strand of nationalist thought – that of modern nationalism – they have argued that the study of India needs to free itself from a civilizational perspective and that intellectuals need to locate the growth of Hinduism and its study as part of colonial Orientalist perspective. In the fourth section, I analyze the ideas of the contemporary social theorist T. N. Madan to indicate how his perspective continues to derive its position from Orientalist-Eurocentric positions and resonates those elaborated by earlier sociologists (discussed above) not taking into account the work of the critics who have questioned Orientalist-Eurocentrism. Ignoring these arguments implies the legitimation of the latter perspective in the disciplines of sociology/ anthropology.

I conclude by suggesting that a decolonized critique of colonial social science has existed in other regions of the world, including India, and that this perspective needs to be retrieved to social theorists to reformulate the sociological discourse as a study of modern India and to understand religious expressions and religiosities as being to nineteenth-century colonial expressions.

# ANTHROPOLOGY AND THE EPISTEME OF COLONIAL MODERNITY

European modernity analyzed its own birth (through a linear conception of time) and suggested it was produced through the values and institutional system that were universalized in Europe in the last 500 years in its own backyard. It incorporated two master narratives: the superiority of Western civilization (through progress and reason) and the belief in the continuous growth of capitalism (through modernization, development, and the creations of new markets). These master narratives, which Charles Taylor (1995) calls a "culturist approach," are recognized now as ethnocentric in nature. This ethnocentrism assessed its own growth in terms of itself (Europe) rather than in terms of the other (the rest of the colonized world) which was its object of control and through which it became modern. It was a theory of "interiority" (Mignolo, 2002) – that is, a perspective that perceived itself from within rather than from the outside.

A notion of linear time affirmed a belief that social life and its institutions, emerging in Europe from around fourteenth century onward would now influence the making of the new world. In doing so, it "silenced" its own imperial experience and the violence, without which it could not have become modern. These assumptions framed the ideas elaborated by Hegel, Kant, and the Encyclopaedists and were incorporated in the sociologies of Durkheim, Weber, and Marx. No wonder these theories legitimized the control and domination of the rest of the world through the episteme of coloniality. (Dussel, 1993; Mignolo, 2002; Quijano, 2000).

This discourse of modernity presented a universal set of axioms in which time as historicity defined its relationship to space. To put it differently, because it saw its own growth in terms of itself and defined it through its own specific and particular history, that which was outside itself (the place) was perceived in terms of its opposite: lack of history and thus inferior. Henceforth all knowledge was structured in terms of the master binary of the West (which had history, culture, reason, and science) and the East (which was enclosed in space, nature, religion, and spirituality). This binary linked the division and subsequent hierarchization of groups within geo-spatial territories in the world in terms of a theory of temporal linearity: the West was modern because it had evolved to articulate the key features of modernity as against the East which was traditional. Dussel thus says:

> Modernity appears when Europe affirms itself as the 'center' of a *World* History that it inaugurates; the 'periphery' that surrounds this center is consequently part of its self-definition. The occlusion of this periphery ... leads the major thinkers of the 'center' into a Eurocentric fallacy in their understanding of modernity. If their understanding of the genealogy of modernity is thus partial and provincial, their attempts at a critique or defence of it are likewise unilateral, and in part, false. (Dussel, 1993, p. 65)

This binary oppositions constructed the knowledge of the two worlds, the West and the East, and placed these as oppositions, creating hierarchies between them and thereby dividing them in terms of "I" and the "other", positing an universality for "I" and particularities for the "other." "Maintaining a difference under the assumption that we are all human" (Mignolo, 2002, p. 71) was part of the normative project of modernity and subsequently of its sociological theory. These were the "truths" of modernity and the modern world; these truths were considered objective and universal (Dussel, 1993; Mignolo, 2002; Quijano, 2000).

These seminal assumptions were embodied in the framing of the disciplines of sociology and anthropology in India in the late eighteenth century. Sociology became the study of modern (European-later to be extended to western) society while anthropology was the study of (non-European and non-Western) traditional societies. Thus, sociologists study how the new societies evolved from the deadwood of the old; a notion of time and history were embedded in its discourse. Contrarily, anthropologists studied how space/place organized "static" culture that could not transcend its internal structures to be and become modern.

These frames also constructed the academic knowledge of India as elaborated by colonial anthropologists and administrators who further divided the East that they were studying in separate geo-spatial territories with each territory given an overarching cultural value. In the case of India, it was religion: Hinduism. The discourse of coloniality collapsed India and Hinduism into each other (Patel, 2006, 2007). The collapse of India into Hindu India is not new. The genealogy of the collapse goes back to the nineteenth-century colonial constructs which assumed two principles. The first assumption was geographical and distinguished between groups living in the subcontinent from the spatial-cultural structures of the West, thereby creating the master binary of the West and the East. Later those living in the subcontinent were further classified geographically in spatial-cultural zones and "regionally" sub-divided.

The second assumption is related to the internal division and relationship between these groups within India. All groups living in the subcontinent were defined by their relationship with Hinduism. Those that were directly related to the constructed notion of Hinduism as now understood, such as castes and tribes, were termed the "majority" and organized in terms of distinct hierarchies (castes were considered more superior than tribes who were thought to be "primitive"), while those that were not, were conceived as "minorities"; these being mainly groups who practiced Islam and Christianity (Patel, 2006). Evolutionist theories were used to make Hinduism the "Great tradition" and anchored into a timeless civilization and its margins, the folk cultures, the "little traditions".[6]

Anthropologists/sociologists researching on South Asian religions have oftentimes uncritically accepted this logic, and thereby become trapped in this discourse. The geographically vast subcontinent of South Asia with its thousands of communities having distinct cultural practices and ideas have lived and experienced existence in various forms of unequal and subordinate relationships with each other. In the nineteenth century, anthropological/ sociological knowledge dissolved these distinctions and re-categorized them into four or five major religious traditions thereby constructing a master narrative of the majority and minority. This logic homogenized distinctions between groups, but it also naturalized the Orientalist-Eurocentric language as the only language to comprehend the unequal distribution of power and resources.

British civil servants and anthropologists and later Indian anthropologists placed the debate of identifying and designating these as "caste" or "tribes" within the discussion of "stocks" or "races" in relation to other "stocks" and "races" in the Western world. In order to formulate these categories, they took the help of evolutionary theory, and also Victorian social thought associated with "race science." In this they were aided through a theory of the "Aryan" (white or fair-skinned) invasion of India, which grew out of the discovery of the Indo-European language family in the late nineteenth century. Hence, linguistic classification merged with racial classification to produce a theory of the Indian civilization formed by the invasion of fair-skinned, civilized, Sanskrit-speaking Aryans, who conquered and partially absorbed the dark-skinned savage aborigines.

This theory was critical in producing the theory regarding distinctions between groups in India into Aryan and non-Aryan races, now termed "castes" and "tribes." What is of interest is the fact that while "castes" were defined in the context of Hinduism, as groups who cultivated land, had better technology and a high civilizational attribute, "tribes" were defined in contrast to castes, who practiced primitive technology, lived in interior jungles, and were animistic in religious practices. Such classifications and categorization were not peculiar to India. They also found manifestation in the African continent, as British officials used this knowledge to construct categories of social groups in Africa and retransferred these newly constructed classifications back again to India, as happened in the case of the term "tribe" as a lineage group based on a segmentary state.

In the process, "caste" (and "tribe") was made out to be a far more pervasive, totalizing, and uniform concept than ever before and defined in terms of a religious order, which it was not always so. In fact, ancient and medieval historiographers now inform us that those whom we identify as castes and tribes were groups that were shaped by political struggles and processes over material resources. In pre-colonial India, multiple markers of identity defined relationship between groups and were contingent on complex processes, which were constantly changing and were related to political power. Thus, there were temple communities, territorial groups, lineage segments, family units, royal retinues, warrior subcastes, "little as opposed to large kingdoms," occupational reference groups, agricultural and trading associations, networks of devotional and sectarian religious communities, and priestly cables. Marxist historical analysis retrieved these sources to affirm that colonial knowledge has standardized and homogenized these diversities into an Orientalist perspective.[7]

112 SUJATA PATEL

# SOCIOLOGICAL VISIONS OF G. S. GHURYE AND D. P. MUKERJI

The historian Sumit Sarkar affirms this orientation when he suggests that the historical consciousness of the Indian intelligentsia in the late nineteenth and early twentieth centuries was oriented to the valorization of culture against the colonial state to which they were opposed as (proto-)nationalists. This attribute he contrasted with the intelligentsia of the West who wrote modern (Western) history in terms of the nation-state. He states the following about Indian intellectual thought:

> In this period *samaj* (society, community) came to be counterpoised to *rashtra* or *rajshakti* (state, the political domain). The real history of India, it was repeatedly asserted, was located in the first, not the second, for *samaj* embodied the distinctive qualities peculiar to the genius, culture and religion of the Indian people. (Sarkar, 1997, p. 21)

And

> ... *samaj* was simultaneously all too often conceptualised in Hindu, high caste gentry, and paternalistic terms .... (Sarkar, 1997, p. 23)

Indigenous intellectuals needed to express a utopia on which to build the foundation of a new modernity. However, they were caught into a double bind: on one hand, modernity was understood as freedom and liberty and on the other hand it was experienced as colonialism, as being subordinated. Thus, as Partha Chatterjee has stated, unlike the Europeans for whom, "the present was the site of one's escape from the past," for the indigenous Indian intellectuals "it is precisely the present [given the colonial experience] from which we feel we must escape." Thus, the Indian indigenous intellectuals transposed the desire for a new modernity to the past of India, a past ironically constructed by colonial knowledges of modernity. As a result, Chatterjee argues, "we construct a picture of "those days" when there was beauty, prosperity and healthy sociability. This makes the very modality of our coping with modernity radically different from the historically evolved modes of Western modernity" (Chatterjee, 1997, p. 20).

What were the attributes of this different experience? For the nationalists, the most important attribute of this experience was the material and ideational decadence and degeneration of the country. British domination allowed it to extract and control India's rich material resources. Simultaneously, colonialism also destroyed India's vitality by supplanting its rich heritage of ideas with modern Western ones. For the nationalists, the question was: how does one reflect on ways to transcend these barriers. What ideas, ideologies, and values allowed "us" to confront the might of the colonial state and its control of the Indians through the organization of knowledge?

There were divisions among the nationalists about the solution of these problems and three groups provided three different answers.[8] On one side there were the "modernists" who believed that the solution lay in emulating the Western civilization. They argued that the problem was with India's past, especially its culture which had made the "Indian" people passive, lifeless, and non-productive. They advocated the path set by Europe earlier and wanted India to have a new industrial economy, free from agrarian dependencies. It is no coincidence that these ideas became the source for building a new discipline of economics and later of its intervention in the planning and developmental process inaugurated by independent India. This voice remained a minority, for a large number felt that modernity had little emancipatory potential for a society that was destroyed by a modern nation-state through colonialism.

The "traditionalists" argued for a need to draw out theories from the past – from that of India's rich histories and its civilization. Though this civilization had suffered a decline, it was essentially fundamentally sound and was embodied with much strength. These strengths had kept the "Indian" people together over centuries (except in the interregnum of the Muslim period) and these ideas will continue to bind them together in the future. Indian civilization and thus its society had a distinct history which had evolved in interaction with its people and its agencies. Indians and its social sciences needed to mobilize this creativity for its regeneration without losing its coherence and inner balance. Imitating the West, taking its language and its values will not serve India or its people. India has to work out its own salvation in its own terms – its temperaments, traditions, and circumstances (Bhattacharya, 2011).[9]

The traditional nationalists suggested that India was a civilization and thereby borrowed and reinterpreted Orientalist knowledge to articulate an Indian version. The notion of civilization has a long history in orientalism. In the late eighteenth and early nineteenth century, Orientalists generalized on the basis of the Greek and Egyptian civilizations. Later with the discovery of "Indian" civilization the study of India was absorbed into the existing discourse about antique civilizations. Early British Orientalists used Sanskrit texts to study this civilization and to place it within the linear theories of history. Some even argued that the high culture of Hindu civilization emerged from Greek influence. However, the traditional

114 SUJATA PATEL

nationalists inverted this argument to suggest that Greek culture has learnt its science from India.
These ideas are best reflected in the civilizational approach popularized by the "father" of Indian sociology, G. S. Ghurye (1893–1983), who was Head of the Department of Sociology at the University of Bombay for 35 long years and who trained most of the next generation of sociologists in India.[10] Even today, his theories are considered to have foundational implications for the study of Indian society. How did he understand civilization and how did this affect the sociological study of India?

For Ghurye, culture and civilization were understood as being the same: as a complex of ideas, beliefs, values, and social practices (Upadhya, 2000, p. 44). His work rarely mentions any material practices. He eschews any discussion on livelihoods, control over resources, or classes. Briefly, Ghurye argued that India was a civilization. He suggested that Indian civilization drew its unity from Hinduism and that Brahminism and its ideas and values provided the core values of this Hindu civilization. Brahmins were considered "natural" leaders, the torch bearers, and bearers of this civilization and its "moral guides." As a result, sociology in India was initiated with the Orientalist idea that the territory of the nation-state is equivalent with its culture.

Ghurye reproduced a design of Indian society as it was represented in Orientalist language.[11] Thus for him, Hindu civilization was structured around the caste system wherein if Brahmins were the most civilized, the tribals were the most backward. Other religious groups, such as Muslims, Zorastrians, and Christians were deviants from this norm and needed to be assimilated into the Hindu fourfold system. The most difficult to assimilate would be the Muslims who were perceived to be separate from Hindus, in culture, ideas, and values, and who were responsible for the current social evils of India. Indian society was seen as a set of rules which all Hindus followed and Ghurye's understanding of law was based on a compendium of Hindu laws. No wonder Upadhya can state:

Ghurye's sociology adopted almost wholesale the Orientalist vision of Indian society as a Vedic civilisation and ultimately of the 'Aryan invasion'. And of Indian civilisation as Hindu .... (Upadhya, 2000, p. 47)

As against Ghurye, D. P. Mukerji's (1894–1961) sociology was significantly different. His ideas were akin to modern-traditionalist views. Unlike the traditionalists, the latter intervened in the "future" to construct a sociological language best suited to bring in transformation of Indian culture. While for the "traditionalists" the goal was to create the language from the "past" and carry it forward to the "present" and the "future," for the modern-traditionalists, it was to use the language of the "past" in order to focus on the "future."

Mukerji's sociology was oriented to the "future" in this sense. Because he was trained as an economist, his sociology was of the present and oriented to an interdisciplinary approach. Mukerji visualized a sociology that combined culture and economics in a symbiotic relationship with each other. He viewed the problem of India in terms of reconciliation between the forces of continuity and of change, of tradition and modernization, for which he postulated a need for a holistic view of society.

D. P. Mukerji was constantly troubled by the question: how does one understand India's current economic problems, and what social science language does one need to construct in order to examine and evaluate them? This question led D. P. Mukerji to engage with the ideas of contemporary economists and sociologists in the West, and position these against the traditions in place in India. D. P. Mukerji's difference with his colleagues in Lucknow and within the country related to an understanding and acknowl-edgement of the role played by colonial domination in constructing theories of European modernity[12] and thus for a need to create a new theory of modernity on indigenous epistemic positions. Two attributes distinguished his ideas from R. K. Mukerjee. The first was his effort in reconstituting the "traditionalist" debate mentioned above in order to create a new sociological language based on *Indian* conditions, circumstances, and civilization which elaborate a sociological theory of and for *India*. The second was Mukerjee's use of Marxist methodology (he called for a mix of Dilthey and Marx) to organize and structure this episteme (Hegde, 2011; Joshi, 1986; Madan, 1994, 2007).

This approach was significantly different from what was embedded within the sociology of Ghurye. Both the content of his sociology (in terms of concepts) and his epistemic position emerged from a reconstructed understanding of the past, thus being akin to the traditionalist perspective. In the case of Mukerji, the content was focused on the language of the present: the plight of agricultural labourers, forms of bondage, migrants and their problems, and the contradictory impact of the processes of urbanization and industrialization in the context of colonialism. Even his call to draw an epistemic position of sociology from Indian traditions was related to his assessment of the present and the needs for the future. His argument was not against Eurocentric approach per se. Rather his plea for a "culturist" sociology guaranteed formulations that can grapple with new processes and novel innovations that planned change was inaugurating for India. He called for an assessment of the "Indian path" of social change.

Mukerji argued that sociology needs to be understood as a unified and holistic interdisciplinary discipline that is culture-specific, that is, it represents theories that capture particular practices as these are experienced by a group bound as a nation living in a territory – in this case India. These practices relate to specific ideals, and the indigenization of social sciences should thus be based on understanding of these values (Hegde, 2011). Mukerji not only argued for the growth of new theories and perspectives that reflect particular practices, but also called for the development of new methodological and epistemological precepts to assess them, because these remain frames for relating to new changes taking place.

Mukerji believed that cultural symbiosis is the outstanding feature of India's history. Change in India has proceeded on the lines of acceptance, adaptability, accommodation, and assimilation rather than on that of conflict. The British tried to forge a unity by expanding the market within the territory. But it did not work because there are other principles that have structured the culture of India. These are *shantam* (harmony – that which sustains the universe amidst all its incessant changes), *shivam* (welfare – being the principle of coordination with the social environment), and *adavaitam* ("unity of unity" or synthesis). Madan (1994, p. 9) suggests that Mukerji's sociology is sustained on these three principles.

Both Madan (1964, 2007) and P. C. Joshi (1986) argue that the notion of synthesis allowed Mukerji to combine ideas regarding socialism with those involving Indian traditions, to "Indianize" socialism, and to root itself in the Indian cultural traditions of syncretism. Here one can distinguish his approach from G. S. Ghurye. Though Mukerjee used indological texts to ground a culturist episteme, he affirmed a syncretic position:

> Indian culture represents certain common traditions that have given rise to a number of general attitudes. The major influences in their shaping have been Buddhism, Islam, and Western commerce and culture. It was through the assimilation and conflict of such varying forces that Indian culture became what it is today, neither Hindu nor Islamic, neither a replica of the Western modes of living and thought nor a purely Asiatic product. (Quoted in Madan, 2007, p. 274)

Mukerji's emphasis on the present, his sensitivity to the inequalities and divisions within Indian society, and his efforts to combine economics and state planning with sociology through an interdisciplinary perspective gave his sociology a modern character and placed it in opposition to the one popularized by G. S. Ghurye. And yet, did his sociology make a clear break with the ideas of Orientalist-Eurocentrism? The key issue through which he retains his affiliation with the traditionalists and thus to this perspective is his conception of culture and his use of indological methods to construct it. Many of his arguments can be termed a precursor of the later positions elucidated by Charles Taylor (1995) who called for a culturist theory of modernity and are also resonated in the work of Shmuel Eisenstadt (2000a, 2000b) on multiple modernities and axial civilizations.

## A CRITIQUE OF ORIENTALIST-EUROCENTRIC ANALYSIS: THE CONTRIBUTIONS BY HISTORIANS

In a book now acknowledged as a classic (Bhattacharya, 2008), *The Culture and Civilisation of Ancient India,* Kosambi (1907–1966) asserts three points that are of significance to our argument. The first is the assertion that ancient India was a civilization. However, unlike Mukerji who drew his understanding and perception from indological sources and presented a "unity of unity" or "syncretic" understanding of India, Kosambi termed the ancient culture and civilization of India "diverse" and emphasized on its "diversity in unity", rather than a "unity in diversity," an idea and thematic propagated by Jawaharlal Nehru, India's first prime minister. Second, he elaborated this diversity as being grounded in ecological and material forces and also explained its growth and its ultimate demise in material and ecological terms. For Kosambi the history of ancient India cannot be extracted from texts written by "Brahmins" and reconstructed during the colonial period as part of its project to codify "ancient Indian civilization." Rather it was related to material conditions and political processes. Third, Marxism was thus seen as a tool to assess and understand this material and environmental history. It was not perceived as an all pervasive ideology, nor a positivist theory that structured the debates of historical sociology.

The difference between Mukerji and Kosambi comes out clearly in the following extract:

A dispassionate observer who looks at India with detachment and penetration would be struck by two mutually contradictory features: diversity and unity at the same time. The endless variety is striking, often incongruous. Costume, speech, the physical appearance of the people, customs, standards of living, food, climate, geographical features all offer the greatest possible differences. Richer Indians may be dressed in full European style, or in costumes that show Muslim influence, or in flowing and costly robes of many different colourful Indian types. At the lower end of the social scale are other Indians in rags, almost naked but for a small loincloth. There is no national language or alphabet; a dozen languages and scripts appear on the ten-rupee currency note. There is no Indian race. People with white skins and blue eyes are as unmistakably Indian as others with black skins and dark eyes. In between we find every other intermediate type, though the hair is generally black. There is no typical Indian diet, but more rice, vegetables, and spices are eaten than in Europe. The north Indian finds southern food unpalatable, and conversely. Some people will not touch meat, fish, or eggs; many would and do starve to death rather than eat beef, while others observe no such restrictions. These dietary conventions are not matters of taste but of religion. In climate also the country offers the full range. Perpetual snows in the Himalayas, north European weather in Kashmir, hot deserts in Rajasthan, basalt ridges and granite mountains on the peninsula, tropical heat at the southern tip, dense forests in laterite soil along the western scarp. A 2,000-mile-long coastline, the great Gangetic river system in a wide and fertile alluvial basin, other great rivers of lesser complexity, a few considerable lakes, the swamps of Cutch and Orissa, complete the sub-continental picture. (Kosambi, 1970, p. 1)

Kosambi (a renowned mathematician and an historian by choice) argues that this "diversity" is part of a collective memory of the people of India. Oftentimes this is legitimized by using scriptures that elaborate theories of this "diversity" and thereby allowed certain classes and the elite to relive these precepts as values and ideals. Instead as a Marxist historian, he would argue that material conditions organizing ancient Indian civilization stagnated and died out, leaving only its "culturist" memories in place. A society, according to Kosambi, is held together by bonds of production. The philosophic individual cannot reshape a mechanized world nearer to heart's desire by the "eternal" ideologies developed over 2000 years ago in a bullock-cart country (Kosambi, 1956, p. xiii).

As a result, historians in India have lauded and appreciated Kosambi's efforts to use a wide variety of historical sources rather than indological texts to outline the nature and content of ancient Indian civilization. These include archaeological, numismatics, and literary sources to indicate the long history that organized the social life of India since the third century B.C.[13] Most commentators now agree that this book was a debate with the nationalist traditionalists who made civilizational analysis their core frame for organizing an assessment of contemporary modernity.

Kosambi's protracted mission was to indicate that India like Europe had a long history. This history was organized through the interface of material and political changes with human potential and that the reconstruction of the past as culturist collapsed this history and time into space. He also suggested that each region has a different history and that Indian history unlike that of Europe was not structured around episodes. This innovation was a sign of departure from Eurocentrism. No wonder Bhattacharya argues:

> In some respects, there was a poor fit between Indian history and the classical scheme of Marxism. But he consequently used Marx's method as a tool. In using Marxist method in his own lights, in his effort to construe the civilization in India, in the convergences and divergences between his approach and the nationalist discourse of civilization, Kosambi has left much for us to try and understand and evaluate (Bhattacharya, 2008).

Kosambi argued that the Marxist theory of linear time needs to be displaced but also criticized Marx's "ideological" understanding of India as comprising of "self sufficient small villages":

> Most villages produce neither metals nor salt, the two essentials that had mostly to be obtained by exchange, hence implied commodity production .... The villages did not exist "from times immemorial". The advance of plough-using agrarian village economy over tribal India was a great historical achievement by itself. Secondly, even when the size of the village unit remains unchanged, the density of these units plays a most important role; the same region with two villages, or two hundred, or twenty thousand cannot bear the same form of superstructure, nor be exploited by the same type of state mechanism. (Kosambi, 1956, p. 11)

Kosambi's theories displaced the episteme of colonial modernity which coupled place/territory with cultural identity (India as civilization). This position together with his assertion that India had a long history allowed contemporary Marxists (henceforth) to wholly disregard the "culturist" language that structured conservative, liberal, and some parts of the modernist nationalist discourse. In many ways Kosambi's historiography allowed the discourse of modernist nationalism to be reconstituted in terms of what Chatterjee (1997, p. 10) argues was Kant's understanding of enlightenment and modernity. For Kant, modernity and its language concerned itself with the present and "with those exclusive properties that define the present as different from the past." He asserts "[w]hat is remarkable about Kant's criteria of the present is that they are all negative. Enlightenment means an exit, an escape from tutelage, coming out of dependence."

D. D. Kosambi focused his critique on indological[14] assumption that India did not have a continuous history, that its history was a series of episodes, that the sources of this history can be located within the written texts rather than non-written sources, and that culture and religion organize the unity of India's territory, rather than its diverse material and ecological experiences. He inaugurated a paradigm shift from colonial and nationalist frameworks and the centrality of dynastic history to a new framework integrating social and economic history that related the cultural dimensions of the past to these investigations.

For Kosambi the history of ancient India cannot be extracted from texts written by "Brahmins" and reconstructed during the colonial period as part of its project to codify "ancient Indian civilization." Rather what was needed was the use of combined methods inputting linguistics, archaeology, anthropology, and sociology together in the perspective of the materialistic social theory of history (Thapar, 2008). Third, Marxism was thus seen as a tool to assess and understand the material and environmental history. It was not perceived as an all pervasive ideology or a positivist theory that structured the debates of historical sociology. Given the phenomenal diversity of India, Kosambi completely rejected any unilinear sequence of "modes of production" and argued for the simultaneous presence of several modes of production at any given time in India's long history (Thapar, 2008).

A society, according to Kosambi, is held together by bonds of production. The philosophic individual cannot reshape a mechanized world nearer to heart's desire by the "eternal" ideologies developed over 2000 years ago in a bullock-cart country. (Kosambi, 1956, p. xiii).

Following him historians of ancient India have tried to demystify the ways in which the past was constructed by indologists and then used as political ideologies. Thapar (1989) argues that contemporary manifestation of Hinduism has not emphasized first, the different premises that structured various religions in pre-colonial India. This implies that the Semitic model cannot be applied to India. Second, in the codification of religion, texts received preference over other sources of understanding the religious expressions. Third, these expressions can be seen in the diversity of rituals that expressed religion rather than in its manifestation as theological texts. Fourth, the variety of non-textual sources attests to the fact that these diverse rituals were part of the groups who practiced popular religion called Sramanism rather than Brahminism. And lastly, both these religious expressions changed over space and time as state consolidation took place differentially across the sub-continent; this unevenness and thus practices that became institutionalized as being diverse characterized the experience of religion within pre-colonial India.

Thus, Thapar states:

> The modern construction of Hinduism is often acclaimed as in the following defence of Orientalism: "The work of integrating a vast collection of myths, beliefs, rituals and laws into a coherent religion and of shaping an amorphous heritage into a rational faith known now as "Hinduism" were endeavours initiated by Orientalists." Given that religious traditions are constantly reformulated, the particular construction of Hinduism

in the last two centuries has an obvious historical causation. Deriving largely from the Orientalist construction of Hinduism, emergent national consciousness appropriated this definition of Hinduism as well as what it regarded as the heritage of Hindu culture. Hindu identity was defined by those who were part of this national consciousness and drew on their own idealized image of themselves resulting in an upper-caste, brahmana-dominated identity. (Thapar, 1989, p. 229)

## THE RE-AFFIRMATION OF ORIENTALIST-EUROPEAN EPISTEME: RELIGION AND SOCIAL THEORY IN THE WORK OF T. N. MADAN

It is in this context I examine the writings of T. N. Madan, a contemporary sociologist, and ask why has he not debated with the ideas presented by these historians and why is he continuing to draw his precepts from the perspective of the earlier thinkers? Madan's work has been critically evaluated by his colleague such as Andre Beteille (1994). While agreeing generally with these criticisms, I want to expand this appraisal to include a criticism of his use of methods, methodologies, and perspectives.

In the introduction to his edited book *India's Religions* (2004), Madan, a student of D. P. Mukerji, starts the discussion on religions in India by using the census. Thus, he suggests that the Hindus are the largest community followed by the Muslims, Christians, Sikhs, Buddhists, and lastly Jains. He uses the numbers listed in the census to understand the proportionate strength of each religious group, and the first question that needs to be asked whether the census is the correct representative document, for as Nandini Sundar argues that the census "was significant as numbers were fetishized and became objects of government action in themselves." She continues, "statistics on identities became important as communities demanded entitlements on the basis of numbers, in a politics which conflated representation (standing on behalf of) with representativeness (coming from a particular community)" (Sundar, 2000, p. 113). The second issue relates to the concept of "tradition." Since the mid-nineteenth century there had been attempts to codify "tradition." Again, as stated earlier, indological texts were used in devising theories regarding Hinduism and the caste system in addition to "native informants" (generally Brahmins) to obtain information regarding placements of castes within the hierarchy. Earlier the Brahmins had elaborated the theory of the fourfold classification. Later they reinterpreted it in order to legitimize it, when they became the informants in helping the British to codify practices and classifying castes.

As a result, in the census, castes were placed in different positions on the basis of *varna* categories. And because the *varna* categories were related to Hinduism, religion became a key reference in the first classification of groups (Cohn, 1997).

Madan's position as those of many other contemporary sociologists, I would argue, has continuity with this perspective and remains etched in this discourse. He considers "four out of five Indians," Hindus reiterating the use of numbers to define the majority (Madan, 2004, p. 1). Like the earlier indologists he looks at the scriptures and especially the *Manusmriti* for guidance in assessing the constituents of religion. Later his argument collapses all Indians (including the one out of five) into being Hindus when he states that though Islam and later Christianity "broke the bond between India and her indigenous traditions"

> ... from a cultural perspective, anthropologists and sociologists have provided details of the many components of culture and aspects of social structure of the non-Hindu communities that have either been borrowed from the Hindus or are survivals from their pre-conversion Hindu past with or without significant alterations. (Madan, 2004, p. 1)

In a profound sense Madan was influenced by Louis Dumont who reconstructed the binaries into an elaborate theory of the sociology of hierarchy for the East and contrasted it with the sociology of equality in the West. While sociologists like Srinivas had used the empirical method to demystify some of the received Indological assumptions and had distinguished between *varna* and *jati* (Srinivas, 2002), Dumont made a critique of this empirical position by insisting that not only does "a sociology of India lie at a point of confluence of sociology and indology" (Dumont, 1957, p. 7); he also argued that Vedic Hinduism is the most ancient religion and defines the organic character of India. "The very existence and influence of the traditional higher Sanskrit civilisation demonstrates without question the unity of India ... it does not demonstrate but actually constitutes it" (Dumont, 1957, p. 10).

Madan continues this assessment when he asserts that religion has "immense importance ... in the lives of the people of South Asia" (Madan, 1994, p. 395). No wonder he argues that

> ... religion in India is not discrete element of everyday life that stands wholly apart from the economic and political concerns of the world ... the religious domain is not distinguished from the secular, but rather the secular is regarded as being encompassed. (Madan, 2004, p. 2)

What is this critical holistic notion that unifies all religious activity in India? For Madan, this is Dharma. Dharma connotes for Madan, the maintenance and sustenance of moral virtue. This broad strand of a self-sustaining cosmo-moral order runs through all the religions in India, especially Buddhism, Jainism, and Sikhism which incorporated Hindu principles with subtle difference of nuances. He thus asserts a continuous and a long tradition of Hinduism. This tradition he argues was never a source of conflict, for "the scope of interreligious understanding is ... immense and it is no way contradicted by the holism of the religious traditions of mankind" (Madan, 2004, p. 385). The differences that are there within Hinduism are part of this long history.

No wonder in the introduction to an edited volume, titled *India's Religions: Perspectives from Sociology and History* (2006), Madan characterizes Hinduism as inherently plural and uses the concept of "pluralism" to depict its traditions and values. The argument of pluralism obviously draws from the North American tradition. In the United States, religious pluralism is a loosely defined term concerning peaceful relations between different religions. Pluralism acknowledges the diversity of interests and considers it imperative that members of society accommodate their differences by engaging in good-faith negotiation. It is connected with the hope that this process of dialogue will lead to a re-definition of conflict in terms of a realization of a common good that is best for all members of society. This implies that in a pluralistic framework, the common good is not given a priori. Rather, it is constructed a posteriori. For the pluralists the common good does not coincide with the principles of one religion; these evolve later as negotiations happen between religions.

By suggesting that Hinduism is an immanent tradition, Madan accepts the construct of Orientalist-Eurocentrism that indigenous "Hindu traditions" determine its essence. In this chapter, I am not debating whether Hinduism is essentially plural in nature. Rather, I am questioning the epistemic moorings of Madan's understanding of Hinduism. These moorings are located in the nineteenth-century principles of Orientalist-Eurocentrism which defined every aspect of social life to be circumscribed by Hindu traditions. Can this form of Hinduism be plural in nature? Such a pluralism can evolve only if there is economic equality among individuals and groups of different religious affiliations.

Madan together with many of his contemporaries who argue the indigenous position and uphold "traditions" seem not to recognize that "traditions" are a construct of modernity and part of the binaries of Eurocentric positions. In their logic, India particularly and South Asia more generally live in a world which is steeped in tradition and which has the "native" resources to mitigate religious conflicts. Thus, he states,

"... for in truth, it is the marginalisation of religious faith, which is what secularisation is, that permits the perversion of religion" (Madan, 1991, p. 396).

But is secularism and modernity the source of religious conflicts? Or is the source of conflicts the knowledge process by which religion and religious affiliations has become part and parcel of the politics of identity construction? If it is these processes, how and in what contexts have these processes developed? In being critical of secularism and secularists, and particularly the imposition of European notions of secularism, Madan elides the questioning of Orientalist-Eurocentrism and the way its knowledge is intrinsic to the politics of religious conflicts in South Asia. Surely we should have the sociological language to assess the way these processes have taken place and to explicate the manner in which knowledge construction, including our own, helped to construct and build these identities that have been articulated through these processes? Andre Beteille (1994) has critically appraised Madan's use of the concept of secularization as a process related to secularism and indicated the need to dissociate these two terms. And commenting on Madan's use of scriptures to evolve a position on India's religions, Beteille has reminded us that theological analysis need not be the sole criterion for assessing religion and for making a sociological assessment of religion.

## CONCLUSION

This chapter was written with two goals. First it wanted to explore how sociology/anthropology is enmeshed in Eurocentric ideas. Second, it has suggested that historians from India have initiated a debate on this episteme and that a historical perspective can help to displace it. Third, the chapter contends that methodological nationalism (being the ways theories, methodologies, and methods naturalized the nation and the nation-state as the organizing principle of modernity) has played contrary roles as it designed the disciplines of history and anthropology/sociology differentially within post-independence India. In the discipline of history, it helped to create a critique of colonial modernity while in anthropology/sociology nationalist thought reasserted its affiliations with colonial constructs of traditions and thereby Orientalism. Sociologists need to reframe their disciplinary focus and introduce historical perspective in order to free themselves from inherited colonial epistemes.

# NOTES

1. Instead of using the concept of postcolonial, which is tangled in many conceptual and theoretical questions (see, for instance, Perry, 1997), I use the two attributes of Orientalism-Eurocentrism with which postcolonialism is associated to deconstruct contemporary sociological language of the Indian subcontinent.

2. I recognize that Orientalism is of many kinds; the British version is different from the French and the German one. Also its various elements need to be studied in varied phases and the domains in which it, as a body of ideas, finds representations, such as in art (especially paintings) and literature but also in the writing of diverse histories of the Orient (the Arab world, Africa, Asia, and the Far East) in the nineteenth and twentieth centuries. This chapter is concerned with the way Orientalist ideas were incorporated in the sociological language that described India during early twentieth century. To be more specific, it is not about how Orientalist ideas were evolved in any part of Western Europe or even in India. Rather its focus is on the way *these were received and incorporated in the language of sociology* in India from the 1930s and 1940s onwards.

3. In this chapter, I use colonial modernity interchangeably with Orientalism-Eurocentrism.

4. I use the term derivative in the way elaborated by Partha Chatterjee (1986).

5. I follow the footsteps of Hobsbawm and Ranger who has discussed 'the invention of tradition' in arguing that in the case of India, colonialism constructed 'traditions'. These were cultural constructs to structure an (Orientalist) identity extracted from the past.

6. The colonial state, the chapter argues, codified a history of amorphous religious practices and that of conflicts and contestations regarding religious ideas and religiosities into a discourse that argued that Hinduism was a set of "philosophical ideas, iconology and rituals." In this version Hinduism was reduced to Brahmanism (ideas and rituals practiced by groups who are pure, such as upper castes, who believed that its fundamentals are elaborated in ancient scriptures and who performed sacrifices). What was ignored by this discourse was the relevance of Sramanism, groups having affiliation to non-Brahmanic religions and who practiced diverse forms of religiosities, including animism. Thus, it is necessary to distinguish between culture and religion as life worlds and practices from its association as an ideology and a discourse. Even Brahmanic religious discourses are part of everyday life of a significant section of the population of India, and of course, those cultural expressions and life worlds need to be studied as practices. Given that ideology and discourse have increasingly become part of contemporary politics of the rightist movements, it is important for sociologists to understand and examine its links with colonialism. The chapter suggests that the incorporation of Orientalist thought in sociological language reduces the experience of "fluidities" and diversities of religious practices, a heritage of the Indian subcontinent and asserts only a homogenised model of Hinduism.

7. See the third section for an elaboration of these arguments.

8. On the three kinds of nationalism, see Bhiku Parekh (1995).

9. Parekh (1995) distinguishes between two groups of "traditionalists," one whom he calls the "real" traditionalists and the other called "modern-traditionalists." The

latter's goal was to intervene in the "future" and construct a sociological language best suited to bring in transformation of the specific culture that they were studying: India. For the former the goal was and has been to create the language from the "past" and carry it forward to the "present" and the "future."

10. Ghurye addresses the question of civilization in his magnus opus, *Caste and Race in India* (1932).

11. This chapter is of course not arguing that such discourses are limited to the theories of sociology in India. Ghurye's perspective is resonated in other theories.

12. Mukerji distinguished between Western culture and British colonial culture and reiterated that the first cannot be collapsed into the second.

13. J. D. Bernal (1966, p. 1024), the historian of science, had the following to say about Kosambi's historiography: "Kosambi introduced a new method into historical scholarship, essentially by application of modern mathematics. By statistical study of the weights of the coins, Kosambi was able to establish the amount of time that had elapsed while they were in circulation and so set them in order to give some idea of their respective ages."

14. In India Orientalist thought was defined as indology, a field that laid out the theory and methodology of the study of language, religion, and history of India's past through textual sources.

# REFERENCES

Beteille, A. (1994). Secularism in place. *Economic and Political Weekly*, *29*(10), 559–566.

Bhambra, G. K. (2007). *Rethinking modernity: Postcolonialism and the sociological imagination*. Basingstoke: Palgrave Macmillan.

Bhattacharya, S. (2008). Kosambi and the discourse of civilization. *The Hindu*, Opinion, July 31.

Bhattacharya, S. (2011). *Talking back: The idea of civilization in the Indian nationalist discourse*. New Delhi: Oxford University Press.

Chatterjee, P. (1986). *Nationalist thought and the colonial world: A derivative discourse*. Delhi: Oxford University Press.

Chatterjee, P. (1997). *Our modernity*. Rotterdam/Dakar: SephisCodesria Publication.

Cohn, B. S. (1997). *Colonialism and its forms of knowledge*. Delhi: Oxford.

Dumont, L. (1957). For a sociology of India. *Contribution to Indian Sociology*, *1*, 7–22.

Dussel, E. (1993). Eurocentrism and modernity (Introduction to the Frankfurt lectures). *Boundary 2*, 20(3), 65–76.

Eisenstadt, S. (2000a). Multiple modernities. *Daedalus*, *129*(1), 1–29.

Eisenstadt, S. (2000b). The civilizational dimension in sociological analysis. *Thesis Eleven*, *62*(1), 1–21.

Ghurye, G. S. (1932). *Caste and race in India*. Bombay: Popular Prakashan.

Hegde, S. (2011). Searching for bedrock: Contending with the Lucknow school and its legacy. In S. Patel (Ed.), *Doing sociology in India: Genealogies, locations and practices* (pp. 47–71). New Delhi: Oxford University Press.

Joshi, P. C. (1986). Founders of the Lucknow school and their legacy: Radhakamal Mukerjee and D. P. Mukerji: Some reflections. *Economic and Political Weekly*, *21*(33), 1455–1469.

Kosambi, D. D. (1956). *An introduction to the study of Indian history.* Bombay: Popular Prakashan.

Kosambi, D. D. (1970). *The culture and civilisation of ancient India in historical outline.* New Delhi: Vikas Publishing House.

Madan, T. N. (1991). Secularism in place. In T. N. Madan (Ed.), *Religion in India* (pp. 394–412). New Delhi: Oxford University Press.

Madan, T. N. (1994). *Tradition and modernity in the sociology of D. P. Mukerji, pathways: Approaches to the study of society in India.* New Delhi: Oxford University Press.

Madan, T. N. (2004). Introduction. India's religions: Plurality and pluralism. In T. N. Madan (Ed.), *India's religions. Perspectives from sociology and history* (pp. 1–36). New Delhi: Oxford University Press.

Madan, T. N. (2006). *Images of the world. Essays on religion, secularism and culture.* New Delhi: Oxford University Press.

Madan, T. N. (2007). Search for synthesis: The sociology of D.P. Mukerji. In P. Uberoi, N. Sundar, & S. Deshpande (Eds.), *Anthropology in the East: Founders of Indian sociology and anthropology* (pp. 256–289). Delhi: Permanent Black.

Mignolo, W. D. (2002). The geopolitics of knowledge and the colonial difference. *The South Atlantic Quarterly, 101*(1), 57–96.

Parekh, B. (1995). Jawaharlal Nehru and the crisis of modernization. In U. Baxi & B. Parekh (Eds.), *Crisis and change in contemporary India.* New Delhi: Sage.

Patel, S. (2006). Beyond binaries. A case for self reflexive sociologies. *Current Sociology, 54*(3), 381–395.

Patel, S. (2007). Sociological study of religion: Colonial modernity and nineteenth century majoritarianism. *Economic and Political Weekly, 42*(13), 1089–1094.

Patel, S. (2010). Seva, sangathana and gurus: Service and the making of Hindu nation. In G. Mahajam & S. Jodhka (Eds.), *Religion, community and development: Changing contours of politics and policy in India* (pp. 102–128). New Delhi: Routledge.

Patel, S. (2011a). Ruminating on sociological traditions in India. In S. Patel (Ed.), *Doing sociology in India: Genealogies, locations, and practices* (pp. xi–xxxviii). New Delhi: Oxford University Press.

Patel, S. (2011b). Social anthropology or marxist sociology. In S. Patel (Ed.), *Doing sociology in India: Genealogies, locations, and practices* (pp. 72–99). New Delhi: Oxford University Press.

Perry, B. (1997). The postcolonial: Conceptual category or chimera? *The Yearbook of English Studies, 27,* 3–21.

Quijano, A. (2000). Coloniality of power, eurocentricism and Latin America. *Nepantla: Views from South, 1,* 553–800.

Rodriguez, E. G., Boatca, M., & Costa, S. (Eds.). (2010). *Decolonizing European sociology: Transdisciplinary approaches.* Surrey: Ashgate.

Sarkar, S. (1997). Kaliyuga, chakri and bhakti. In S. Sarkar (Ed.), *Writing social history* (pp. 282–357). New Delhi: Oxford University Press.

Srinivas, M. N. (2002). *Collected essays.* Delhi: Oxford.

Sundar, N. (2000). Caste as a census category: Implications for sociology. *Current Sociology, 48*(3), 111–126.

Taylor, C. (1995). Two theories of modernity. *The Hastings Center Report, 25*(2), 24–33.

Thapar, R. (1989). Imagined religious communities? Ancient history and the modern search for a Hindu identity. *Modern Asian Studies*, *23*(2), 209–231.

Thapar, R. (2008). Early Indian history and the legacy of D. D. Kosambi. D.D. Kosambi: The man and his work (Special Issue). *Economic and Political Weekly*, *43*(30), 43–51.

Upadhya, C. (2000). The Hindu nationalist sociology of G. S. Ghurye. *Sociological Bulletin*, *51*(1), 28–57.

# PART III
# SCHOLARLY CONTROVERSIES:
# RAEWYN CONNELL'S
# *SOUTHERN THEORY*

# A SOCIOLOGICAL BREAKTHROUGH, NOT A SOCIOLOGICAL GUILT TRIP

Mustafa Emirbayer

## ABSTRACT

*This essay critically examines Raewyn Connell's* Southern Theory. *Limitations of the work include a tendency to overgeneralize about "Northern Theory" and to leave some claims about the power of "Southern Theory" unsubstantiated.* Southern Theory's *most important contributions include its insights into the problematic tendencies and patterns of knowledge production in the Global North and its insistent plea to make social theory more dialogic.*

Social thinkers have criticized the unacknowledged assumptions in one another's work since at least the beginnings of disciplined social inquiry more a century and a half ago, when Marx took on the bourgeois political economists for mispresenting as universal truth what happened to be their own particular, class-bound perspective on the social world. As time went by, critiques based on race, gender, sexuality, nationality, and a whole host of other important principles of social division supplemented those based on

Decentering Social Theory
Political Power and Social Theory, Volume 25, 131–136
Copyright © 2013 by Emerald Group Publishing Limited
All rights of reproduction in any form reserved
ISSN: 0198-8719/doi:10.1108/S0198-8719(2013)0000025011

class position. Now Raewyn Connell adds yet another dimension to this effort at reflexive critique in her recent work, *Southern Theory*. According to Connell, most social science "picture[s] the world as seen from the rich capital-exporting countries of Europe and North America – the global metropole" (p. vii). "On close examination," she writes, "mainstream sociology turns out to be an ethno-sociology of metropolitan society. This is concealed by its language" (p. 226). But what has been concealed must be laid bare, for mainstream sociology's "theorising is vitiated whenever it refuses to recognise its ethno-sociological being – or, to put it another way, its situation in the world and its history in the world" (p. 226).

Connell presents her ideas in a frankly experimentalist spirit (p. xiii). As she acknowledges, these ideas mark only the beginnings of a critique of Northern theory – and "a shaky beginning at best" (p. xiv). Her hesitant tone is appropriate, for while there is a good deal to learn from this stimulating and often insightful work, much also remains to be puzzled over. First I shall offer some words of criticism; then I shall turn to why this nonetheless is an important work for social thinkers on both sides of the global divide.

In the background to *Southern Theory*, of course, stands an earlier statement by Connell (1997), published in *American Journal of Sociology* and reproduced as the book's opening chapter, together with an infamous rejoinder to that paper by Randall Collins (1997). Collins's criticisms are defensive and dismissive in tone: he characterizes Connell's arguments as a "sociological guilt trip." However, Collins also offers some effective and compelling counter-arguments, particularly in defense of an internalist reading of the history of Western sociology. As he demonstrates, the internal problems and challenges posed by European social transformation indeed were an important stimulus to the development of classical sociology, far more so than Connell claimed. Connell, too, however, partly is right in suggesting that an externalist perspective, one highlighting the importance of global developments such as imperialism and colonialism, can shed light on important aspects of the history of European social thought. In hindsight, each party to this important debate pushed too hard for his respective one-sided position; a more balanced, multidimensional interpretation was the way to go. But in *Southern Theory*, Connell's arguments remain unchanged from their original formulation.

Another of Collins's complaints was that "Connell ignores the analytical contents of theories" (Collins, 1997, p. 1560). Whether or not this was true then, it certainly is not the case now. In fact, Connell devotes another of her early chapters to examining the theoretical approaches of three important

Northern thinkers: James Coleman, Anthony Giddens, and Pierre Bourdieu. In each case, she argues that the work in question exemplifies distinctive features of metropolitan theory, namely, its tendencies to claim universality; to read from the center; to exclude ideas from the periphery; and to erase the experiences of people from the global South. Again, there is much to this critique. It is instructive, for instance, to learn that objectivism and subjectivism, long regarded as encompassing the entire universe of options for social thought, hardly seem so universal in the eyes of colonial thinkers, being "alternative ways of picturing oneself at the centre of a world, alternative models of actions or systems with no external determinations" (p. 45). As Connell astutely points out, "a general social theory shaped around the objectivism/subjectivism problem necessarily constructs a social world read through the metropole – not read through the metropole's action on the rest of the world" (p. 45). Arresting insights of this sort are to be found throughout her interpretations of Coleman, Giddens, and Bourdieu. In the future, Northern social thinkers will ignore them at their peril.

There also is, however, something a bit tendentious about some of Connell's readings. Just to provide a couple of examples regarding Bourdieu, whose sociology I know best, her claim that he found "no reason to search out colonial voices" (p. 44) while working on Algeria is perplexing in light of his close collaborations with Abdelmalek Sayad and many other "colonial voices." Connell's suggestion, too, that Bourdieu's sociology sought to "escape specific settings and speak in abstract universals" (p. 206) is oddly off-target, given his longstanding insistence that researchers aim to particularize their objects of inquiry, that is, to immerse themselves in their specificities and understand them as particular cases, while simultaneously generalizing or universalizing them and seeking to discover, "through the application of general questions, the invariant properties [they conceal] under the appearance of singularity" (Bourdieu & Wacquant, 1992, p. 234). (Connell's charge might be truer of Giddens and, especially, of Coleman than it is of Bourdieu.) Northern theory is divided, not united, in its approach to such issues. Regrettably, we see here yet again a tendency on Connell's part to paint her picture with too broad a brush, to develop often valid, even acutely perceptive arguments in too undifferentiated a fashion, without sufficient nuance. Perhaps at moments, too, we notice a tendency (which Connell, to her credit, resists most of the time) to proceed in a romanticizing fashion with invidious, stylized comparisons: Northern theory as falsely universalizing, decontextualized, and ungrounded; Southern theory as its more appealing opposite – itself a pernicious binary.

Finally, let me touch on two other (closely related) difficulties with Connell's critique.[1] One is that the critique concerns itself more with exposing the social unconscious of particular authors and approaches than it does with laying bare their disciplinary assumptions. To consider but one example, Connell accepts a taken-for-granted disciplinary binary in which "theory," or "general theory," is distinguished from "empirical work" and treated as a domain unto itself. An artifact of mid-twentieth century American sociology, this schema now has been exported to Western Europe and much of the global South, but it inscribes a division, both mental and social-organizational (including curricular), that we ought to question rather than accept uncritically. To be fair, Connell underscores that much of the work she discusses in the core chapters of *Southern Theory* actually is not "theory" in the limited sense of that term, nor is it always located within sociology per se. Yet the idea of "theory," or "general theory," organizes much of the critical analysis in her work; indeed, it finds its way into its very title. I do not mean to suggest that this is a deep flaw in Connell's reasoning. I mean only to point out that, once critiques such as Connell's have exposed an unrecognized social unconscious, the tougher task remains of uncovering the blind spots created by longstanding disciplinary ways of seeing and not-seeing: a disciplinary, rather than a social, unconscious.

There also remains the even tougher challenge of exposing the scholastic assumptions behind social thought, that is, the hidden influence on social inquiry of occupying a position marked by scholastic leisure. As Bourdieu pointed out, a disposition toward pure, disinterested thought, detached intellectuality, and a playful, "as-if" mode of engagement with the world and its problems is shared by many who enjoy the privilege of being able "to withdraw from the world so as to think it" (Bourdieu, 2000 [1997], p. 49). Like fish in water, they remain less than fully aware of how their own thinking as scholars is shaped by these conditions of relative leisure. "There are many intellectuals who call the world into question, but very few who call the intellectual world into question" (Bourdieu, 2008, p. 23). Perhaps certain of the features of Northern theory itself, at least as depicted by Connell, are due less to its being "Northern" than to its being grounded in a scholastic condition of freedom from social and economic constraint. Connell has no way of parcelling out the two potential kinds of causal influence, conflating as she does two things – the social and scholastic unconscious – that ought analytically to be kept distinct.[2]

Despite these perplexities and difficulties, *Southern Theory* remains a breakthrough work, one that will deeply challenge sociology (and social science more generally) for years to come. In particular, there is much to its charge, developed at length throughout the work, that social thinkers in the global North have failed to take seriously the analytic innovations and substantive insights of Southern authors. While perhaps the claim that "[c]olonised and peripheral societies produce social thought *about the modern world* which has as much intellectual power as metropolitan social thought" (p. xii, italics in original) is, again, an overreach – in my view, the book does not produce sufficient evidence to back up such a sweeping claim – the central chapters of the work do provide fascinating accounts of rich and interesting lines of theorization and research emanating from different regions of the global South. Whether speaking of sub-Saharan Africa, Iran, Latin America, or India, Connell is right to call attention to the highly monologic fashion in which Northern authors have engaged with ideas and perspectives coming from different regions of the periphery. Northern theory, she forcefully argues, "works through categories produced in the metropole, and does not dialogue with the *ideas* produced by the colonised world" (p. xi, italics in original). It relies "exclusively on the metropole for [its] intellectual tools and assumptions, and therefore treat[s] the majority world as object" (p. 68). Metropolitan thinkers subsume the concepts and insights of Southern authors into their own systems – an unthinking appropriation – and do not engage with them on an equal footing. Often they do not even cite them (p. 64). Their categories are "read outwards to societies in the periphery, where the categories are filled in empirically" (p. 66). Southern writings become, at best, low-level grist for Northern thinkers' mill. Connell's most important contribution in *Southern Theory* is to highlight these tendencies and patterns – and to do so time and again – whether in the context of great thinkers' sociological discourse or in that of the burgeoning field of globalization studies, whether in relation to Australian sociology or to the study of "land rights" and colonial dispossession.

Compelling and persuasive, too, are Connell's insistent calls for a more genuine dialogue, "a mutual learning process on a planetary scale" (p. 222). Connell speaks of a reconstituted – and reinvigorated – social science in which "an interconnected set of intellectual projects ... proceed from varied social starting points into an unpredictable future" (p. 228). In this ideal, alternative future, the metropole learns "at least as actively as the periphery" (p. 224) and engages with the global South on a basis of "critique, respect, and recognition" (p. 224). As Mikhail Bakhtin (1986 [1970], p. 7), for whom dialogue also was a central concept, once expressed it, "Such a dialogic encounter ... does not result in merging or mixing. Each

retains its own unity and open totality, but they are mutually enriched."
The great achievement of Connell's *Southern Theory* is that it helps to bring
that ideal an important step closer to realization.

# NOTES

1. The arguments in this and the following paragraph are drawn from Emirbayer
and Desmond (2012); see also Bourdieu 2000 (1997).
2. Connell is aware of the importance of scholastic conditions of knowledge
production; see, for example, her discussion of "Production and Circulation of
Knowlege" (pp. 217–220) in the concluding chapter. But the critical strategy of the
work as a whole does not distinguish with sufficient analytic clarity between social
and scholastic conditions. Not without accident does the title of the book refer, not
just to "theory," but to *Southern* theory.

# REFERENCES

Bakhtin, M. (1986 [1970]). Response to a question from the Novy Mir editorial staff. In
    V. W. McGee (Trans.), C. Emerson & M. Holquist (Eds.), *Speech genres and other late
    essays*. Austin, TX: University of Texas Press.
Bourdieu, P. (2000 [1997]). *Pascalian meditations*. Stanford, CA: Stanford University Press.
Bourdieu, P. (2008). *Sketch for a self-analysis*. Chicago, IL: University of Chicago Press.
Bourdieu, P., & Wacquant, L. (1992). *An invitation to reflexive sociology*. Chicago, IL:
    University of Chicago Press.
Collins, R. (1997). A sociological guilt trip: Comment on Connell. *American Journal of
    Sociology, 102*, 1558–1564.
Connell, R. W. (1997). Why is classical theory classical? *American Journal of Sociology, 102*,
    1511–1557.
Emirbayer, M., & Desmond, M. (2012). Race and reflexivity. *Ethnic and Racial Studies, 35*,
    574–599.

# CRITICAL INTERVENTIONS IN WESTERN SOCIAL THEORY: REFLECTIONS ON POWER AND *SOUTHERN THEORY*

Patricia Hill Collins

## ABSTRACT

*This essay critically assesses Connell's* Southern Theory. *Operating from the premise that knowledge is a "project" embedded in power relations, the essay suggests that while the scope of ideas surveyed in* Southern Theory *is an important accomplishment, two main dilemmas can be found. The first is that* Southern Theory *inadvertently puts "Northern theory" at the center. The second is that the southern theorists examined tend to be educated elites from the Global South, thereby overlooking other actors in the Global South and their ways of doing theory. Struggling to change, not just the ideas, but also the ownership, vested interests and institutional actors of social theory as knowledge project might create space for much needed dialogues across differences in power.*

Decentering Social Theory
Political Power and Social Theory, Volume 25, 137–146
Copyright © 2013 by Emerald Group Publishing Limited
All rights of reproduction in any form reserved
ISSN: 0198-8719/doi:10.1108/S0198-8719(2013)0000025012

I try not to, but I see the workings of power everywhere. Western social theory is no different. Given the involvement of Western social theory in upholding power relations of imperialism, colonialism, and their aftermath, I find it useful to ask three core questions. *First, whose knowledge project is this?* I see social theory as a *knowledge project*. A sociology of knowledge framework suggests that knowledge is socially constructed and transmitted, legitimated and reproduced by social mechanisms that emanate from and shape systems of power. My understanding of the term "project" parallels Michael Omi and Howard Winant's definition of racial projects (Omi & Winant, 1994). I broaden these understandings of *knowledge* and *project* to conceptualize social theory produced in the "North" or in the "South," to use Connell's framework, as knowledge projects that are differentially positioned within social formations of inequality.

Second, *whose interests does this knowledge project serve?* In other words, who benefits and who is penalized within particular knowledge projects? This question suggests that vested interests, whether conscious or not, shape social theories. Different social groups will benefit and/or be penalized by social theories that represent the interests of dominant groups.

My third question drills down into these broader social relations of social inequality to take a look at intellectuals and the politics of intellectual production that shape social theory. I ask, *who are the main social actors who advance this knowledge project and what accounts for their involvement?* In prior periods where knowledge projects were crafted within stark politics of exclusion, scholars, academics, and intellectuals came from homogenous social groups that decided what would be best for everyone else. Blacks, women, indigenous people, poor people, and all individuals who could be identified as "other" were routinely excluded from literacy, schooling, jobs, and publication venues that legitimated knowledge. In a contemporary period with more fluidity of individuals but not necessarily a fluidity of structural power relations, it becomes more difficult to tell whose vested interests are represented by which intellectuals.

This question of social actors speaks to the conditions under which social theory is produced. From within privileged positions of the West, the power dynamics that make social theory possible in the first place are rarely questioned. When it comes to interrogating their own practice, Western social theorists rarely engage my three questions. Instead, they seem distracted by smaller questions of whether one can get a job of teaching social theory; whether one's work can be published in an elite journal or by a top-notch press; or internecine debates about what Michel Foucault meant under all that dense prose or why Judith Butler remains so hostile to identity politics.

Intellectuals creating social theory in non-elite settings, especially if they are using non-traditional tools to do so, have no such distractions. Education is more than one's individual property whose main purpose is for personal enrichment or career advancement. Intellectuals and/or thinkers on or from the bottom understand what need really is, and regardless of their answers to my questions, they are more apt to confront these questions in trying to do intellectual work within devalued social locations.

These three interconnected themes of ownership, vested interests, and institutional actors can be applied to any knowledge project. These three themes also provide guidance concerning which questions, themes, content, and methodologies are deemed to be legitimate within a given knowledge project, and which are not. This framework provides me with a quick snapshot of where to start in thinking through the works of a particular thinker or of Western knowledge writ large.

## CRITICAL INTERVENTIONS IN WESTERN SOCIAL THEORY

Connell's *Southern Theory* aims to be a critical intervention in power relations that vests the "West" with producing social theory and the "rest" with knowledges that remain derivative if not mimetic of the West's accomplishments. It is important to read this volume not as a definitive text on Southern theory but rather as a preliminary outline of one way that a knowledge project whose goal is to decenter or decolonize Western social theory might proceed. Connell's five chapters each constitutes a critical intervention in Western social theory. How often do courses and texts of Western social theory focus on indigenous knowledge and debates about African philosophy, an Iranian analysis of how Islam might serve as a site to resist Western domination, the significance of Latin American social science in theorizing core/periphery economic relations, how Subaltern Studies emerged in India to grapple with the transitions from colony to national independence, and the relationship of Aboriginal peoples to the land? By itself, the scope of ideas surveyed in *Southern Theory* is an important accomplishment.

The issue is less the existence of many knowledge projects produced by non-Western peoples, but rather the theme of how knowledge projects that do gain some power and notoriety are received within Western social theory.

140 PATRICIA HILL COLLINS

Recall that this is an unequal power relation where Western theorists have held most if not all of the cards. Despite a history of exclusion, a range of "Southern" knowledge projects have been developed beyond the reach of Western social theory (Connell's contributions lie in highlighting selected projects). Alternately, a series of similar "Southern" projects have been catalyzed *within* the boundaries of the West. Wherever it is developed, Southern social theory expresses a shared set of concerns. Grappling with being subordinated within Western hierarchical power relations has been the core existential question of Southern theory.

None of the spaces in which Southern theory is created were or are comfortable. Here I want to focus on the tensions of doing social theory in these *outsider within* social locations, as I suspect that the thinkers on whom Connell focuses most likely worked in such spaces. They were insiders to the varying knowledge traditions of their respective areas, whether they were living in the West or not. Yet, when it came to gaining the power that accrues to Western social theorists, they stood as outsiders and were able to see how power relations operated.

Connell's discussion of early work in Subaltern Studies provides an excellent example of how outsiders within social locations shape knowledge projects. Subaltern Studies occupied an outsider within space between eroding colonial practices and Indian national independence that made room for native intellectuals. Thinkers working in this border space could see power relations above and below. Their then startling insight was that a shared culture existed among the oppressed or subaltern groups that, while it could catalyze political practice, was routinely misrecognized by dominant groups. What is striking for me is how the radical potential of the early writings of authors within Subaltern Studies became transformed into decontextualized ideas that then could be inserted into academia as "Postcolonial Studies" within English departments. Although anthropologist James Scott gets much of the credit for this theme with his work on "weapons of the weak," it is useful to remember that this provocative idea that subordinated groups might produce political knowledge projects using different epistemological criteria for legitimation was a core feature of Subaltern Studies.

The transformation of Subaltern Studies into Postcolonial Studies and its acceptance within Western social theory can be seen as a success story in that the ideas of a group of non-white, non-Western thinkers gained visibility within academic settings. One wonders, however, how profoundly the imperial center of Western knowledge has been shaken by arrival of this and other dissident discourse. Subaltern Studies has traveled, but has the cost been its appropriation and annexation to another agenda? Subaltern Studies may also have fallen victim to the impulse to reject past patterns of exclusion by carefully managing the terms of inclusion concerning the ownership, vested interest, and institutional actors of this competing knowledge project. Given these challenges, how effective is Connell's critical intervention within power relations such as these?

## CONNELL'S CRITICAL INTERVENTION: TWO DILEMMAS

Western theory is a particular kind of knowledge project, engaged in by a short list of social actors, under particular power relations. People doing Southern theory understand this social context – the issue is finding ways to challenge, reform, and transform if not destroy these relations. Just because thinkers cannot yet envision alternative and more democratic ways of producing social theory does not mean that those who continue to be harmed by Western theory are satisfied with the status quo.

Despite repeated references to imperialism and power relations as *topics* of conversation, Connell ignores how patterned *practices* of ownership, vested interest, and institutional actors that are associated with the production of Western social theory shape this project. Connell wants this text to be taken seriously as a work of social theory and, for *Southern Theory*, that means embracing the legitimation practices of Western social theory. Connell wants this work to "rise" to the level of theory and, as a result, relies upon conventions from Western social theory that are designed to foster that legitimacy. Reflecting the epistemological constraints of working within this confining intellectual space, *Southern Theory*'s critical intervention confronts two main dilemmas.

One dilemma concerns how to negotiate the inequalities among the multiple knowledges that have been created by unequal power relations. Despite Connell's goal of decentering social theory as a Northern knowledge project by expanding it to incorporate many other knowledges – I appreciated *Southern Theory*'s chapters on Africa, Iran, Latin America, and Australia – the structure of the book follows the all too familiar setup of putting the ostensibly most important knowledge in the beginning, thereby centering it and positioning all other knowledges as "critique." This framework goes by many names – the "other voices" model and, in this volume, the "West and the rest" framework.

My sense is that Connell knows fully well that the marginalization of multiple knowledges discussed in *Southern Theory* is a direct reflection of their status within the contested power relations of global capitalism and imperialism. Yet, at the same time, Connell also knows that this familiar, quasi-hegemonic and comfortable trope permeates college classrooms and edited volumes. This is the frame that readers bring to the project and a cardinal rule of teaching and scholarship is to know your audience. The interpretive framework of placing the normal, normative, and universal at the center of analysis and positioning its critics on the margins functions in hegemonic ways by incorporating opposition to a dominant discourse into the terms of the dominant discourse itself. Structuring the argument so that readers encounter Southern theory through the eyes of the dominant discourse itself constitutes a twenty-first-century variation of William E. B. Du Bois's insightful "double consciousness."

These issues become especially difficult when dealing with social theory, a discourse that has been so central to the power relations that created this "West and the rest" thinking in the first place. Lest we forget that neoliberal market relations matter, the gloomy environment for textbook publishing has made the industry especially risk-aversive. Market surveys of what consumers want to see in their textbooks often drive what actually ends up being published.

I do not fault Connell because I know how difficult it is to negotiate this narrow epistemological space and pushback against this "West and the (undifferentiated) rest" framework. When I first taught a graduate seminar on contemporary social theory, I used this framework, putting Foucault, Bourdieu, and other generally accepted theoretical heavy weights at the beginning of my syllabus. The holism of their thought – done by one man what couldn't even be covered in a week – was followed by several weeks of theories by multiple "others," each of whom had many people jockeying for a slot on the syllabus. Who would I assign for the feminism week, or for the critical race theory session? Who best represented queer theory?

The next time I taught the course, I added Franz Fanon's *The Wretched of the Earth*, a text that was written within the same social conditions as those facing the French postmodernists (primarily the insight that many French postmodernist scholars had varying connections to the colonial struggle in Algeria). But I included Fanon after Foucault and Bourdieu, again as a "critical" voice that ironically reified Foucault's and Bourdieu's authority. What a disservice to Fanon. The next time I taught the course, I switched the order of the sessions. I no longer organized the course into two starkly divided sections – the West and the rest. Instead, I created a more fluid, borderland space in the middle. My students read *The Wretched of the Earth* before being exposed to the French postmodernists. They then used Fanon's provocative ideas from this archetypal text from Southern theory to engage dominant Western theorists. Postmodernism certainly reads differently when keeping Fanon's analyses in mind. There was pushback. As one talented yet clearly annoyed young white male student asked, "Why do we need to read this stuff?" He meant Fanon – apparently the utility of reading Foucault, Bourdieu, and the others was obvious.

A second dilemma that Connell confronts concerns Western epistemo-logical standards that are used to legitimate social theory, and some would argue, Western knowledge projects overall. When one is trying to write a project as expansive as global social theory, criteria for legitimation become especially significant. Connell uses a standard epistemological practice within Western theory, namely, grounding *Southern Theory*'s analysis in the works of a few hand-picked intellectuals. While I see the merits of this editorial strategy, this common practice of identifying a short list of thinkers within a canon as the carriers of bona fide social theory for that canon is limiting. Recognizing these standard legitimation patterns, *Southern Theory* excavates forgotten and/or unknown intellectuals from non-elite national settings as a critical intervention. Yet this is a first step. The focus on individual intellectuals from continental Africa, Australia, Iran, India, and Latin America, whose literacy and educational credentials most likely separates them from the masses in the bottom of their respective societies, undercuts the broader claim that social groups who are differentially positioned in the South produce social thought that can "rise" to the level of theory. It does so by paying scant attention to individuals who may have produced social thought by other means.

Within Western social theory, this strategy of looking for great books by individual great scholars (intellectuals) rarely produces thinkers who are not white, educated, male, and/or Western. The critical intervention in *Southern Theory* is that there are intellectuals from other parts of the world who are thinking about and working on themes that also concern scholars in the West. Just as Western social theory is always searching for Blacks, or women, or people of color, or poor people, or immigrants that meet its standards of excellence, so too does *Southern Theory* replicate these same standards in its efforts to legitimate itself. Ironically, women are missing from this volume, thus replicating the same critique leveled against Western social theory. Again, I do not fault Connell for this strategy. My goal instead is to point out the ways in which we are all constrained in what we can say and do. Social theory is not simply a constellation of ideas, instead it operates as a discourse of power.

Those of us who struggle to contribute to broader knowledge projects of developing a global social theory that avoids false universals and that adequately analyzes contemporary global phenomena confront these dual dilemmas of being constrained by organizational conventions like the "West and the rest" and by epistemological criteria that tell us in so many ways that Black, female, poor, non-Western, Muslim, Aboriginal people can't think, let alone do complex social theory. These dilemmas point to the constraints that confront those of us who wish to broaden and democratize social theory.

## BUILDING A CRITICAL SOCIAL THEORY

Connell desperately wants to create space for a new "global" social theory that transcends both the limitations of a narrow Western social theory that has managed to elevate its ideas as "universal" and the uneven success of "Southern" knowledge projects that remain neglected, appropriated, or ghettoized. Like Rodney King's famous statement after the 1992 L.A. riots, *Southern Theory* seems to be asking social theory from the West and the rest, "Can't we all just get along?"

Wishing for collaboration because we all have so much to learn from one another is a noble sentiment. In one of the book's concluding sections titled "Reconfiguring Knowledge on a World Scale," Connell argues: "I think it is helpful to think of social science not as a settled system of concepts, methods and findings, but as an interconnected set of intellectual projects that proceed from varied social starting points into an unpredictable future" (p. 228). Connell's suggestion of moving forward by putting Southern theory in dialogue with its Northern counterpart simply didn't ring true for me, precisely because the power relations that produce the "varied starting points" within intellectual production remain absent.

Crafting relations across differences in power such as those framing imperial knowledge projects will be difficult to achieve, precisely because so much is at stake. I think that the next step in drafting global social theory will be far more difficult than creating space for dialogue. I, for one, would find it especially refreshing if privileged Western intellectuals magically recognized the myriad ways that the privileges associated with race, gender, class, sexuality ability, age, religion, citizenship status, and literacy in the approved national language promoted their success, including why they are drawn to some forms of social theory and avoid others like the plague. Sadly, there appears to be too much at stake for those who have a vested interest in sustaining the status quo to challenge it. The abstractions of social theory can be a wonderful place to hide from the messy political practices that replicate social inequalities, precisely because theory ostensibly is about what theorists think and not what we do. Conversely, for intellectuals who have been disadvantaged, erased, marginalized, and oppressed by these same power relations, walking away is not an option. In a global context, there's nowhere to run. There's nowhere to hide.

It remains difficult and often extremely disheartening to produce social theory across such vast differences in power that separate thinkers who are privileged within the North from intellectuals in the South. Grappling with this situation will take far more than a Gentleman's agreement to engage in friendly conversation. Quite frankly, I don't see how debates that originate solely *within* the contours of Western social theory will have much to say about power relations that shape their own practice. Western social theorists have a vested interest in not seeing these power relations, much as whites in an ostensibly post-racial America have a vested interest in remaining colorblind.

Connell certainly is no rookie when it comes to power relations, yet has chosen not to focus on these contested power relations. Instead, *Southern Theory* follows the seemingly safer path of speaking to the concerns of two primary audiences who might be persuaded to start the dialogue: (1) teachers, scholars, and graduate students who both already participate in Western social theory and who are already predisposed to see these power relations; and (2) thinkers and intellectuals from the South who remain outsiders because they have been excluded from the corpus of Western social theory. Let us not forget that these exclusions have affected pretty much everyone outside the West as well as selected populations within it.

Academics certainly put their faith in dialogues, but within contemporary global power relations much more is needed than talk. People in privileged positions routinely propose slow, evolutionary understandings of social change, suggesting that thoughtful dialogue will eventually bring about social justice. People in disadvantaged positions remain far less sanguine about the benefits of dialogue, especially those who have participated in a barrage of conversations that go nowhere. For example, African Americans and their allies ignored the "go slow" talk that counseled patience because America wasn't ready for racial integration, bringing the much-talked about quest for civil rights into the public area through actions. Sometimes action brings about desired results quicker than endless conversations. In this case, struggling to change not just the ideas, but also the ownership, vested interests, and institutional actors of social theory as a knowledge project might create space for much needed dialogues across differences in power. Perhaps we all need a better balance between talk and action.

## REFERENCE

Omi, M., & Winant, H. (1994). *Racial formation in the United States: From the 1960s to the 1990s*. New York, NY: Routledge.

# CONNELL AND POSTCOLONIAL SOCIOLOGY

## Raka Ray

### ABSTRACT

*This essay argues that* Southern Theory *kick-started a conversation long overdue in sociology about the colonial bounds of the sociological canon and its implications. It makes the case that* Southern Theory *can be used as a jump-off point to reflect on what the contours of a postcolonial sociology might look like since it argues that postcolonial difference can be used to extend theory, point to earlier theoretical misrecognitions, and to illuminate hitherto unseen logics of social organization by shifting the center.*

With the publication of *Southern Theory*, and before that, with her essays on Northern Theory, Raewyn Connell kick-started a conversation long overdue in Sociology about the colonial bounds of the sociological canon (in Connell's words, "metropolitan sociology") and its implications. In short, without actually embracing the term, Connell initiated a dialogue between postcolonial theory and American sociology. While others might suggest that what Connell initiated was actually a particular form of global sociology, I would like to make the case here for Connell's contribution to the postcolonial sociology, and to use *Southern Theory* as a jump-off

Decentering Social Theory
Political Power and Social Theory, Volume 25, 147–156
Copyright © 2013 by Emerald Group Publishing Limited
All rights of reproduction in any form reserved
ISSN: 0198-8719/doi:10.1108/S0198-8719(2013)0000025013

point to reflect on what the contours of a postcolonial sociology might look like.

As Stuart Hall (1996) has astutely put it, colonialism was simultaneously a system of rule and knowledge production. A project which desires to create a dialogue between postcolonial theory and American sociology thus must take on both the substance of the theory – a consideration of the constitutive effects of colonial rule on colonizer and colonized – as well as its challenges to the epistemological foundations of the field. The absence of the first (the constitutive effects of colonial rule) has to do with America's refusal to see itself as an imperial power. The absence of the second (challenges to epistemology) with American sociology's very firm attachment to a certain narrative of capitalism and modernity. In *Southern Theory*, Connell challenges American sociology on both grounds.

As practiced in the contemporary United States, sociology bears a particularly knotted relationship to questions of universality and difference – therein lies the crux of the discipline's problem with the postcolonial. In many ways, sociology has two others: anthropology with which it was originally twinned, and economics. Economics retains resolutely the figure of the universal rational preference maximizing person as its unit of analysis. The difference that interests economics is the difference in outcome that accrues to similarly universally rational persons which must then be attributed to institutional structures such lack of property rights and poorly developed markets. Anthropology on the other hand was predicated on the very assumption of difference. Along its history it has confronted itself and its colonial fascinations with hyper-difference but remains devoted to that central problematic. Sociology, Janus-faced, facing both anthropology and economics, resorts to seeking out difference but only if it can be explained by relatively universal principles. In other words, sociology is interested in *reconcilable differences*.

Postcolonial theory, which considers seriously the continuing impact of colonialism on the social, cultural, and economic development of both colonial powers and the colonies, has yet to make its way into the theoretical arsenal of American sociology because the difference that postcolonial theory addresses is not seen to be reconcilable with sociological universals. The price for this omission is high and the creation of this dialogue is hard, for one must specify the analytical contributions that postcolonial theory can make to the field of sociology. I am grateful to Raewyn Connell for taking that first gigantic step.

*Southern Theory* is a direct critique of the parochial nature of sociology in America, highlighting its method of addressing the issue of difference, and of the origin story that the discipline tells itself. The book serves as both critique and mission statement, for it wants to create a sociology that takes the interconnected history of the world more seriously than it does now. It recognizes that such sociology must be open to theoretical ideas from a wider range of places than today, and is attentive both to alternative knowledges that exist in the global south and to the ways in which those knowledges are being increasingly marginalized. *Southern Theory* seeks, in short to decenter American sociology in terms of its objects of research, its epistemologies and methodology, its theoretical interlocutors, and its need for reconcilable differences. And it does so with the idea that such a sociology is a better sociology.

## THE HISTORY OF METROPOLITAN SOCIOLOGY

The textbook story of the creation of the discipline of sociology has to do with the French Revolution (new ideas), the Industrial Revolution (new conditions of living therefore new problems), and the ascendancy of science. Seldom is the less savory relationship between the rise of sociology and imperialism explored – as if that is a burden we have relegated to anthropologists (cf., Go, 2013; Steinmetz, 2013). Anthropology took on its colonial origins (Lévi Strauss (1966) famously declared "Anthropology is daughter to an era of violence"), went under for a period, and re-emerged a stronger discipline. When it re-emerged, it was not to repudiate its origins, but to recognize both the complicity of its field with colonialism *as well as* its many radical contributions to world of knowledge. Sociology has yet to undergo that transformation. Indeed, there is in sociology what Stuart Hall has identified as a "powerful unconscious investment" in its Western categories. *Southern Theory* challenges both the categories and the means by which they came to be central to the discipline.

Raewyn Connell argues that global difference – translated as backwardness and development – was a core feature of early sociology, more so than industrialization. Durkheim and others freely borrowed between ancient civilizations and contemporary places elsewhere in making their arguments, underscoring a lack of history in those places, moving across what Anne McClintock (1995, p. 37) has called the assumptions of *panoptical time* and *anachronistic space*. Yet all the while, colonialism shaped the way these thinkers experienced the world in ways they did not acknowledge. Writing at the height of French colonialism, for example, Durkheim refers to many other societies (which he learns about through the knowledge created by the colonial mission) but sees no reason to relate them to France's development as a society – he sees them only as different and backward as compared to France. The development of the comparative method, now core to the discipline, was premised not only on difference, but also on the "capacity to examine a range of societies from the outside, and an ability to move freely from one society to another – features which all map the range of colonial domination (Connell, 2007, p. 12)". Indeed, the discipline managed the contradictions between liberal thought and empire by relying on abstraction and ideas about social evolution. With specific reference to the United States, Connell (2007, p. 20) suggests that while the origins of the discipline lay in global difference, by the 1920s, the issue of difference had left the global stage and moved to those *within* the nation. In other words, the US sociology between 1920 and 1950 focused increasingly on difference within the metropole.

The managing of difference through abstraction and principles of social evolution enables a universalism that then comes to mark contemporary Northern theories. These theories, Connell argues, read the world from the center outwards, excluding that which does not fit and erasing those very histories of colonial struggle through which both the North and the South were made. These erasures, she argues, lead to a misguided focus for contemporary theories of globalization.

These erasures and exclusions enable the form of universalization that lies at the heart of the problem for the discipline today. As Gurminder Bhambra argues, "the western experience has been taken both as the basis for the construction of modernity and, at the same time, that concept is argued to have a validity that transcends the western experience (2007, p. 4)." So, for example, the analytic stories of the unfolding of modernity as narrated by Marx, Weber, and Durkheim assumed a self-contained Europe which formed the empirical crux from which they generated their theories (French armies were in full imperial mode at the time Durkheim wrote, as Connell reminds us, but this does not seem to have affected his understanding of French society). While contemporary sociology, by and large, assumes the same self-contained Europe and the United States – with most explanations about phenomenon in the United States tending to favor exclusively internalist logics – historians and postcolonial theorists have demonstrated that neither Europe nor the United States was as self-contained as previously imagined. Historian Dipesh Chakrabarty (2000) reminds us that Europe was a specific place with a specific colonial history, and that we have universalized the European story to create a single model of historical progress comes with great costs. If Western Europe developed certain forms of capitalist modernity it did so because of its particular history, which makes its replication unlikely in other parts of the world. Thus, he suggests we "provincialize" rather than universalize Europe. This would mean that we move away from our belief in one model of the history of capitalism and of modernity to accepting multiple models, and to seeing the sociology of the world as interconnected rather than seeing a world divided into those nations that are modern and those that have failed to becomes so. By ignoring these possibilities, the sociological stories we know, tell, and act upon, how we understand the constitutive parts of entire societies, or the roots of social problems, or even the consequences of social and political action are at best incomplete and at worst inaccurate.[1]

The question of the history of the discipline has not surprisingly taken a different turn in postcolonial countries. I refer you here to Satish Deshpande's (2001) wonderful essay on the creation of sociology in India where he considers the effects of British social anthropology, American funding for area studies and social sciences during the Cold War, and the Indian nation's embrace of the development project on shaping a post-colonial sociology. I do not know of an attempt prior to Connell's to understand the history of American sociology through a similar global lens. She issues a challenge to decolonize and democratize the parameters of knowledge production.

## THE PRODUCTION OF KNOWLEDGE

Dipesh Chakrabarty belongs to a group Connell highlights in her work – the subaltern studies collective of India – whose work was marked by simultaneous attention to questions of power, culture, and the politics of the dispossessed. Their work on the politics of knowledge production speaks directly to questions of power in sociology by asking about whose narratives contribute to a "universal" truth and whose authorial voices are given more credibility.

In *Provinicalizing Europe* (2000), arguably the strongest statement about the subalternity of knowledge production, Chakrabarty argues that the very production of South Asian history occupies a subaltern position given the asymmetries of power in global knowledge production and circulation. "Third world-world historians feel a need to refer to works in European history; historians of Europe do not feel any need to reciprocate .... The problem, I may add in parentheses, is not particular to historians (Chakrabarty, 2000, p. 28)." Edward Said poignantly refers to this phenomenon as a "dreadful secondariness (1989, p. 207)". Thus, subaltern and postcolonial theorists join Connell in the call for the decolonization and democratization of the parameters of knowledge production.

Yet, how should we make the case for democratizing knowledge? It is here that I diverge from Connell's approach. In the part of the book labeled "Southern Theory," Connell brings in thinkers from Iran, the continent of Africa, Latin America, Australia (which is without doubt a strange inclusion), and India to show us that there were in those countries intellectuals who had different ideas from those which circulated in the metropole. The problem is that there is no real systematicity in her exposition of the depth and range of argument and debate in those countries. We do not know why these scholars, and not others, are brought to our attention. Neither are we told by Connell what we gain by dipping into the thoughts of such a wide range of thinkers. In the end her argument about the inclusion of Southern theories feels like a *moral* claim about the importance of democratizing knowledge as an end in itself. Thus, the reason to read them would be not because one's understanding of the world one inhabits would shift with the power of the ideas one would encounter there, but because it was the morally right thing to do to read some non-Western thinkers. It may indeed be so, but ultimately this will be a weak argument. Intellectual work has rarely switched course for the sake of internal democracy. Postcolonial theories will matter either if they offer a more satisfactory explanation of events or characteristics of the Global South than existing theories, or even more centrally if they are seen to illuminate phenomena that matter in the North. Our theorizing has to make clear why theories that emanate from the South refocus theorizing of the North in the North – that is the task that remains unfinished. In other words in order to produce a truly global sociology we must simultaneously provincialize the United States and deprovincialize the South. This is the task that Connell brings to our attention but leaves unfinished.

## BETTER KNOWLEDGE

If we return to Stuart Hall's remark about colonialism being both a system of rule and of knowledge production, how might taking colonialism seriously improve sociological knowledge? Cross-national comparative work occupies a central place in the sociological enterprise. Yet, unlike in anthropological work such as by Jim Ferguson (1990) or Ann Stoler (2002), the impact of colonial histories on the institutions being compared is seldom recognized.[2] I would suggest that colonial histories might usefully factor into our understandings of a range of issues in the contemporary historical moment, from the urban problems of New York, Paris, or Johannesburg to the women's movements of Mexico and India. Indeed, while my preference would be for a deeper historical understanding of the effects of colonial rule, for the more positivist inclined colleagues I would advocate that colonial histories be added to the arsenal of key independent variables that we assemble when we consider a sociological problem.

Colonial histories can correct our working assumptions of race and gender, for as scholars such as Anne McClintock remind us, categories of race, class, and gender – the usual triumvirate that sociologists work with – may be formed in interaction with colonial histories. Let us reflect upon the banning of the *burqa* in France, for example. While many in this part of the world see it either as a mistake because it will alienate Muslims further and others think France has stood up for women's rights, being attentive to colonial histories will direct us to understand that the ban is in line with French assimilationist policies core to French colonialism and which continue with regard to immigrants today. We may also consider an example closer to home which reinforces the problematic of colonial knowledge production: While Nicholas Kristof (Kristof & WuDunn, 2009) has garnered praise and popularity for his recent writings on women in the third world, his analysis entirely misses the effects of colonialism on gender relations in Africa. It also replicates in a quite startling way, a 19th century savior mentality where the active agents of liberation come only from the West, where women not-of the-West are victims and their men the oppressors. In so doing, Kristof both *misrecognizes* the nature of the crises he discusses and *replicates* a power equation that is inherited from a colonial view of the world. But because both these problems are normalized in absence of a recognition of colonialism, he is much feted.

In general, in our comparative work, we take the United States or England as the unquestioned standard against which phenomena are to be compared. What would it do to our understanding of social phenomena in the North if the North were not, in fact, the frame of reference?[3] In most classic works that are global in their scope, it is the rest of the world which gets problematized in comparison to the United States, which remains the norm. The rest of the world, then, is the difference which must be reconciled to abstract sociological principles that have been created precisely through, and yet with the denial of, the colonial encounter. This point is, of course, central to Connell's critique.

But what intellectual exercise does decentering the West provide the global sociologist? My 2009 book, *Cultures of Servitude* (coauthored with Seemin Qayum), foregrounds ideologies and practices of paid domestic work, pointing to the home as a site infused with relations of inequality in which gender and class play a unique role. Through the examination of Kolkata's culture of servitude, located in the interstices of the social imaginaries of feudalism and capitalist modernity, the book traces the constitution and reproduction of the employing middle classes in dialectical relation with the serving classes. In examining middle-class reliance on domestic servants, we suggest that classes come into being not just through practices of consumption or production outside the home but also through labor and intimate practices within the home. Our central argument is simply this: the institution of paid domestic work is both constitutive of, and a marker of, class.

With a few exceptions, the literature on paid domestic work emanating from the United States and Europe, however, focuses on the contribution of the contemporary care "crisis" in advanced industrialized countries on global circuits of care. In other words, the literature is based on an assumption that the increased labor force participation of middle class and affluent women in the North has led to a crisis of care and thus to the increased reliance on imported labor for the performance of cleaning and childcare work. The institution, relationships, and arrangements of paid domestic work are thus treated as new phenomena brought about by the increased labor force participation on middle class women.[4] Our study departs from this assumption of paid domestic work as a response to a new need by focusing on a country with a relatively low women's labor force participation (11.9% in urban India) and in which domestic service has a very long and unbroken history. In other words, our work shows that there is no *necessary* relationship between the employment of domestic workers and middle-class women's labor force participation. This difference enables us to shift the conversation from one about the *actual* needs of "modern" dual career couples to the *assumption* of what constitutes household needs. Middle-class women in India who do not work outside the home feel they absolutely cannot do without domestic workers. The issue of working women employers can thus be seen as an instantiation of the status-based ability to transfer reproductive work to a lower class and not necessarily the logical outcome of a crisis of care. Centering the experience of servitude in India, and taking that explanation as the one to contend with, can actually provincialize the experience of the United States. Using India as the center of comparison, then, what would need to be explained is why, in the United States today, paid domestic work is *not* seen as constitutive of a class culture (except as parody in the *Nanny Diaries*) but as a market response to a new demographic and social need. What does this lens reveal about US society? This, I suggest, opens, rather than closes, avenues of intellectual inquiry.

## CONCLUSION

*Southern Theory* is a call to action and a reminder that for too long we have behaved as if the *space of the universal* has already been occupied by the North – which leaves only the *space of the particular* for the South. What I have tried to show here, however briefly, is not only that the theories of the North may have validity in a restricted geographical domain but that the theories from the South we seek to work with do not have solely a restricted geographical domain; they too can scale and travel. *Southern Theory* enables us to work toward a sociology which can use postcolonial difference to extend theory, point to earlier theoretical misrecognitions, and to illuminate hitherto unseen logics of social organization by shifting the center.

## NOTES

1. Wallerstein and the world systems theorists were an exception. They do indeed read from the center out, but they are far less guilty of the erasures of which Connell speaks. They can be accused, if anything, of being too monocausal in their explanatory focus. Yet dependency theorists such as Cardoso and Falletto (as Connell acknowledges) and their more sophisticated and contemporary exponents in both the South and North in the North (such as Peter Evans) do stand apart, and I want to acknowledge that.

2. George Steinmetz, "The Colonial State as a Social Field: Ethnographic Capital and Native Policy in the German Overseas Empire before 1914," and Julian Go, *Patterns of Empire: The British and American Empires, 1688 to the present*, are two welcome exceptions.

3. The feminist version of this challenge is, of course, the understanding of men as the norm and women as the difference.

4. Earlier works on the history of the institution, such as Evelyn Nakano Glenn's, emphasize the relationship between the racial history of the United States and domestic servitude.

## REFERENCES

Bhambra, G. (2007). *Rethinking modernity: Postcolonialism and the sociological imagination*. Basingstoke: Palgrave Macmillan.

Chakrabarty, D. (2000). *Provincializing Europe: Postcolonial thought and historical difference.* New Delhi: Oxford University Press.

Connell, R. (2007). *Southern theory: The global dynamics of knowledge in social science.* Malden, MA: Polity.

Deshpande, S. (2001). Disciplinary predicaments: Sociology and anthropology in postcolonial India. *Inter-Asia Cultural Studies, 2*(2), 247–260.

Ferguson, J. (1990). *The anti-politics machine: 'Development,' depoliticization, and bureaucratic power in Lesotho.* Cambridge, MA: Cambridge University Press.

Go, J. (2011). *Patterns of empire: The British and American empires, 1688 to the present.* Cambridge, MA: Cambridge University Press.

Go, J. (2013). Sociology's imperial unconscious: Early American sociology in a global context. In G. Steinmetz (Ed.), *Sociology and empire* (pp. 83–105). Durham: Duke University Press.

Hall, S. (1996). When was the "postcolonial"? Thinking at the limit. In I. Chambers & L. Curti (Eds.), *The postcolonial question: Common skies, divided horizons* (pp. 242–258). London: Routledge.

Kristof, N., & WuDunn, S. (2009). *Half the sky: Turning oppression into opportunity for women worldwide.* New York, NY: Vintage.

Lévi-Strauss, C. (1966). Anthropology: Its achievements and future. *Current Anthropology, 7*(2), 126.

McClintock, A. (1995). *Imperial leather: Race, gender and sexuality in the imperial context.* London: Routledge.

Said, E. (1989). Representing the colonized: Anthropology's interlocutors. *Critical Inquiry, 15*(2), 205–225.

Steinmetz, G. (2008). The colonial state as a social field: Ethnographic capital and native policy in the German overseas empire before 1914. *American Sociological Review, 73*, 589–612.

Steinmetz, G. (Ed.). (2013). *Sociology and empire.* Durham: Duke University Press.

Stoler, A. L. (2002). *Carnal knowledge and imperial power: Race and the intimate in colonial rule.* Berkeley, CA: University of California Press.

# THEORETICAL LABORS NECESSARY FOR A GLOBAL SOCIOLOGY: CRITIQUE OF RAEWYN CONNELL'S *SOUTHERN THEORY*

Isaac Ariail Reed

## ABSTRACT

*This essay considers the relationship between global sociology and sociological theory through an examination of the critique of Northern Theory developed by Raewyn Connell. The author accepts many of Connell's criticisms of the formation of the Northern Theory canon, and of the false universalism of contemporary Northern Theory, but disputes the degree to which Connell has succeeded in finding a replacement for the "ethnosociology of the metropole" provided by current sociological theory. In particular, the author suggests that, in* Southern Theory, *Connell pursues an intellectual history of world philosophies instead of the development of theoretical concepts that could provide a more adequate global sociology from a Southern perspective. Connell leaves the reader with a reconstructed canon of classics, but without a new repertoire of middle-range explanatory and interpretive concepts with which to*

Decentering Social Theory
Political Power and Social Theory, Volume 25, 157–171
Copyright © 2013 by Emerald Group Publishing Limited
All rights of reproduction in any form reserved
ISSN: 0198-8719/doi:10.1108/S0198-8719(2013)0000025014

*reconstruct our understanding of history itself. The former may be the*
*necessary first step toward the latter, however, rendering* Southern
Theory *an important moment in the global turn in sociological theory.*

# THE GLOBAL CHALLENGE TO SOCIOLOGY, AND
# TO SOCIOLOGICAL THEORY IN PARTICULAR

Circling through different sociological discourses of the last 25 years has
been the possibility of a refounding of the discipline, a kind of epistemic
contestation. Patricia Hill Collins has raised questions about how race and
gender inflect and influence "the kinds of questions that could be asked and
the explanations that would be found satisfying," and thus argued for a
black feminist sociology (1989, p. 752); Andrew Abbott (2007) has argued
for a lyrical sociology to complement or perhaps displace the dominant
causal narratives given by positivist or variable-driven sociology; Frederic
Vandenberghe (1999) and Mustafa Emirbayer (1997) have both called for a
relational sociology, influenced by the methodology of network analysis and
Bourdieu's concept of "field." Each of these individual authors are
exemplars of broader movements within the discipline to challenge the
basic conceptual methodology of sociology; their arguments are arguments
about how empirics and theorization intersect, about how data about the
world, assembled via various methods – from survey research to interviews
to ethnography – informs, and is organized by, the sociological concepts
that are used to explain what happens in the world at various levels of
specificity.

One of the most complex and contentious of these epistemic challenges
has been that of global sociology, and, in particular, the question of how a
sociology unencumbered by methodological nationalism and Western/
Northern bias can be developed. A certain way of addressing these global
questions has an elective affinity with – or perhaps a particularly effective
critique of – historical sociology and social theory. This is because historical
sociology and social theory in the global North would be unrecognizable to
many of its most fervent practitioners without the concept of "modernity";
simultaneously, the social theory that operates from the standpoint of the
global South articulates an argument that the blindnesses of Northern
Theory are intrinsically related to the oppression and exclusion that
accompanied and accompanies modernity, and in particular the modern
colonial encounter and its aftermath, and various neo-imperial formations.

Raewyn Connell's *Southern Theory: The Global Dynamics of Knowledge in Social Science* can, I think, be understood as part of this global challenge to sociology. It is an important argument, and, stands out, along with Gurminder Bhambra's *Rethinking Modernity*, as specifically aimed at *sociological theory* as those in the Anglophone academic world tend to understand it. It thus has the potential to be a signpost for a new generation of sociological theorists. While postcolonial theory, debates about empire and neo-imperialism, and a global perspective on power relations are by no means new to academic work in the metropole, a focused attack on and reformulation of *sociological* theory as a rather delimited set of discourses has been much less well-developed.[1]

The global challenge to Northern Theory, then, points out problems that have long structured the discipline of sociology in the metropole, and are just now coming to be recognized as problems; Connell's book is a symptom of, and active participant in, this shift. What follows here is an immanent critique, structured by my reading of the book and my reaction to it, which can be summarized quite simply as the view that Connell has correctly and rigorously identified, as have others, a clear set of problems for sociological theory and, more broadly, sociology, but that Connell's attempt, in *Southern Theory*, to ameliorate these problems does not succeed. The way in which this lack of success plays out, however, is a bit more subtle and requires me to build an interpretation of what is going on in Connell's extraordinarily learned book. So I hope the reader will bear with me. My argument will be, as this introduction suggests, epistemological. Specifically, I will argue that Connell has missed, in her reconstructive project, what are in fact the core conceptual developments required to rewrite sociological theory – namely, concepts that help build limited generalizations, effective comparative explanations, and new middle-range interpretations. She has attacked meta-theoretical presuppositions, and she has offered new intellectual histories that could bring a radical shift in the canon. But she has not yet made southern theory into the sort of theoretical repertoire that would create, and win, the contestation of concepts that she suggests must take place if sociology is to reform itself.

# WHAT IS THE THEORETICAL LABOR NECESSARY FOR A NEW GLOBAL SOCIOLOGY?

The conceptual encounter Connell offers her reader in *Southern Theory* is about sociology's past (the construction of the canon, other intellectual histories outside the metropole) and the future (imagining a new sociology on a global scale), but it is also quite clearly about the present. The sharpness of the challenge to the present of sociological *theory* is made clear by the chapter on Coleman, Bourdieu, Giddens, and Beck. The theories that she takes on in that chapter are active and developing research programs for explanation-building in social science; the authors that Connell focuses on are iconic tags for the more fundamental and collective labor of doing sociology in one way or another. So we have, in *Southern Theory*, a theoretical challenge that reaches out to the production of knowledge in the discipline at large.

Given this ambition, certain aspects of Connell's proposed program for sociology and sociological theory are worth pausing to examine. In particular, it is important to note that Connell's fourfold critique of Northern Theory, including her attack on its claim to universality, is paralleled by a strong argument *for* generalization. In her call for a "permanent revolution in social science, based on the empirical dimension in the collective learning process," Connell writes provocatively that:

> To speak of social science is ... to presume a capacity for generalization. How generalization works is a delicate and difficult question, but the fact of generalization is vital. A drive towards generalization is constitutive of science, and this is why we need theory, why science can never be simply a heap of facts. Theory is the way we speak beyond the single case. (p. 225)

A delicate and difficult question indeed; I agree with the broad strokes painted here by Connell. Many sociologists reference the dialogue of theory and data; the question is how seriously one takes the metaphor – does it just indicate an offhand way of talking about hypothesis testing, or does it indicate a deep hermeneutic commitment? One senses that Connell is reaching for a version of theory and generalization that takes the idea of dialogue extremely seriously. And it is in the terms of this project – that is, theory as dialogue-driven generalization and critique, with a particular eye to the global distribution of power and the way such power is encoded into sociological knowledge itself – that I will attempt to criticize her book.

How *would* we change the concepts with which we do sociology, in a "permanent revolution" or learning process that takes place on a global scale? At several points in the text Connell reveals that she views theorization to be a kind of labor, and specifically, a kind of labor that is undervalued if it is done in the global south, and overvalued if it is done in the metropole (pp. 105, 109, 136, 207, 223, 229; the concept of "dirty theory" on page 207 is particularly evocative). This over and undervaluation is no doubt exercised via mechanisms of material transfer, institution-building, and prestige-mongering with which we are all familiar. But implied in Connell's text is an understanding of theoretical labor as creative sociality, constituted by the intersubjectivity achievable between human beings. I agree. But what is the particular theoretical labor Connell thinks will make for a better sociology?

There is an argument to be made that Connell is imagining a theoretically driven format of sociological research that reaches for the best concepts possible to build explanations of the social world. Of course, what makes for an explanation in sociology is itself a power-laden issue that must be addressed in part through the sociology of knowledge. But note that Connell disavows "postmodernism" (e.g., pp. 172, 226) and embraces its counterpoints (e.g., "Guha's structuralism," and "Chaterjee's orginal conceptualization of power"; "We do try, as researchers, to make our statements agree with realities in other people's lives that are independent of our statements"). And note also that she maintains quite clearly that, in "risky" social science, "not only do data criticize theory, theory also criticizes data" and thus that "in this continuous argument, one tries to arrive at a configuration of knowledge that *reveals the dynamics of a given moment in human history*" (italics added, p. 207). She also notes, in the chapter wherein she engages the debate over Akiwowo's "Contributions to the Sociology of Knowledge from an African Oral Poetry," that

> what is at stake here is not just the ethnographic interpretation of a local culture. The question is the grounding of concepts that are intended to circulate beyond Yoruba culture, and as Akiwowo's 1986 paper put it, "contribute to a general body of explanatory principles for sociology across the world." (p. 95)

With this vision of reconstructing the toolkit for building good sociological explanations I agree wholeheartedly; in *Southern Theory*, Connell moves toward what I view as an emerging form of sociological epistemology which, having dispensed with the false universalisms of a previous era, nonetheless seeks to develop intellectually powerful, histori-cally delimited, causal explanations. What this epistemology is called is less important than its effects on research and the construction and critique of truth claims in sociology. And it seems to me that Connell is participating in this epistemic shift, thus connecting a global sociology to an epistemic break in conceptual methodology. And yet, something goes awry; the promise is never fulfilled, indeed it is displaced by something else.

# THE CONNELL HERMENEUTIC: ENCOUNTER, TRANSLATION, AND THE GROUNDED INTELLECTUAL HISTORY OF THEORY

First, let us examine how Connell herself pursues the theoretical labor necessary for the transformation of sociology. The model that her text follows is that of the intellectual encounter, and this is made clear by the moments where her own subjectivity enters the text directly, via descriptions of her use of translations, reactions upon reading a text for the first time, and so on. And in bringing Southern Theory – and its history – into the orbit of the sociological theory of the metropole, Connell creates, or attempts to create, a dialogue of concepts. These concepts do not meet on neutral ground, but rather on the ground of the history of colonial and neo-colonial domination, which she shows us.

This encounter with "other" traditions of thought is meant to replace the relation to which she objects so fervently, wherein the metropole produces theory and the periphery is either erased entirely from the metropole's knowledge project, or, at best, supplies metropolitan theory with data. In arguing this way, and in her reconstruction of the intellectual histories of Southern Theory, her encounters become an argument for a new theoretical canon. This new canon's construction will be informed by better knowledge of world history, reflexivity about the relationship between sociological theory and its points of origin, and, finally, an understanding of the task of social theory that includes the project of social critique. Connell's encounters are necessarily selective, and her selections, in each case, involve the examination, interpretation, and elaboration of key texts. This is canon work. In between the lines of *Southern Theory*, I detect the possibility, and perhaps the intention, that the reinterpretation of classics as a way of doing theory could take a new form. Why not a dissertation comparing the intellectual trajectory of Subaltern studies toward postmodernism with the reception of the modernist/postmodernist divide in Canclini? Or an exegetical dissertation on the conceptualization of power and solidarity in Akiwowo and Chatterjee? And so on. Connell's text implies that this is the knowledge-production sequel to *Southern Theory*.

However, the format of encounter-with-intellectual-history that Connell has developed so well does contain a major risk. By reinterpreting "traditions" of thought, and in suggesting a shift at the level of sociology's theoretical canon, *Southern Theory* does not *directly* push us toward the nuts and bolts of a global sociology, or toward explanations build upon the conceptual foundations of Southern Theory. I fear, in fact, that *Southern Theory* is slightly misguided about how to attack, change, and reconstruct Northern Theory, and, in turn, sociology itself. In what follows, I will try to explain why I think this is so.

## CONNELL'S CHALLENGE AND THE SPECTRUM OF GENERALIZATION

Connell's reconstruction of canon formation is instructive, and her argument about what Northern Theory effaces is compelling. From there, she proceeds to reconstruct intellectual traditions from around the world, a process that introduces her reader to a series of intellectuals and their big ideas. Prima facie, this is a valuable process, as I stated above. However, it must be said that this intellectual reconstruction occurs at two extreme ends of a spectrum of generalization. Her chapters reconstruct:

(1) "Metaconcepts" or "orienting concepts" that frame the core ideas of sociology and sociological theory, and "big debates" from the global south. At this level, the critique is that while what Durkheim or Homans thought that the study of society was about is highly consequential for what we think sociological theory is in the metropole, what Shariarti or Prebisch thought that the study of society was about is not consequential. Collins (1997) does not think this is a problem. Connell (1997) and I do think this is a problem.

(2) The *particular intellectual history* of such metaconcepts and debates, with occasional references to specific empirical studies that they informed or that informed them. Here the encounter is with the basics of the intellectual history of theory. So, again, the point is made, and made well: American graduate students in sociology are probably forced to learn something about, say, Weber's life and times, but not about, say, Akiwowo's life and times.

But something massive is missing in all of this. We do not get mechanisms or models, new definitions or classifications, a set of semi-general propositions, or a reconstructed theory of anything in particular. We do not even get an epistemological account of how the concepts under scrutiny would reorient analysis, or how an explanation that is informed by *Southern Theory*, as opposed to by Northern Theory, would work. The text, then, appears to fall into a dilemma: *Either* we get stories of intellectual history from the global periphery, *or* we get an overarching critique, suggesting a reorientation of presuppositions, and assumptions about who is or should be in the classical and modern canon. Connell's argument repeatedly alternates between these two poles of reconstruction, moving from the presuppositional level of "what is sociology?" (or even "what is the social?") to case-based empirical detail, often detail on the origins of the canonical texts that aid the reconstruction at the presuppositional level. Although space is limited, I want to give one example of how this works in *Southern Theory* in a bit more detail.

# FROM SOCIOLOGICAL CONTROVERSY TO PHILOSOPHY IN CONNELL'S READING OF AFRICAN SOCIAL THOUGHT

Consider Chapter 5, "Indigenous Knowledge and African Renaissance," a forceful argument that leads off Part III of *Southern Theory*. We begin this chapter with a reconstruction of the debate around Akinsola Akiwowo's argument for an indigenous sociology, which is to say, his argument for a sociology constructed out of the insights gleaned from Yoruba poetry. Akiwowo developed various sociological propositions out of his readings of this oral poetry tradition, and Connell reproduces some of them, such as "The unit of social life is the individual's life, being, existence, or character ..." and "Since the social life of a group of individual beings is sustained by a spirit of sodality, any form of self-alienation for the purpose of pursuing a purely selfish aim is, morally speaking, an error or sin ..." (p. 91). Connell then traces with tact and sophistication the critiques of Akiwowo that emerged, including that of Olatunde Baoyo Lawuyi and Olufemi Taiwo who argued rather fiercely that while Akiwowo has discovered the *possibility* of a Yoruba sociology, he has not in fact developed any usable sociological theory; indeed he has mostly done a "search for Yoruba-language equivalents for English-language sociological terms" (p. 93). Connell then traces Akiwowo's replies, accounts for her own difficulty in interpreting this controversy, and notes its similarity to controversies in Australia.

Then, in an abrupt turn, the text moves on to the controversial question of whether or not there is a distinctly "African" philosophy, giving a theoretically informed account of debates about the culture of European colonialism in Africa and the reception of Placide Tempels' *Bantu*

*Philosophy*. And here we get a cycle of argument that is by now well-worn and well-established in the humanities, about false universals, the possibility or impossibility of a universal philosophy, and the counterpoint of ethnophilosophy. This is important stuff, and perhaps not all sociologists know it. However, it is also a radical displacement of the precise problem that the first half of Chapter 5 ends with, namely, whether one can develop, by pursuing sociology in "African idioms" a set of explanatory concepts. This displacement, from the problem of sociological theory to the cultural politics of ethnophilosophy, is the problem I see with *Southern Theory*, and I will try to explain why.

Connell engages African sociology for extremely general presuppositions – presuppositions reminiscent of, or perhaps usable as a counterpoint to, the writings of Karl Marx in *Economic and Philosophical Manuscripts of 1844* that form the backbone of so many classical theory courses. Indeed, these propositions address the problem of what society is, and suggest furthermore, in broad strokes, how humans in society can become alienated from each other. Hence, as I argued above, Connell's book can be read as attempting to reconstruct the canon. And in doing this work, Part III of the book functions at the *most general level*, and links this level to the particular intellectual histories that make up the background for understanding this general level.

However, left untouched when Connell moves from sociological con-troversy to philosophy are the concepts that form the sinews of most sociological explanations. And, what this reveals, I think, is that Connell has *radically misunderstood where the social and political power of metropolitan sociology is really encoded*. The power of Northern Theory in sociology is not really located in the classical theorists, in canon construction, or in reinterpretation of intellectual histories; it is, rather, encoded in the "theories of the middle range," the analytical schemas, and the well-honed, widely accepted explanations that are used to construct sociological understandings of certain well-established social phenomena. These phenomena are also defined in terms of such working concepts.

To change sociology, the global challenge must articulate itself this level. How could this be done? Can we also build Southern Theory that contains concepts useful for constructing explanations? When paradigms are shifting, radical critiques are being made, and the very possibility of a global sociology is at stake, seeking semi-general concepts that explain some actions, some of the time, may seem a bit mundane. *But this is an illusion.* "Theories of the middle range" are the lifeblood of prestige and power in sociology in the metropole (in so far as it extends beyond mere cronyism and institutional inertia). Lately metropolitan sociology has been captivated by "mechanisms," and, to a certain degree, the intellectual movement of analytical sociology. This is, however, just one turn in a long history of quasi-generalization, and I believe that the actual identification of certain mechanisms, and their ensuing use in the construction of bounded sociological explanations, could do more for global sociology than mechanism-allegiance has done for the ever-recurring ideal of putting sociology on firm scientific foundations.

Given this, it would seem that the theoretical work for building global sociology is not in "encounters" with traditions, but rather in the development of a series of abstract terms, semi-general in their intended application, that throw into relief causal processes that account for the sociohistorical production of global inequalities. Some of these may come directly from the theoretical and philosophical texts Connell encounters in *Southern Theory*. But they may come from elsewhere as well, and they surely go beyond the super-general, ontological meditations on the nature of the social that Connell places at center stage.

Furthermore, Connell's book appears to separate traditions and concepts from each other into different intellectual silos, thus eliminating the whole question of which theoretical constructs can be usefully applied, and where. Connell's search for global difference in southern theory, then, does not operate via conceptual contestation, radical reinterpretation, and successful explanation. It presents, instead, a pluralized set of voices or philosophical "letters from the South." This articulation of voices distracts from the contestation and reinterpretation that makes explanations in global sociology really work – I refer, for example, to arguments about hybrid habitus (Decoteau, 2013); global fields and imperial forms (Go, 2008); servitude and class (Ray & Qayum, 2012).

## GLOBAL SOCIOLOGY, EPISTEMIC SHIFT, AND THEORY

Does this mean that, in the end, global sociology should just be an addendum to analytical sociology or that Robert Merton is in fact its founding father? No. But it does mean that to take on Northern Theory, global sociology must replace Merton and not Marx. Connell's critique of Northern Theory holds. But to complete the challenge, conceptual development has to occur at the level of explanation and comparative description; and here Connell's book is suggestive, but not forceful enough, and often misdirected. Her three-page discussion of "social knowledge as science" touches on the importance of generalization, the limits of social scientific knowledge,[2] and argues that there is one social theory with many different voices (pp. 225–226). Then, returning to her critique of Northern Theory, Connell writes that, "[o]n close examination, mainstream sociology turns out to be an ethno-sociology of metropolitan society." This fact is concealed by metropolitan sociology's universalist rhetoric. Praising this sociology for its "profound insights, well-honed methods, well-defined concepts and lots of skilled practitioners" (p. 226), Connell then argues that "its theorizing is vitiated whenever it refuses to recognize its ethno-sociological being." This leads to "major incompleteness, and a profound problem about the truthfulness of arguments framed as universal generalizations" (p. 226).

What does it really mean for mainstream sociology to recognize its "ethno-sociological being"? I understand that Northern Theory ends up being a theory of the urban centers of the North. But, given this critique, we are left wondering, after reading *Southern Theory*, what this new global social science will really look like, or what the means are for achieving it. I thus posit that there is a kind of displacement going on here, which I referenced in my discussion of the two halves of Chapter 5 above, but which I think applies to the whole book: Connell *substitutes* the comprehension of other voices for a genuine solution to the problem of developing explanations that incorporate the history of colonialism, or, more broadly, the global history of racism, violence, and exploitation, and the continued operation of empire in new forms.

Rather than a sociology of world philosophies, Connell should consider when and how abstraction-inflected interpretations are, and are not, accepted as sociological explanations. Instead of disowning "models" as pragmatist-postmodernist claims "only to usefulness not to truth" (p. 226) she should criticize which models, in which studies, get labeled "explanations" and which ones become "just interpretations," and develop a sociological explanation of why they get (mis)labeled in this way. The process of developing, and then effectively performing in the intellectual sphere, a successful sociological explanation is precisely how the intellectual hegemony of certain Northern theories is maintained, and it is also precisely where a better global sociology can force itself onto the scene. A global sociology should develop new concepts, critique the middle-range theories produced to account for well-researched phenomena the world over, and rewrite the sociohistorical explanations of what happened in Paris, in Chicago, and in Port-au-Prince, at different points in human history.

The metropole may need to recognize its ethno-sociological being. But perhaps it must also be forced to recognize that it has *bad middle-range theories*. And for all of the conceptual encounters on offer in *Southern Theory*, I cannot help but feel that Connell has not taken global sociology in this direction.

The move away from the false universalism, imperial complicity, and blind spots of Northern Theory is necessary, and this move will coincide with an epistemic shift in how we think about sociological knowledge. Connell's gestures toward such a shift made me, as a reader, enthusiastic. The world of social causality is multitudinous, complex, and strange, and our concepts for comprehending it are narrow. The models we have inherited from sociological theory for giving explanations are reductive and overawed by physics, while the models we need are those that can comprehend, render understandable, and ultimately be used to explain the contradictions of human experience and their consequences for action. The achievement of such an enriched sociology could, it seems to me, dovetail with Connell's goals. But the problem is that this is not the kind of work that is lauded by Connell as the essence of Southern Theory. The possibility of these new, better, more informed explanations never emerges, nor does a new compendium of concepts and types, mechanisms and models, interpretations and explanations. Instead we get the question of whether and how there is an African philosophy, the question of Islam and the West stated in highly general terms, and an intellectual history of, rather than a reconstruction and restatement of, dependency theory.

To create a different sociology, what is needed is not only a reconstruction of the intellectual history of the discipline, but also, and more urgently, a reconstruction of history itself (Bhambra, 2013, pp. 311–312). How will this happen? By getting into the thick of the fight over which concepts have the most explanatory torque. Ironically, attempts at building such concepts are on display in Connell's chapter on Northern Theory, and her critique of them as insufficient is perspicacious. But we never get their fully developed alternative. And it is thus possible that this lack, in the reconstruction of *Southern Theory*, undermines the very project to which Connell has dedicated herself. For she risks reproducing an imbalance she wishes to critique: in *Southern Theory*, the metropole produces explanatory theories, while the periphery produces philosophy and interesting intellectual history. That this encodes global power seems to me indisputable, and thus I fear *Southern Theory* substitutes multicultural politics for the explanation of neo-imperialism, and in so doing constructs a global sociology that subtly undermines the very project of global critique in whose name it is written.

## CONCLUSION

In a recent article in *Political Power and Social Theory*, Gurminder Bhambra (2013) discusses how, in a variety of different literatures, allowance has been made for global difference, and that these allowances are often viewed as having provided "sufficient modifications" to meet the global challenge. Bhambra disagrees. When multiculturalism is given as the answer to the problems of Northern Theory, she argues, it is too easily dismissed as "political, or politically correct," and the hardest epistemological issues are not addressed. Bhambra wants a *postcolonial* challenge to sociology that will lead to a global sociology that goes "beyond a simple multiplicity." And she worries that in the current intellectual configuration of sociology, "new voices are allowed to *supplement* the already existing truths about a Eurocentered modernity, but not to *reconstruct* them" (Bhambra, 2013, pp. 303, 305, 306, 311).

To use Bhambra's terms, Connell has, in *Southern Theory*, engaged in a project of reconstruction that risks veering into supplementation. She has reconstructed the theory canon, and placed that reconstruction on a geographical and historical map of modern imperialism and colonialism. She has compellingly rendered her own interest in, and difficulties with, texts that we should all learn our way through. But somewhere in this process the cutting edge with which she went after Coleman, Bourdieu, Giddens, and Beck was lost, and the chorus of many voices replaced the fierce contestation of concepts. We do not leave *Southern Theory* with a new repertoire with which to replace the explanation-generating concepts that appear in high-status research.

It may be that we have to change our general presuppositions and philosophical concepts of the social before we can get around to articulating new models and concepts; that we have to replace our Weber stories with other stories. In this sense *Southern Theory* could be read as a prolegomena to a global sociology. That is, in my view, a generous and partially justified reading of the text. But the less generous reading is important as well: The book falls short because Connell's interpretation of the new canon stops where explanations would begin. Only by making it clear why different concepts manage to provide interpretations that are also better explanations and comparative descriptions of the social world in various times and places, can the global challenge accomplish its goals. These goals are, in my view, essential, and they are founded on a problem diagnosed well by Connell – the complicity with empire, effacement of the periphery, and the radical misunderstanding of modernity that characterized the foundations of sociology in the West.

To reach these goals, the global challenge must make clear that it is not "just an interpretation." And here I fear Connell has erred. Despite her disavowal of postmodernism, she has fallen into the trap of a certain complacence of multiple interpretations. Has she made "available to us answers that others, guarding other sheep in other valleys, have given" (Geertz, 1973, p. 30)? Yes. Has she contextualized these answers by placing them within the history of modern imperial domination? Yes. But has she shown us the concepts that can provide the true analysis of this domination, and thus replace the false universals of an unknowing ethnosociology in the West? Not yet.

# NOTES

1. The challenge may be a bit late in coming, but it is given weight by the fact that, in the politics of truth and science in the Western academy, sociology as a discipline (albeit a hybrid and fragmented one) occupies a place of some prestige on the ladder of money-making, science-claiming knowledge production projects. Inferior to economics and political science in this regard, it nonetheless leverages more grant money and policy relevance than many of the disciplines we have come to characterize as "the humanities," and retains the purchase on truth implied by the term "social science." Thus the stakes of the postcolonial challenge are, if not new, highly significant in sociology, as well as taking on a different character than such a challenge takes in anthropology or English literature. Sociology claims some sort of scientificity; simultaneously it still allows a theoretical framing of itself in terms of big conceptual problems, qualitatively stated, and still forces its undergraduate and graduate students to read some of the classical theory canon, while of course turning to the grant-generation game to support itself during the neoliberalization of the academy. In this intensely fragmented and high-pressure context, *any* coherent and well-supported attack on the canon would likely make for interesting reading. But Connell's attack and rearticulation goes far beyond the interesting.

2. Connell is willing to limit social scientific ambition, including social science as she imagines it. Drawing on Veena Das, she recognizes that there are aspects of, or processes and events in the world that, despite tremendous hermeneutic effort, cannot be adequately theorized or explained. This is an interesting, and under-addressed issue, in sociology (pp. 177–182).

# ACKNOWLEDGMENTS

The author thanks Julian Go, Gurminder Bhambra, Claire Decoteau, and Kristen Schilt for reading and/or discussion of earlier versions of this text.

# REFERENCES

Abbott, A. (2007). Against narrative: A preface to lyrical sociology. *Sociological Theory, 25*(1), 67–99.

Bhambra, G. (2013). The possibilities of, and for, global sociology: A postcolonial perspective. *Political Power and Social Theory, 24,* 295–314.

Collins, P. H. (1989). The social construction of black feminist thought. *Signs, 14*(4), 745–773.

Collins, R. (1997). A sociological guilt trip: Comment on Connell. *American Journal of Sociology, 102*(6), 1558–1564.

Connell, R. W. (1997). Why is classical theory classical? *American Journal of Sociology, 102*(6), 1511–1557.

Decoteau, C. (2013). Hybrid habitus: Toward a post-colonial theory of practice. *Political Power and Social Theory, 24,* 263–293.

Emirbayer, M. (1997). Manifesto for a relational sociology. *American Journal of Sociology, 103*(2), 281–317.

Geertz, C. (1973). Thick description: Toward an interpretive theory of culture. In C. Geertz (Ed.), *The interpretation of cultures* (pp. 3–30). New York, NY: Basic Books.

Go, J. (2008). Global fields and imperial forms: Field theory and the British and American empires. *Sociological Theory, 26*(3), 201–229.

Ray, R., & Qayum, S. (2012). *Cultures of servitude: Modernity, domesticity, and class in India.* Stanford, CA: Stanford University Press.

Vandenberghe, F. (1999). 'The real is relational': An epistemological analysis of Pierre Bourdieu's generative structuralism. *Sociological Theory, 17*(1), 32–67.

# UNDER SOUTHERN SKIES

## Raewyn Connell

### ABSTRACT

*This essay responds to comments on* Southern Theory *by Mustafa Emirbayer, Patricia Hill Collins, Raka Ray, and Isaac Reed as part of a larger discussion about the future of postcolonial sociology. It clarifies aspects of* Southern Theory *that are commented upon while stressing the big claim of* Southern Theory, *which is that the periphery produces social theory that sociology should take seriously in order to make for a more global and democratic intellectual project of social change.*

The University of Sydney, where I work, has just "re-branded" itself. The advertising people created a university logo by redrawing the old coat of arms and deleting the university's motto. No doubt they reasoned that the fee-paying Asian students they want to attract don't understand Latin any more. But in doing so they deleted a good joke. For the University's motto, written by colonial intellectuals in the 1850s, is "Sidere Mens Eadem Mutato" – "Under Changed Skies, the Same Mind." Or, as I used to translate it for the First Year students, "We Aren't Going to Learn Anything New Here."

Learning something new under changed skies *is* on the agenda in this symposium. I'm delighted, and honored, that four excellent sociologists have engaged with *Southern Theory* and given us so much to think about.

Decentering Social Theory
Political Power and Social Theory, Volume 25, 173–182
ISSN: 0198-8719/doi:10.1108/S0198-8719(2013)0000025015

I don't agree with all their arguments, and will reply to some of the debatable points below, but I do want to register the importance of holding a discussion about the postcolonial future of sociology. Such discussions are developing in other forums too, including the International Sociological Association, where there is an upsurge in attention to the "diverse sociological traditions" (to quote the title of Sujata Patel's 2010 handbook) across the world, and the troubled relations between them.

Debates about the coloniality of knowledge have happened in other social sciences: Anthropology, as Mustafa Emirbayer notes, and History, as Raka Ray notes, mentioning Dipesh Chakrabarty's splendid *Provincializing Europe*. They have even happened in Economics, for example, in the work of Raúl Prebisch at the formation of CEPAL, or the work of Celso Furtado in Brasil, though the neoclassical revival has gone far to erase that memory.

Sociology isn't alone, then, in grappling with the politics of knowledge in an unequal world. But I have a feeling our discussion will work differently. Sociology, from its Comtean days, has a lingering ambition to be a unifying science – and why not try? – but it also has, in the critical sociology of knowledge, tools for thinking about the issues that all knowledge projects encounter. These tools must themselves be reexamined in postcolonial times, with the aid of scholars such as Paulin Hountondji and Veena Das.

I wasn't being modest when I described the chapter on world-scale social science at the end of *Southern Theory* as "a shaky beginning at best." These are genuinely difficult issues and the terrain is enormous. The book was fourteen years in the making, and at the end I felt as Isaac Newton did when he pictured himself as a child playing with shells and pebbles on the beach, while the great ocean of truth rolled undiscovered at his feet. And the difficulties are not just what one doesn't know, but what can happen when one does know something. Patricia Hill Collins describes a striking example, the gritty knowledge project of *Subaltern Studies* being decontextualized and absorbed into the metropole's academic system as a branch of literary postcolonial studies.

Raka aptly describes *Southern Theory* as both critique and mission statement, and she is right about the ambitious nature of the mission. For the project is not just about amending a reading list or creating a new specialization within sociology. We are talking about a collective project for a refounded social science. This involves what Isaac Ariail Reed accurately calls an "epistemic shift"; and a whole series of practical shifts, too, required to subvert the structures of Northern hegemony in world social science.

For that reason I thought it essential to start with an extended critique of mainstream Northern sociology – its self-understanding through history, its high-prestige forms of general theory, and its attempt to reconnect with the world through theories of globalization. This is what currently occupies the commanding heights in the institutionalized discipline of sociology. I'm happy for that critique to be corrected; though I have to say, in response to Mustafa's commentary, that *Southern Theory* itself points out the striking contrast between Bourdieu's knowledge of Algeria and cooperation with Abdelmalek Sayad, and the complete absence of colonial voices in his formulation of the general problems of social theory. It is the reproductionist Eurocentric formulations that are the "Bourdieu" now most influential in mainstream sociology. On the other hand, I think Mustafa is right in suggesting I have underplayed the disciplinary mechanisms and institutional privilege that also shape Northern theory.

It's a very important fact that the mainstream formation of knowledge and institutional practices in the metropole have tremendous influence in the periphery. My chapter on Australia shows how deeply sociology in one part of the periphery is shaped by its dependence on the metropole, and I could have (and perhaps should have) documented the same point from other continents. It's the pattern Hountondji (1997) names "extraversion," where science in the colony and postcolony are structured by the authority and techniques of the metropole.

I admit the irony, which Patricia points out, of reproducing the order of exposition in imperialist science, putting the discussion of Northern theory first. I love her example of the theory course where putting Fanon before, rather than after, changed the students' experience. But I wasn't putting "the ostensibly most important knowledge in the beginning ... and positioning all other knowledge as 'critique'." The book puts the *critique* first, trying to show why orthodox Northern social science is not tenable as a framework for world social science. Until that critique is made and driven home, the machinery of metropolitan science continues to function undisturbed – and all the passion, work and knowledge of the periphery goes for nothing, so far as the future of social science is concerned: corralled by extraversion, subsumed as area studies or postcolonial exotica, or (most often) simply ignored.

Yet the critique is only one moment of change. A tremendous task of making and remaking is also involved. What would motivate the intellectual workforce of the social sciences to undertake a project on that scale? Here we come to the political purpose of writing *Southern Theory*, because the book also contains an argument about the role of social science in the world. In fact it starts with this argument: "The purpose of this book is to propose a new path for social theory that will help social science to serve democratic purposes on a world scale." It explores many political uses of social science in the substantive chapters; and comes back to the issue in the final chapter. I entirely agree with Patricia about the importance of power relations in the realm of knowledge and knowledge institutions. And I'm disturbed by her evident feeling that my emphasis on South–South dialogue is depoliticizing or somehow opposed to action for social justice. I can't have made this clear enough, but a great deal of the work discussed in the book is activist knowledge: the work of Sol Plaatje who was one of the founding organizers of what became the ANC, Paulin Hountondji who was involved in two revolutionary movements in Benin, Ali Shariati who was imprisoned as a dangerous radical by the Shah, al-Afghani who fought British imperialism all his life, Ariel Dorfman who was on the death list, Teresa Valdés who was in the opposition to the Pinochet dictatorship and has worked for continental feminism since, Mick Dodson who has been a national leader in Aboriginal social justice struggles, and more.

Further, the "dialogue" isn't just casual conversation. The idea here is an educational process, a mutual learning on a planetary scale. I should have been more explicit about this, but I don't think education is a bland affair; it's deeply bound up with questions of social justice (Connell, 1993). The "better knowledge" (as Raka puts it) that we want is not just technically improved academic formulations. It's deeper and more powerful knowledge, that's fit for democratic use, and its production and circulation involves social struggle. *Southern Theory* ends on exactly this note (pp. 230–232).

The central parts of the book, the chapters about social thought from Australia, sub-Saharan Africa, Iran, Latin America and India, and about the place of the land, are in a different style, as the commentators have noted. Indeed the book is unorthodox in its literary form, and these chapters are far from the analytic-treatise format in which we usually package "theory." There is a lot of story telling and backgrounding, some musing and personal reflection, some description of country, even some jokes. I wanted readers to enjoy this stuff, to get a sense of the verve and passion of the people I was writing about, to the excitement as well as the complexity of the intellectual and political project. Romanticizing? Well perhaps; though I'd also want to do the same for good Northern theorists.

There is also a more conventional reason for this method of writing, which speaks to Isaac's dissatisfaction with these parts of the book. It's characteristic of the Eurocentric – latterly North-Atlanto-centric – world knowledge economy that raw material from the periphery is imported, processed, and transformed by theoretical work in the knowledge factories of the global North. (That's a large part of the history of science, as Mustafa recognizes). The big claim that the book makes is that despite the operation of this economy, the periphery *does* produce theory, lots of it. The colonial and postcolonial encounter, in its many forms and its myriad social consequences, does receive an intellectual response from the colonized, and from within settler populations.

Now, if I am going to convey that understanding to readers who are not familiar with the periphery's intellectual production – and the book is written mainly for people who aren't already readers of Shariati, Guha, Valdés, Hountondji or Dodson – I *cannot* process their work into a synthetic abstraction in the style of Northern theory. I have to try to understand and present their work *on its own terms*, in its integrity. That's an important reason for the story-telling, to put the readers in touch with the circumstances in which the texts were produced, the problems to which this knowledge production was a response. I tried to give the texts a respectful reading, to approach authors from the periphery with the care that sociologists would use in approaching Lord Giddens or Professor Bourdieu. That's why the book took fourteen years, and I still haven't done everybody justice, I'm sure.

That purpose involves not only single authors but whole skeins of argument. I have tried to follow, in different parts of the book, the development of lines of thought among groups of authors in specific colonial and post-colonial contexts; for instance the debate about indigenous knowledge in sub-Saharan Africa, the relationship of Australian indigenous society to the land, or the meaning of peripheral development in Latin America. I wanted to show debates and collective or sequential discussions as part of the panorama of Southern social thought, not just individuals.

This means that each chapter covers different ground and deals with different dramas; the cast list therefore seems unsystematic, as Raka observes. It's a little less arbitrary than it seems. The imbalance between women and men, for instance, reflects the gender imbalance in the intelligentsias involved in these debates. (It is not, *pace* Patricia, an absence of women: the book highlights Das, Valdés and Montecino, discusses Australian women in sociology, Indian feminists, and more.) But my main purpose wasn't to sample a population of intellectuals, it was to show the range of vigorous intellectual work that has come out of the colonial encounter. Yes, I think there is a moral claim here: that as social scientists we *should* be inclusive in our reading and work towards the democratisation of knowledge. There is also a professional claim: that one can't now be a good sociologist – if one ever could – without knowing about imperialism and encountering southern theory.

178                                               RAEWYN CONNELL

Is this an exercise in canon formation? That wasn't my intention, though
I agree it might be an effect. I certainly wanted to encourage my readers to
go and read the originals, to understand these texts in their integrity. And
then to go on and read more.

The book therefore had to discuss many texts that were possible for
Anglophone readers to access. That brought into play the selectivity of
publishers, translators, editors, librarians and database managers; and the
patterns of privilege that are all too familiar in the sociology of education.
Yes, the people I have written about are mainly from the more privileged
classes of their regions, though rarely from the rich. Some have elite
education, some write with state support, many have international
connections. Indeed they are the kind of people who might have been
complacent, buying into the system. Instead they produced this amazing
outpouring of critical thought, and some were engaged, as I noted earlier, in
demanding and dangerous activism. This isn't a "social reproduction" story!

Isaac gives us a beautiful formulation when he poses the key question,
what kind of theoretical labour is required to rewrite sociological theory,
and transform sociology. I actually share his enthusiasm for work on the
Mertonesque scale, for the patient building of analyses, concepts and
generalizations around concrete problems and empirical findings in the
famous middle-range. That's what I've tried to do in my own research on
educational inequality, masculinity, class structure, and intellectuals; and so
have people discussed in *Southern Theory*.

The difficulty is that Isaac's critique supposes this is the *only* kind of
theoretical labour that will allow us to progress. Thinking that, he sees Parts
II and III of *Southern Theory* as misguided, a substitute for the true course;
and thinks there is "something massive" that has gone missing as the text
pursues its stories of intellectual history. There is actually more of the
Mertonesque in the book than he allows. The case he treats in detail, the
discussion of African literature on indigenous knowledge in Chapter 5, is
one example. It doesn't involve an "abrupt turn" away from sociology and a
"displacement" of the issues. Rather, the chapter examines the roots of
Akiwowo's strategy for sociology in the discourse of African philosophy,
and shows how the critique of that discourse produced, particularly in the
work of Hountondji, an important new sociology of knowledge. (That's
actually flagged in the section subtitle: "From 'African philosophy' to the
sociology of post-colonial knowledge.")

The more important point, however, is that the kind of work that
Isaac eloquently describes and urges, is only *one* of the multiple kinds of
labour a transformation of sociological thought requires. There is also the

reexamination of intellectual history in the light of colonialism, both North and South; the respectful as well as critical study of texts that haven't been considered canonical; the new fieldwork projects that will generate conceptual revision, such as Raka's work on domestic service and her earlier work on women's politics; the contestation and change of power operating through knowledge institutions, as Patricia mentions; the articulation of ideas in social movements; the trying-out of alternative general frameworks, such as the exploration of Gandhian perspectives by Ashis Nandy and more recently Vinay Lal (2002); and the exploration of method for knowledge formation in the South, opened by Linda Tuhiwai Smith (1999) in *Decolonizing Methodologies* and now being pursued by the journal *Method(e)s*.

That is the spectrum of transformative labours, *already under way*, that I hoped to picture in *Southern Theory*. It's a large and messy terrain, the resources are often far less than in the universities of the North, the incoherence and struggle doesn't make for a neatly organized text, and the process doesn't produce a single model that we can easily teach in our courses. But that's the complexity we expect in a global insurgency and transformation.

I'm writing this text at 34° South, and I'm about to e-mail it to 42° North. The difference does matter. Raka comments humorously that Australia is a "strange inclusion" in the panorama of southern theory. Australia (the name, invented by British colonizers, means literally "South-ia") is in the book for a specific reason – apart from the fact that I live here. The spectrum of colonial history includes settler colonialism, and distinctive intellectual problems and projects arise in that context.

Modern Australia is a settler-colonial society, the product of a European invasion of Aboriginal lands that started in the late eighteenth century and continued into the twentieth; arguably the conquest has never stopped. (The cover of *Southern Theory* is a painting by an Aboriginal elder representing Bow River country in the northwest of the continent.) The Australian economy is organized around primary exports, agriculture, pastoralism and above all mining. Multinational corporations effectively dominate the economy and keep the local state well under control. What allows Australia to pass for part of "The West" – a trope in local politics – is its white ethnic majority, its institutionalized racism, and the wealth from that export economy. Few of the indigenous people share in the wealth.

Contemporary Australian social science is mostly what Hountondji calls "extraverted" knowledge, constructed in postcolonial dependence on metropolitan thought and in weird denial of the reality all around. Yet

critical intellectual work also develops and the colonial encounter is
discussed in new ways. This includes the Aboriginal-led debates about land,
on which Chapter 9 of *Southern Theory* is based, and which is now
generating a sociology of indigenous issues; and work by white intellectuals
including Chilla Bulbeck's (1998) *Re-Orienting Western Feminisms*, Peter
Beilharz's (1997) *Imagining the Antipodes*, and Kay Anderson's (2007) *Race
and the Crisis of Humanism*.

That Australian work is only a small part of a growing field, and I will
finish with some notes on resources now available for sociologists, in
addition to the work mentioned by Raka and Isaac. Published just before
*Southern Theory* was a book from Singapore with a very similar agenda,
Farid Alatas's (2006) *Alternative Discourses in Asian Social Science*, which
has rich material from the Arabic-speaking world, south and southeast Asia.
Published just after, was Wiebke Keim's (2008) *Vermessene Disziplin* [Daring
Discipline], which looks in close focus at industrial sociology in South Africa
as a counter-hegemonic knowledge project, and compares it with South
American work. (There is an English-language summary of Wiebke's work in
*International Sociology*, Vol. 26, No. 1.) There are reexaminations of the
history of social thought from the periphery such as Oliver Kozlarek's (2009)
study of Octavio Paz, my study of Paulin Hountondji (Connell, 2011), and
João Maia's (2008) *A Terra como Invenção*, on space and coloniality in
Brasil. (Good for *International Sociology*! see Vol. 26, No. 3 for a summary
of João's work.) There's a continuing philosophical discussion about
alternative knowledges, linked to antiglobalization and decolonial movements (e.g., Santos, 2007).

There are increasing numbers of conferences and publications that bring
together social thought from the periphery. Examples are Sujata Patel's
(2010) volume already mentioned; Burawoy, Chang and Hsieh's *Facing an
Unequal World* (2010); the international conference "Perspectives from the
Periphery" on the history of social science held in Umeå (as far north as you
can get!) in 2008, and the forthcoming Danell, Larsson and Wisselgren
volume *Social Science in Context*; and volumes currently being published
under the auspices of ISA and Sage such as Arjomand and Reis (2013)
*Worlds of Difference*. Very unevenly, there are more republications of
significant primary texts from Southern thinkers, such as the essays on
Pacific Island society by the remarkable Epeli Hau'ofa (2008) collected in
*We Are the Ocean*, the original letters of the pioneering Javanese feminist
Kartini (2005) and the articles of the pioneering West African feminist
Mabel Dove (2004). There is a growing critical and agenda-setting litera-
ture about postcoloniality and Northern sociology. This can be found in

Gutiérrez Rodríguez, Boatcă, and Costa's (2010) *Decolonizing European Sociology*, and Reuter and Villa's (2009) *Postkoloniale Soziologie*, as well as Gurminder Bhambra's (2007) important monograph *Rethinking Modernity*, and our editor's very recent and detailed argument for a postcolonial sociology (Go, 2012).

Significantly there is also a growing *applied* literature, which takes southern-theory and postcolonial perspectives into fields where social science is put to use in professional and social-movement practice. Helen Meekosha's (2011) work on decolonizing the social model of disability is generating international interest, including a recent special issue of *Third World Quarterly* on disability and the global South (Vol. 32, No. 8, 2011). There is a literature on social dimensions of education, including gender, which makes a postcolonial critique of the field of knowledge and explores Southern knowledge formation (Epstein & Morrell, 2012; Fennell & Arnot, 2008; Gulson & Fataar, 2011). There are applications of southern-theory ideas in youth studies (Nilan, 2011), health sociology (Henderson, 2012), even counselling (Burns, 2008), and of course development studies (Schech, 2012).

There is more; I hope these examples are enough to show the growing resources for remaking social science on a world scale. *Southern Theory* argues for undertaking this task and illustrates an approach to it – not the only one, and not a definitive one as this symposium well shows, but perhaps a useful one. I wrote in the introduction to the book: "If I can convince readers it is a beginning that should be improved on, then the book is serving its purpose." I think it has done some of that.

# REFERENCES

Alatas, S. F. (2006). *Alternative discourses in Asian social science: Responses to Eurocentrism.* New Delhi: Sage.

Anderson, K. (2007). *Race and the Crisis of Humanism.* London: Routledge.

Arjomand, S. A., & Reis, E. (Eds.). (2013). *Worlds of difference.* Thousand Oaks, CA: Sage.

Beilharz, P. (1997). *Imagining the antipodes: Culture, theory and the visual in the work of Bernard Smith.* Cambridge: Cambridge University Press.

Bhambra, G. (2007). *Rethinking modernity: Postcolonialism and the sociological imagination.* Basingstoke, UK: Palgrave Macmillan.

Bulbeck, C. (1998). *Re-orienting Western Feminisms: Women's Diversity in a Postcolonial World.* Cambridge: Cambridge University Press.

Burawoy, M., Chang, M.-k, & Hsieh, M. Fi-yu (Eds.). (2010). *Facing an unequal world: Challenges for a global sociology* (3 vols). Taipei: Academia Sinica.

Burns, E. (2008). How can a "southern theory" perspective contribute to New Zealand counselling? *New Zealand Journal of Counselling, 28*(2), 10–24.

Connell, R. (1993). *Schools and Social Justice. Toronto: Our schools ourselves*. Philadelphia, PA: Temple University Press.

Connell, R. (2011). Paulin Hountondji's postcolonial sociology of knowledge. In R. Connell, *Confronting equality* (pp. 119–135). Sydney: Allen & Unwin

Danell, R., Larsson, A., & Wisselgren, P (Ed.) (in press). *Social science in context: Historical, sociological and global perspectives*. Lund: Nordic Academic Press.

Dove, M. (2004). *Selected writings of a pioneer West African feminist*. Nottingham: Trent Editions.

Epstein, D., & Morrell, R. (2012). Approaching Southern theory: explorations of gender in South African education. *Gender and Education, 24*(5), 469–482.

Fennell, S., & Arnot, M. (2008). Decentring hegemonic gender theory: the implications for educational research. *Compare, 38*(5), 525–538.

Go, J. (2012). For a postcolonial sociology. *Theory and Society*. 10.1007/s11186-012-9184-6

Gulson, K. N., & Fataar, A. (2011). Neoliberal governmentality, schooling and the city: Conceptual and empirical notes on and from the Global South. *Discourse: Studies in the Cultural Politics of Education, 32*(2), 269–283.

Gutiérrez Rodríguez, E., Boatcă, M., & Costa, S. (Eds.). (2010). *Decolonizing European sociology: Transdisciplinary approaches*. Burlington, VT: Ashgate.

Hau'ofa, E. (2008). *We are the ocean*. Honolulu: University of Hawai'i Press.

Henderson, J. (2012). Southern theory: Health in the periphery. *Health Sociology Review, 21*(2), 138–140.

Hountondji, P. J. (Ed.) (1997 [1994]). *Endogenous knowledge: Research trails*. Dakar: CODESRIA.

Kartini, R. A. (2005). *On feminism and nationalism: Kartini's letters to Stella Zeehandelaar, 1899–1903*. Clayton: Monash University Press.

Keim, W. (2008). *Vermessene disziplin: Zum konterhegemonialen Potential afrikanischer und lateinamerikanischer Soziologien*. Bielefeld: Transcript Verlag.

Kozlarek, O. (2009). The sociology of Octavio Paz. In O. Kozlarek (Ed.), *Octavio Paz: Humanism and critique* (pp. 137–154). Bielefeld: Transcript Verlag.

Lal, V. (2002). *Empire of knowledge: Culture and plurality in the global economy*. London: Pluto.

Maia, J. M. E. (2008). *A Terra como Invenção: O espaço no pensamento social brasileiro*. Rio de Janeiro: Zahar.

Meekosha, H. (2011). Decolonising disability: Thinking and acting globally. *Disability & Society, 26*(6), 667–682.

Nilan, P. (2011). Youth sociology must cross cultures. *Youth Studies Australia, 30*(3), 20–26.

Patel, S. (Ed.). (2010). *International handbook of diverse sociological traditions*. London: Sage.

Reuter, J., & Villa, P.-I. (Eds.). (2009). *Postkoloniale Soziologie: Empirische Befunde, theoretische Anschlüsse, politische Intervention*. Bielefeld: Transcript.

Santos, Boaventura de Sousa (Ed.). (2007). *Another knowledge is possible: Beyond northern epistemologies*. London: Verso.

Schech, S. (2012). Development perspectives from the Antipodes: an introduction. *Third World Quarterly, 33*(6), 969–980.

Smith, L. T. (1999). *Decolonizing Methodologies: Research and Indigenous Peoples*. London: Zed Books.